BECKETT AND BUDDHISM

Beckett and Buddhism undertakes a twenty-first-century reassessment of the Buddhist resonances in Samuel Beckett's writing. These reverberations, as Angela Moorjani demonstrates, originated in his early reading of Schopenhauer. Drawing on letters and archives along with recent studies of Buddhist thought and Schopenhauer's knowledge of it, the book charts the Buddhist concepts circling through Beckett's visions of the 'human predicament' in a blend of tears and laughter. Moorjani offers an in-depth elucidation of texts that are shown to intersect with the negative and paradoxical path of the Buddha, which she sets in dialogue with Western thinking. She brings further perspectives from cognitive philosophy and science to bear on creative emptiness, the illusory 'I', and Beckett's probing of the writing process. Readers will benefit from this far-reaching study of one of the most acclaimed writers of the twentieth century who explored uncharted topologies in his fiction, theatre, and poetry.

ANGELA MOORJANI is Professor Emerita of Modern Languages and Intercultural Pragmatics at the University of Maryland (UMBC). She has extensively explored the multidimensional writings of Samuel Beckett in her many publications. In her other books and articles, she investigates the effects of trauma and mourning on modernist writers and artists.

BECKETT AND BUDDHISM

ANGELA MOORJANI

University of Maryland

UMBC

CAMBRIDGE
UNIVERSITY PRESS

CAMBRIDGE
UNIVERSITY PRESS

University Printing House, Cambridge CB2 8BS, United Kingdom

One Liberty Plaza, 20th Floor, New York, NY 10006, USA

477 Williamstown Road, Port Melbourne, VIC 3207, Australia

314–321, 3rd Floor, Plot 3, Splendor Forum, Jasola District Centre, New Delhi – 110025, India

103 Penang Road, #05–06/07, Visioncrest Commercial, Singapore 238467

Cambridge University Press is part of the University of Cambridge.

It furthers the University's mission by disseminating knowledge in the pursuit of education, learning, and research at the highest international levels of excellence.

www.cambridge.org
Information on this title: www.cambridge.org/9781316519691
DOI: 10.1017/9781009024082

First published 2021

A catalogue record for this publication is available from the British Library.

ISBN 978-1-316-51969-1 Hardback

For Kishin

Contents

Figures

Acknowledgments

For many years I had wanted to explore in greater depth the sources of Buddhist echoes in Beckett's fiction and theatre, so on receiving an invitation to lecture on a topic of my choice at the 2016 Samuel Beckett Summer School at Trinity College Dublin, I set to work on a paper entitled 'What the Archive Tells Us about Beckett and Buddhism'. I owe a debt of gratitude to Sam Slote and Nicholas Johnson for their invitation and hospitality and to the audience of students, faculty, and summer school participants from around the globe for their questions, comments, and interest in knowing more about the topic of my lecture. Special thanks to Rónán McDonald, a fellow lecturer at the summer school that year, whose suggestion that I expand the lecture into a book led to my seriously considering this project. I remain grateful to Minako Okamuro, whose invitation to teach a seminar on Beckett's theatre at Tokyo's Waseda University in 2008 brought with it opportunities to interact with the Samuel Beckett Research Circle of Japan and to experience Japan's Buddhist-imbued culture, especially in the theatre and the arts. But it is the unfailing support, forbearance, and solicitude of Kishin Moorjani that made possible the years of intense research and writing for both the lecture and the book. His involvement with my passion for Beckett's oeuvre dates to the time of the writing of my doctoral dissertation in the late 1960s and my always renewed attempts to grapple with the work's multidimensionality. One could not wish for a more sympathetic, astute, and witty conversation partner through it all, for whose unfaltering encouragement and kindness, not to forget his reading of an earlier version of the manuscript, there are no adequate words of gratitude.

I have greatly profited from the encouragement and expertise of friends and colleagues. Much appreciation is due to Paul Lawley for casting a critical eye over the entire manuscript and over sections of it as it was in progress. His learned recommendations and exchanges about Beckett's oeuvre over many years are ever treasured. My thanks to Danièle de

Ruyter for her unfailingly perceptive comments on parts of the manuscript
and for raising probing questions; to Peter Gidal for expert feedback on
selections of the study and mind-opening dialogue over the years; to my
UMBC colleagues Thomas Field and John Sinnigen for discussions on the
transformative potential of intercultural research for teaching and writing;
and to my then colleagues on the editorial board of *Samuel Beckett Today/
Aujourd'hui*: Matthijs Engelberts, Sjef Houppermans, Mark Nixon,
Danièle de Ruyter, and Dirk Van Hulle, who discussed the project early
with me and helpfully answered subsequent queries. Other fellow
Beckettians, too many to set down here, with whose investigations mine
have been in conversation are cited throughout the present study and in
the notes. Even though we don't always agree, their work has acted as a
constant ferment of mine.

The attentive interlibrary loan staff at UMBC's Albin O. Kuhn Library
and the archivist librarians at the Bibliothèque Nationale de France, the
Beckett International Foundation at the University of Reading, and at
Trinity College Library Dublin greatly facilitated the preparation of this
study. Much gratitude is owed to the many people who provided and
helped with illustrations, foremost Zen artist, scholar, and peace activist
Kazuaki Tanahashi, who generously provided an image of one of his Zen
circles and permission to use it in this study; my cousin Peter Schmidt-
Breitung, who at my request photographed bodhi trees and ancient
Buddha statues on a trip to Sri Lanka; and my niece Priya Moorjani for
her expert assistance with technological queries and illustrations. For their
helpful responses to my requests and generous support of this study, I am
grateful to the staff of the Archive of the Südwestrundfunk (SWR) in
Stuttgart, the Schopenhauer-Archive in Frankfurt, the Zentrum Paul Klee
Archive in Bern, the Brooklyn Academy of Music Hamm Archives, and
the UMBC Albin O. Kuhn Library Archive in Baltimore. I would further
like to acknowledge the recent Open Access policy of the Metropolitan
Museum of Art, New York, which permits the downloading and reprodu-
cing of images of public-domain artworks in the Met's collection.

For his invaluable support and guidance, my gratitude to Ray Ryan of
Cambridge University Press and my thanks to the staff for their helpful-
ness and expertise.

Abbreviations of Editions Used

Works by Beckett

Cc	*Comment c'est* (Paris: Éditions de Minuit, 1961).
Co	*Company* (New York: Grove Press, 1980).
CP	*The Collected Poems: A Critical Edition*, ed. by Seán Lawlor and John Pilling (New York: Grove Press, 2012).
CSP	*The Complete Short Prose, 1929–1989*, ed. by S. E. Gontarski (New York: Grove Press, 1995).
CSPL	*Collected Shorter Plays* (New York: Grove Press, 1984).
D	*Le Dépeupleur* (Paris: Éditions de Minuit, 1970).
Dis	*Disjecta: Miscellaneous Writing and a Dramatic Fragment*, ed. by Ruby Cohn (New York: Grove Press, 1984).
DN	*Beckett's Dream Notebook*, ed. by John Pilling (Reading: Beckett International Foundation, 1999).
Dream	*Dream of Fair to Middling Women*, ed. by Eoin O'Brien and Edith Fournier (New York: Arcade Publishing, 1992).
EB	*Echo's Bones*, ed. by Mark Nixon (New York: Grove Press, 2014).
Eleu	*Eleutheria* (Paris: Éditions de Minuit, 1995).
End	*Endgame* (New York: Grove Press, 1958).
Film	*Film: Complete Scenario/Illustrations/Production Shots* (New York, Grove Press, 1969).
Fin	*Fin de partie*, suivi de *Acte sans paroles* (Paris: Éditions de Minuit, 1957; 1967 ed.).
HD	*Happy Days* (New York: Grove Press, 1961).
How	*How It Is* (New York: Grove Press, 1964).
Ill	*Ill Seen Ill Said* (New York: Grove Press, 1981).
In	*L'Innommable* (Paris: Éditions de Minuit, 1953; 2016 ed.).
LSB I	*The Letters of Samuel Beckett, vol. I: 1929–1940*, ed. by Martha Dow Fehsenfeld and Lois More Overbeck (Cambridge: Cambridge University Press, 2009).

LSB II	*The Letters of Samuel Beckett, vol. II: 1941–1956*, ed. by George Craig, Martha Dow Fehsenfeld, Dan Gunn, and Lois More Overbeck (Cambridge: Cambridge University Press, 2011.)
LSB III	*The Letters of Samuel Beckett, vol. III: 1957–1965*, ed. by George Craig, Martha Dow Fehsenfeld, Dan Gunn, and Lois More Overbeck (Cambridge: Cambridge University Press, 2014).
LSB IV	*The Letters of Samuel Beckett, vol. IV: 1966–1989*, ed. by George Craig, Martha Dow Fehsenfeld, Dan Gunn, and Lois More Overbeck (Cambridge: Cambridge University Press, 2016).
Ma	*Malone Dies*, in *Three Novels* (New York: Grove Press, 1956), 177–288.
Mal	*Mal vu mal dit* (Paris: Éditions de Minuit, 1981).
Mo	*Molloy*, in *Three Novels* (New York: Grove Press, 1955), 7–176.
MPTK	*More Pricks than Kicks* (London: Calder & Boyars, 1970).
Mu	*Murphy* (New York: Grove Press, 1957).
P	*Proust* (New York: Grove Press, 1957).
PA	*Premier amour* (Paris: Éditions de Minuit, 1970).
Pm	*Pas moi*, in *Oh les beaux jours suivi de Pas moi* (Paris: Éditions de Minuit, 1963–1974), 79–95.
Textes	*Nouvelles* et *Textes pour rien* (Paris: Éditions de Minuit, 1958; 2013 ed.), 113–206.
Un	*The Unnamable*, in *Three Novels* (New York: Grove Press, 1958), 289–414.
W	*Watt* (New York: Grove Press, 1959).
WfG	*Waiting for Godot* (New York: Grove Press, 1954).
Worst	*Worstward Ho* (New York: Grove Press, 1983).

Works by Meister Eckhart

CMW	*The Complete Mystical Works of Meister Eckhart*, trans. and ed. by Maurice O'C. Walshe, revised with a foreword by Bernard McGinn (New York: Crossroads Publishing, 2009).
DW	*Deutsche Werke*, vols. 1–5 (Stuttgart: Kohlhammer, 1958–2003).
MEW I	*Meister Eckhart Werke I*, trans. by Josef Quint, ed. and comm. by Niklaus Largier (Frankfurt a. Main: Deutscher Klassiker Verlag, 1993).

MEW II   *Meister Eckhart Werke II*, trans. by Ernst Benz et al., ed. and
             comm. by Niklaus Largier (Frankfurt a. Main: Deutscher
             Klassiker Verlag, 1993).

Works by Fritz Mauthner

BKS I   *Beiträge zu einer Kritik der Sprache*, vol. 1, 3rd ed. (Stuttgart:
             J. G. Cotta'sche Buchhandlung Nachfolger, 1921).
             http: archive.org.
BKS II   *Beiträge zu einer Kritik der Sprache*, vol. 2, 2nd ed. (Stuttgart:
             J. G. Cotta'sche Buchhandlung Nachfolger, 1912).
             http: archive.org.
BKS III   *Beiträge zu einer Kritik der Sprache*, vol. 3, 2nd ed. (Stuttgart:
             J. G. Cotta'sche Buchhandlung Nachfolger, 1912).
             http: archive.org.

Work by Nāgārjuna

MMK   *Mūlamadhyamakakārikā*, in *Nāgārjuna's Middle Way*, trans.
             and comm. by Mark Siderits and Shōryū Katsura
             (Sommerville, MA: Wisdom Publications, 2013).

Works by Arthur Schopenhauer

PP II   *Parerga and Paralipomena: Short Philosophical Essays,* vol. 2,
             trans. and ed. by Adrian del Caro and Christopher Janaway
             (Cambridge: Cambridge University Press, 2015).
WWR I   *The World as Will and Representation,* vol. 1, trans. and ed.
             by Judith Norman, Alistair Welchman, and Christopher
             Janaway (Cambridge: Cambridge University Press, 2014).
WWR II   *The World as Will and Representation*, vol. 2, trans. and ed.
             by Judith Norman, Alistair Welchman, and Christopher
             Janaway (Cambridge: Cambridge University Press, 2018).

Library Archives

TCD   Trinity College Dublin Library, Department of Manuscripts
UoR   Beckett International Foundation, The University of Reading

Notes on the Text

Parenthetical translations from French and German, without
quotation marks, are the author's. On first mention of texts Beckett

wrote first in French and subsequently translated into English, both the French and English titles are given. Because of constraints of space, in subsequent discussion, reluctantly, only the English versions are cited except for comparisons. Diacritics and italics are used to mark transliterated Sanskrit terms, even when these, *nirvāṇa* for example, are in common usage in English. The intent is to defamiliarize such terms in order to draw attention to their meanings in Eastern thought. Among the exceptions are the words 'karma' and 'Upanishads' and the name Shankara, which are commonly transliterated without diacritics. Underlining is used to indicate words or titles underscored by Beckett and others in their letters and drafts.

Introduction
Buddhism, Schopenhauer, Beckett: Influence, Affinity, Relay?

On my asking Beckett how he goes about writing, his answer was unexpectedly brief: 'One decides what elements to use and puts them together'.[1] Audiences and scholars of his work, hard put to keep up with Beckett's erudition, have observed the extraordinary number of elements he stitches into his texts while taking care to conceal them, cast doubt on them, parody, or unravel them. In engaging with Beckett's poetics of indirectness, exegetes have not failed to note the Buddhist threads that pervade his works.

Nevertheless, 'I know nothing about Buddhism', was Beckett's response, when asked about Buddhist parallels in his 1957 mime *Acte sans paroles I / Act without Words I* (qtd. in Shainberg 1987, 111).[2] The query by the Buddhist wife and assistant of the puppeteer who staged a performance of the play in 1981 was no doubt based on the mime's lone contemplative figure who, after being repeatedly flung from the wings into the blinding light of the play's desert setting, ultimately resigns in the face of the whistled cues that frustratingly tempt him with objects arriving from the flies to relieve his suffering. These expedients, such as a small jug of water to satisfy his thirst and a rope to put an end to his existence, are whisked away just as the character is about to get hold of them. Ruby Cohn has pointed out that the French original *Acte sans paroles I* was first entitled *Soif* (thirst), and noting the comic effect of the clownlike figure's pratfalls, she draws attention to the similarity of the mime with the myth of Tantalus whose punishment in Hades consists of Zeus frustrating his desire to quench his thirst (Cohn 2005, 218). Lance St. John Butler, on the other hand, sees the mime as one of several of Beckett's parables for Martin Heidegger's *Geworfenheit*, the 'thrownness' into 'Being'

---

[1] See the account of my conversations with Beckett in Moorjani 2017, 41.
[2] Lawrence Shainberg, an American writer of fiction and nonfiction and a practitioner of Zen, recounts his meetings with Beckett in his 1987 memoir 'Exorcising Beckett'.

(Butler 1984, 37–8). To the mime's scenario of a hellish existence, Beckett, however, added his character's contemplative response. In the brief written script of the mime (*CSPL* 43–6), the figure's reflections, receiving thirty-four mentions, are interrupted fifteen times by the shrill whistle misleadingly alerting him to material relief for his pains. At the end, ignoring the cues, he lies unmoving on his side, looking at his hands.

Encapsulated in this brief mime, if in skeletal form, one can in fact detect parallels to the four noble truths the Buddha taught in his first sermon shortly after attaining enlightenment: life is suffering; the cause is the craving thirst for sensual gratification, for perpetuation of the self, and for extinction; the way to end suffering is emancipation from craving; and the means include contemplation and resignation.[3] And yet, liberation from craving is also taught by the Upanishads, the ancient Sanskrit philosophical texts of which the most ancient predate Buddhism. And just to complicate matters further, the mime and its emphasis on suffering and its causes can also be understood in terms of Arthur Schopenhauer's thought, self-proclaimed to be congruent with that of the Buddha and the medieval mystical philosopher Meister Eckhart (1260–1328) (qtd. in App 2014, 25). It is no surprise, given Beckett's adeptness at secreting allusions into his texts, that after learning about Indian thought and Christian mysticism in his early reading of Schopenhauer and of works by and on Christian mystics, he picked up threads from all three philosophers to wind into his writings, inviting readers to take notice by leaving clues.[4]

Beginning with the elements of Beckett's texts that reverberate with Buddhist concepts, as is the case of his mime, this study probes his Eastern sources and its crosscurrents with related biblical and Christian teachings, mystical and otherwise. The similarities and differences noted between Buddhist concepts, on the one hand, and Upanishadic teachings and Christian mysticism, on the other, lead to the conclusion that, despite similar teachings of a path including resignation and meditation, their views on salvation set them apart, the Upanishads and Christian mysticism

---

[3] This description of craving follows the eminent Buddhologists and translators of Buddhist texts Rhys Davids 1910, 743; and Conze 1959a, 43.

[4] There are, of course, other Christian mystics, besides Eckhart, whose writings advocate a renunciation and quietism similar to that of the Buddha. Lack of space prevents the attention they deserve, which, however, is provided by other Beckett scholars to whom this study refers. To these, David Tucker adds the *Ethics* of seventeenth-century Flemish philosopher Arnold Geulincx, on which he draws to point out the apt resemblance of the figure of Beckett's mime to a puppet cruelly manipulated by an offstage puppet master (Tucker 2012, 162–5).

teaching a fulfilling union, the one with *brahman*, an eternal world principle, the other with divinity, in contrast to the Buddhist ultimate emptiness and unknowable beyond. Shared by Schopenhauer, the latter view is in consonance with Beckett's fascination with the void and his resolute 'perhaps' in the face of an 'unspeakable home' (*CSP* 258).

This study engages with both the Christian and Buddhist views as they emerge from Beckett's writings. They are alternate responses to the oft-evoked Beckettian 'woes' of the world. His distressing depictions of suffering reverberate with both biblical and Buddhist teachings, as evident, on the one hand, in his frequent allusions to the Christian iconography of the Passion, his evocations of Job, and the biblical teaching of the origin of guilt and suffering, but stopping short of the consolatory belief in a merciful God and Christian salvation, and, on the other hand, in the echoes in his oeuvre of the Buddha's meditations on the origin of suffering, karmic rebirth, and the path to an ineffable beyond. It is in order to understand Beckett's fascination with cyclical existence, the 'not I', time-lessness, the 'unborn', and the void that led to this study's exploration of the congruence of his texts with Buddhist thought and its transmission by Schopenhauer.

This study's aim is not to fit Beckett into a Buddhist or mystical mold, but rather to scrutinize the imaginative dialogue between his writing and Indian thought and the apophatic, or negative, mysticism of which he became aware by reading Schopenhauer and books on and by mystical thinkers. It is a matter of transtextuality, or the scrutiny of relations between texts, overt or secret (Hutcheon 1985, 21), and the dialogue resulting from putting into relation texts issuing from several cultures.[5] Emphasis is therefore placed on tracking down the sources of Beckett's allusions to Buddhist and other philosophical and mystical concepts in verifiable extratextual and textual evidence. There were clearly traces of Buddhist influence in Beckett's postwar writings, and when, in his late works of the 1970s and 1980s and in the still later posthumous publication of his early fictions, Buddhist resonances called increasingly for investigation, the recent archival findings substantiating Schopenhauer's knowledge of Eastern thought – Buddhism in particular – coupled with the extraordinary revival of scholarly interest in Mahāyāna Buddhism, as well as enhanced access to Beckett's letters, archival notes and drafts set in motion

---

[5] Such intercultural dialogue is indebted to Mikhail Bakhtin's concepts of 'dialogism' and 'polyglossia' (Bakhtin 1981, 61, 282–3ff.).

this study's twenty-first-century reevaluation of the Buddhist echoes in Beckett's texts and their sources.

Beckett's Buddhist reverberations join the many other transtextual 'elements' that exegetes keep uncovering and exploring in the oeuvre of this omnivorous and receptive reader, despite his protests to the contrary. His 'can't and must' ethical approach to writing, explored in Chapter 4, encompassed forays into fields ranging from literature in his first language and the French and Italian literatures he majored in as an undergraduate at Trinity College Dublin to readings in other ancient and modern European languages, some in the original, some in translation;[6] the Western philosophical tradition from the Presocratics to philosophers of his time; painting, film, theatre, music, and vaudeville; mathematics and the changing world views occasioned by the discoveries of the physical sciences; the new understanding of the human psyche and its and the body's ills by contemporaneous psychological, psychoanalytic, and medical investigations; historical traumas and repressions instigated by colonial powers, monstrous regimes, and world conflagrations, and the miseries and violence inflicted by the powerful on the less so; and the vast domains of mythological and religious writings, Western and beyond, including by such dissident groups as the Gnostics and, after reading Schopenhauer, engaging further with the Buddha's thought as evident from his citing Gautama's 'folle sagesse' (mad wisdom), a few years before the mime, in a postwar piece of art criticism in French (untranslated) that chimes with the postwar resurgence of interest by Western artists in Buddhist thought (*Dis* 146–7). (See Chapter 4.)

The transtextual contact with this wealth of material is shaped by what, in contemporary cognitive terms, the inheritors of the pragmatics of American philosopher Charles Sanders Pierce (1839–1914) term the 'distributed cognition' between minds that occurs in the interpretation of a sender's externalized, or extended, signs into all forms of discourse and artefactual models. Emphasized in pragmatics is that understanding such discourse requires as a first step an overlap of contextual information between sender and receiver, the awareness of an author's cognitive environment thereby making accessible to readers elements that otherwise would remain opaque. To that end, this study engages at some length

---

[6] Born in 1906 in Foxrock, a prosperous Protestant suburb of Dublin, Beckett, as is well known, resided in Paris in 1928–30 and then permanently from 1937 to his death in 1989, accounting, in addition to his education, for his awareness of and engagement with political, cultural, and intellectual developments in France, while maintaining his Irish citizenship and interest in the Irish equivalents as well as in European and world affairs.

with the Eastern thinking and mystical, or spiritual, writings with which Beckett and other modernists of the times were intersecting.[7] In bringing their own cognitive and imaginative environment to such overlapping contexts, every new generation of readers creates different understandings of works such as those by Beckett, who invented techniques to leave much undetermined and open to recontextualization.

Because there has been a tendency in Beckett studies, although not universally shared, and contested by Beckett himself, to focus on finitude and exclude forms of transcendence (theistic or nontheistic) in his writing, this study counters this view by drawing attention to his reiterated explorations of a tentative 'beyond' and 'a way out' in his texts, drafts, letters, and conversations. Thus, in a 1960 letter, he speaks of resurrecting the Proustian 'ideal real', which he analyzed in his 1931 essay on Marcel Proust. For Beckett, in 1960, the writer's task to view 'the "real" of the human predicament' from an ideal and timeless vantage point remains valid. In his early essay, Beckett qualified the resulting 'ideal real' as a 'mystical experience' mingling finitude, or the empirical, with the ideal and the imaginative (*LSB III* 377; *P* 55, 56). (See Chapter 2.) Accordingly, in this study, Beckett's staging of finitude and the 'real' of human dramas, both outer and inner, is investigated along with his simultaneous timeless and imaginative viewpoint in affinity with the Buddha's and mystical thinking. In fact, Beckett consistently produced contrapuntal texts in which four dimensions simultaneously reverberate: the outer world with inner and other worlds concurrently with metareflection on the medium of transmission.[8]

Still adhering to the double vantage point of the 'ideal real' in the last decade of his life, Beckett confided that the excitement of writing for him was a combination of 'metaphysics and technique' (qtd. in Shainberg 1987, 134). Because the word 'metaphysics' startles, as it seemingly did Shainberg who asked for an explanation, Beckett replied that you have to draw on your own experience (134). In this regard, in his 1965 lectures inquiring into the possibility of metaphysics after the horrors of the

---

[7] On 'distributed cognition', see Magnani 2009, xiv, xv, 43–4. Further, the explorations of hypothesis formation by Lorenzo Magnani, a philosopher of cognition, help to engage with the current controversies in Beckett studies on the topic of hypothesis falsification. Counter Popperian neopositivistic rules, Magnani recommends the more current 'negation as falsification', in which hypotheses are discarded in favor of others that prove to be more explanatory when new information or discoveries come to light (Magnani 2009, 98, 415).

[8] Beckett drew on the ancient and Dantean fourfold method of exegesis in his 1929 essay on Joyce's future *Finnegans Wake* and in his 1931 lectures at Trinity College. For further details on Beckett's adaption of this method, see Moorjani 2008, 123–5.

Holocaust, Hiroshima, and ongoing tortures, Theodor Adorno main-tained that 'the dramas of Beckett ... seem to me the only truly relevant metaphysical productions since the war' (Adorno 2000b, 117).[9] And that is, Adorno argues, because after the war 'metaphysics has slipped into material existence' in the form of wretched physicality (117). Similar to Beckett's reaffirmation of the 'ideal real' merging the empirical and the ideal and imaginary, Adorno sees in Beckett's postwar works the mise en scène of the decay and filth of finitude, on the one hand, and, on the other, the turning away from the traditional affirmative theses of metaphysics to the question of 'what nothingness actually contains; the question, one might almost say, of a topography of the void' (2000b, 135–6). For Adorno, metaphysics involves a thinking beyond one's entrapment in finitude and language into an 'openness' (2000b, 68). Agreeing with Adorno, specialist in philosophical and political theory Anna-Verena Nosthoff finds behind the radical negativity in Beckett's works 'a metaphysical remainder' corresponding to an open question (Nosthoff 2018, 49).

Emilie Morin's *Beckett's Political Imagination* (2017) provides over-whelming evidence of Beckett's actions protesting war, oppression, and torture in the political arena of his time and the imaginative ways he found of alluding indirectly to political terror in his writing. Once uncovered in this unsettling book, beyond what was already known, Beckett's political engagement and allusions, which he kept hidden no less than the meta-physical, render increasingly comprehensible the necessity Beckett expressed for an elsewhere from which to contemplate, though not with-out humor, the 'human predicament' at its most hellish and unbearable.

Dialogue with other exegetes and thinkers who have wrestled with Beckett's texts is an important part of this study in preparation for the new readings proposed. Additionally, the question of how much back-ground to include for the anticipated readers of this book was a constant concern. Envisioned is a readership similar to the audience at the 2016 Samuel Beckett Summer School at Trinity College Dublin, consist-ing of undergraduate and graduate students and scholars of Beckett and other fields as well as nonacademic participants with varied backgrounds whose interest in Beckett led to their traveling from around the world to participate in the Trinity program. After my lecture on the topic, the

---

[9] Adorno's transcribed and edited 1965 lectures on metaphysics at the University of Frankfurt were first published in 1998, followed by an English translation two years later.

interest this diverse audience expressed in further exploration of the relation between Beckett and Buddhism is the impetus behind this study.

This book, then, is intended for an academic and nonacademic audience intrigued by one of the most iconic writers of modernism and postmodernism and the extraordinary legacy and ongoing reverberations of his oeuvre across a global cultural field. The astonishing techniques Beckett invented to present his vision in prose, poetry, and drama in several media, which have already added to the global appeal of his creative works and their resonance in the performance and visual arts as well as the literary, will no doubt lead to further dramatic renewals in these domains. It can be anticipated that productions of Beckett's plays and adaptations of his work in other art forms, such as the one-act opera *Fin de partie* by György Kurtág, premiered in 2018 at La Scala, could increasingly be inflected by the new readings proposed in this study. Such was, for instance, the renewed attention paid to Richard Wagner's blending of Buddhist concepts into his operas under the influence of Schopenhauer, which resulted in the New York Metropolitan Opera's 2013 production of *Parsifal*, whose Canadian director François Girard was attentive to both the Christian and Buddhist intertexts serving to intensify the production's spiritual effects. That, for Beckett, such effects are desirable is evident in a number of comments he made about the arts, remarking, for instance, that Franz Schubert's music is 'more pure spirit than that of any other composer' (qtd. in Zilliacus 1976, 38) and commenting to Patrick Bowles: 'People are not in touch with their spirit. What counts is the *spirit*' (qtd. in Bowles 2006, 110; emphasis in the original). Similar effects can be anticipated in the ongoing affiliations of popular culture and new media with Beckett's oeuvre.[10]

Although there is much in this study to engage the attention of an audience alert to the exploration of religion in modernist/postmodernist texts, the book's primary focus is, rather than on the practice of religion, on the influence of the Buddha's thought and its interactions with other domains of religious and philosophical thinking. This study, then, aligns itself more closely with the philosophy of religion, the comparative history of thought, and the explorations of a nontheistic transcendence that Beckett shared with other modernist thinkers and artists under the tutelage

---

[10] See Paul Stewart and David Pattie's 2019 collection of articles, *Pop Beckett: Intersections with Popular Culture*.

of Schopenhauer's relay of Eastern thought.[11] Mindful of the interest of a broader audience in the East–West interconnections between Buddhist thought and comparative religious, literary, performance, and cultural studies, my concern was to make available the necessary contextual information for an engagement with the transtextual elements investigated throughout. As a result, unavoidably, readers acquainted with the fields under scrutiny may find more background information than they need, whereas nonspecialists in one or the other domain may wish for more. My aim was to adhere to a middle path of neither too much nor too little.

To return to Beckett's 'I know nothing about Buddhism', what is one to make of this declaration of ignorance? Knowing nothing is a claim frequently made by Beckett (and his creatures, often quite comically). At the time, for instance, of preproduction rehearsals of *En attendant Godot*, destined to become one of the most celebrated plays of the twentieth century, its author claimed that he knew nothing about the theatre (*LSB II* 316).[12] No doubt Beckett's knowing nothing can be understood in terms of the ignorance born of knowledge, the *docta ignorantia* of mystics and philosophers, including Buddhist thinkers. About Buddhism in *Act without Words I*, Beckett, however, tempered his assertion of ignorance by adding: 'If [Buddhism is] present in the play, it is unbeknownst to me.' In fact, that 'there had always been more in the work than he'd suspected was there' is an admission Beckett made, at age seventy-eight, to Shainberg on another occasion (Shainberg 1987, 133). The implication of unintentionally inscribed elements in creative work, which has always mystified writers, poets, and artists, and which is the subject of current investigations by philosophers and cognitive scientists, is probed in Chapter 6.

There are other possible ways of understanding Beckett's expression of ignorance and the 'unbeknownst to me'. 'Voluntary amnesia' is one scholar's alternative explanation for Beckett's protests of forgetfulness about the intertexts in his writings. Coining the terms 'voluntary' and 'involuntary' amnesia on the model of Proust's two types of memory, Thomas Cousineau argues that in order to deter scholars and audiences from focusing too exclusively on the sources he keeps hidden, Beckett makes use of voluntary amnesia to redirect attention to his own reshaping of the elements he chooses to echo (Cousineau n.d., n.p.). Similarly,

---

[11] See Professor of Philosophy and Religion Charlene Spretnak's *The Spiritual Dynamic in Modern Art* (2014, chs. 4–6).

[12] *En attendant Godot* (*Waiting for Godot*), written in 1948–9, was first performed in Paris on 5 January 1953.

Beckett's future biographer James Knowlson had earlier detected Beckett's fear that audiences will by their attention to his sources be less engaged with his imaginative use of quotations for his own dramatic ends (Knowlson 1983, 23–4). In conversations in the early 1960s with Lawrence Harvey, however, Beckett admitted his tendency to proffer red herrings to his readers and audiences to put them off the trail: 'Of course, I say my life has nothing to do with my work, but of course it does' (qtd. in Harvey 2006, 136). Could it not be likewise, 'Of course, I say I know nothing about the theatre, about Buddhism, but of course I do'? Not to be excluded, though, is that the anxiety of influence contributed to the frequency with which Beckett denied his sources. Whatever the case may be, Beckett was protecting his art of indirectness and his crafty ways of misleading critics and readers to prevent his work from being tied down to ready meanings that put an end to dialogue with his work. This study is intended to prolong the dialogue.

If 'involuntary amnesia' is a possibility, Beckett's remark about knowing nothing about Buddhism coming twenty-five years after the work in question, it is highly unlikely, given obvious allusions to Eastern thought in between. His recognition of the significance attached to resignation in Eastern thinking, for instance, is apparent from the line in *Comment c'est / How It Is* (French, 1961; English, 1964), which is dictated to the fiction's narrating voice: 'an oriental my dream he has renounced I too will renounce I will have no more desires' (*How* 56). Moreover, Buddhist echoes have been identified not only in *Act without Words I* but in *Fin de partie* (1957; English *Endgame*, 1958) with which it was originally performed on a double bill and published in one volume. As a matter of fact, Beckett considered the mime a 'codicil' of sorts to the longer play, in which the characters Hamm and Clov are locked in a conflict of wills (*LSB III* 64). Frequently either directing *Fin de partie / Endgame* or assisting with its direction (in several languages), it is unlikely that Beckett would have forgotten the Buddhist echoes that sound throughout the play.

In his essay on *Fin de partie*'s Buddhist resonance, Emmanuel Jacquart contends that Hamm renounces at the end, as literally stated in the stage directions: '*Hamm renonce*', translated as '*Hamm gives up*' (*Fin* 110; *End* 82; Jacquart 1997, 36). Hamm comments as much by interrupting the story he is composing with the words: 'Moments for nothing, now as always, time was never and time is over, reckoning closed and story ended' (*End* 83). Jacquart associates Hamm's renouncing with the Buddhist concept of a no-self, a fluctuating and illusory collection of physical and mental processes, whose emptiness corresponds to the emptying out at the end of *Fin de partie*. Hamm, for him, follows Buddhism's teaching of detachment from the world and from the desires that make suffering inevitable (Jacquart 1997, 36). To these arguments one can add Hamm's 'moments for nothing' that suggest Buddhist emptiness and its paradoxical view of time, an absolute timelessness ('time was never') coexisting with the linear time of finitude ('time is over'). In the play, Hamm thus proceeds from his opening question – 'Can there be misery – (*he yawns*) – loftier than mine? No doubt'. (*End* 2) – to his renouncing and discarding his connections with the world. With all forms of life, sustenance, and comfort depleted in the shelter or refuge in the skull, Hamm throws away his remaining possessions, his gaff, stuffed dog, and whistle of command. Hamm's gesture resonates with Schopenhauer's denial of the will to life, which, for him, precedes a *nirvāṇa*-like liberation from existence. (See Chapters 1 and 2.)

Unbeknownst or not to the author, audiences and critics have caught Buddhist resonances in both the mime and the play it follows as a codicil. Suggesting an echo that could be both Eastern and Christian Quietist, Beckett explained to Ernst Schroeder, who played Hamm in the 1967 Berlin production under Beckett's direction, that Hamm and Clov 'are both focused on quiet and inner contemplation, but one of them is always disturbing the other' (qtd. in McMillan and Fehsenfeld 1988, 238). As we have seen, such is also the case in *Act without Words I*, in which the contemplation of the figure, identified by Beckett as 'Clov thrown into the desert' (qtd. in *LSB III* 65, n. 3), is continuously disturbed by whistled interruptions.[13] Further, the desert setting of Beckett's mime recalls the increasingly barren setting of *Endgame* as well as Schopenhauer's musings on the feelings of the sublime evoked by the vastness of deserts eclipsing human interests (*WWR I* § 39, 228). In this sense, 'Clov thrown into the desert' echoes Hamm's lines in *Endgame*: 'you'll be like a little bit of grit in the middle of the steppe' or 'a speck in the void' (*End* 36). (For Beckett's adoption of the trope of the desert as a figure of emptiness, see the discussion of *Le Dépeupleur / The Lost Ones* in Chapter 5.)

Was it perhaps similarly voluntary amnesia and/or the anxiety of influence when 'unbeknownst to me' was Arthur Schopenhauer's claim about the influence of Buddhism on his major work *The World as Will and Representation* when it was first published in 1818, a claim coming, like Beckett's, a quarter of a century after composition of the work in question?

---

[13] In the earlier novel *Murphy*, the eponymous character is similarly interrupted while in a meditative trance (*Mu* ch. 1).

In both cases, was it then purely a matter of affinity as Schopenhauer continuously affirmed?

'Affinity', as I will use the term, implies a transtextual relation along the lines of of Ludwig Wittgenstein's 'family resemblances'. In his *Philosophical Investigations*, inquiring what the many types of games have in common to justify the use of the same word for them, Wittgenstein remarks on the similarities and differences between one game and another, asserting that there is nothing to be found that is common to all games, but rather, 'similarities, relationships, and a whole series of them at that'. As a result, he maintains, 'we see a complicated network of similarities overlapping and criss-crossing: sometimes overall similarities, sometimes similarities of detail', and he compares these to resemblances among members of a human family. For him, games 'form a family' (Wittgenstein 1958 [1953], § 66 and § 67). He goes on to compare the investigation of family resemblances to the spinning of a thread in which fiber is twisted on fiber, explaining that, 'the strength of the thread does not reside in the fact that some one fibre runs its whole length, but in the overlapping of many fibres' (§ 67).

Adopting Wittgenstein's apt textile metaphor for the similarities Schopenhauer claimed for his own thought and that of the Buddha and the Christian Neoplatonic Eckhart,[14] this study ventures to associate Beckett's texts with theirs to form a family whose resemblances correspond to the Wittgensteinian crisscrossing and overlapping of similarities, with each strand strengthening the thread of my argument. Yet, despite resemblances among family members or, in Wittgenstein's example, between a game of chess and 'ring-a-ring-a-roses', it is obvious that not all members of a family resemble each other in the same way – there is no one fiber running the length of the thread – so that there are marked differences that do not negate the crisscrossing resemblances. My special emphasis is on the Buddhist thought that is twined into Beckett's texts, interwoven with those of the other two members of the family of thinkers whose overlapping strands of thought make up the thread winding through this study.

There is still another possible way of approaching Beckett's relationship with Buddhist thinking, that is, the insertion of all work in a 'system of relays', as Gilles Deleuze defined the intertextual imbrication of any work

---

[14] Neoplatonism, the idealist philosophical school active in Greco-Roman late antiquity, roughly from the third to the seventh century CE, is known to have considerably influenced Christian theology and Western philosophical thought. Neoplatonic teachings emphasize the priority of mind and a belief in a single higher principle, either divine or the 'One'.

in a number of fields. For Deleuze, then, 'the only true criticism is comparative' across fields (Deleuze 2000 [1986], 367). In other words, could it be a matter of the unmistakable imprints that other fields leave on a work, recognized or not? Most likely, as we shall see, all three – influence, affinity or family resemblances, and relay – are at work in a varied hybrid mix.

To avoid the problem and seemingly unaware of Schopenhauer's transmission of Buddhism to the West, or not giving it heed, most early commentators who explored the Buddhist resonances in Beckett's oeuvre avoided attributing an interest in or knowledge of Buddhist thought to him. My approach is different. As already noted, Beckett, who read Schopenhauer's major works as early as 1930, came under the influence of the German philosopher's passionate embrace of Buddhism as did other major writers, philosophers, musicians, and artists in the late nineteenth and early twentieth centuries. A close analysis of motifs derived from Schopenhauer's transmission of Eastern thought, intertwined with Christian mysticism, sheds light on Beckett's works from the earliest to the last as well as on the works of other modernists similarly influenced.

Much of the evidence concerning Beckett's Buddhist allusions, however, was either unavailable or not easily accessible to early exegetes: Beckett's first novel *Dream of Fair to Middling Women* (*Dream*) and the short story 'Echo's Bones' were published posthumously in 1992 and 2014 respectively; the untranslated piece on Henri Hayden, written in 1952 in French, in which Beckett uses the Buddha's *folle sagesse* (mad wisdom) to discuss Hayden's painting, became readily available only in the 1986 *Disjecta*; and scholars had to wait until the mid-1990s to 2016 to have access to carefully researched biographies, the four volumes of Beckett's letters, an extensive account of the books remaining in his library, and archival riches, including student lecture notes of the courses he taught; his notebooks and reading notes on literature, history, philosophy, science, and psychology and psychoanalysis; his German diaries of the 1930s; and many of the drafts of his works. Without these, my arguments and claims in this study could have been neither formulated nor substantiated. To this treasure trove and the 'archival turn' in Beckett studies and other disciplines must be added the reawakening of philosophical interest in Schopenhauer in the latter part of the twentieth century, the research uncovering his extensive knowledge of Indian thought, and the numerous scholarly studies that began to appear on Mahāyāna Buddhism – the movement of principal interest to Schopenhauer – at about the same time. My plumbing of these recent sources resulted in a broader and deeper engagement with the Buddhist-related strands in Beckett's texts and their 'reapplications' in his works than was previously possible. (In his 1929 defense of James Joyce's 'Work in Progress', Beckett terms 'reapplications' the use Joyce made of his hidden sources.)

In addition to the books entirely or partly devoted to Beckett and Buddhism, a growing interest in the topic is apparent from the more than fifteen essays on the subject published since the year 2000. Strange as it may seem, most commentators addressing Schopenhauer's influence on Beckett make no reference to Buddhism, and others exploring Beckett's affinities with Buddhism largely ignore the source in Schopenhauer or only briefly acknowledge the philosopher's influence. By way of example, there is no mention of Buddhism or other Eastern thought in Ulrich Pothast's frequently cited *Metaphysical Vision: Arthur Schopenhauer's Philosophy of Art and Life and Samuel Beckett's Way to Make Use of It*, an expanded 2008 version of his study first published in German in the 1980s. On the other hand, Schopenhauer receives barely a nod by the three authors of book-length examinations of Zen parallels in Beckett: Paul Foster (1989), John Leeland Kundert-Gibbs (1999), and Junko Matoba (2003). The same can be said of authors that engage in their books with Buddhist reverberations in Beckett's writing: Paul Davies (1994, 2000) and Sandra Wynands (2007). In an earlier study of 1976, *Samuel Beckett and the Pessimistic Tradition*, however, Steven Rosen investigates both Schopenhauer and Buddhism's influence on Beckett's 1931 *Proust* essay, but he does so in separate chapters. Schopenhauer gets short shrift as well in what appears to be the earliest perusal of Buddhist threads in Beckett's works. In his *Beckett*, a slim volume dating from 1964, Richard N. Coe expresses his doubt about the philosopher's influence on the author (Coe 1970 [1964], 17). Defending the view that Beckett is foremost a Cartesian, Coe, who maintains that 'Beckett does no more than toy with Oriental thought', nevertheless proposes provocative Buddhist readings of several of Beckett's texts (26–7). Thirty years later, while acknowledging Beckett's knowledge of Eastern thought, his biographer James Knowlson notes the speculation by scholars on how he may have acquired it, without advancing the likelihood of Schopenhauer (Knowlson 1996, 675, n. 141). In articles appearing over the past ten years or so, however, Schopenhauer as a source of Beckett's knowledge of Buddhism is becoming increasingly recognized, if not explored in depth.[15]

---

[15] In his 2020 book *Still: Samuel Beckett's Quietism*, Andy Wimbush investigates Beckett's knowledge of Indian thought by way of Schopenhauer more extensively than the earlier authors referred to

Of the three book-length studies of Beckett and Buddhism to date that focus on Zen Buddhism, Paul Foster's study examines Beckett's postwar trilogy of novels and *How It Is*, whereas the other two concentrate on Beckett's theatre. As his title intimates, *Beckett and Zen: A Study of Dilemma in the Novels of Samuel Beckett*, Foster limits his 1989 study to the predicaments facing Beckett's characters from the viewpoint of the first two of the Buddha's four noble truths – universal suffering and its origin in craving – but from which Beckett, Foster contends, offers no way out. In his 1999 book *No-Thing Is Left to Tell: Zen/Chaos Theory in the Dramatic Art of Samuel Beckett*, John Leeland Kundert-Gibbs likens Beckett's plays to Zen koans – paradoxical riddles, 'with no rational entrance or exit', as he puts it – that serve to jolt Zen initiates, or, in Beckett's case, audiences, out of their usual frame of mind in the interest of liberation from *doxa*, or received and habitual belief, to attain enlightenment (Kundert-Gibbs 1999, 178). In the most recent of the three, the impressive *Beckett's Yohaku: A Study of Samuel Beckett's Empty Space on Stage in His Later Shorter Plays* (2003), Japanese scholar Junko Matoba explores the affinity between Beckett's empty space in his late work for the stage and the empty space (*yohaku*) in Zen ink painting.[16]

Of the two other authors that comment at some length in their books on Beckett's fiction and theatre from a Buddhist perspective, Paul Davies, in his *Beckett and Eros: Death of Humanism*, argues that Beckett's questioning of self and world and his imaginative explorations of the psyche are congruent with the insights of Dzogchen and Vajrayāna Buddhism of the Tibetan tradition of Mahāyāna (Davies 2000, 54–5). In this study and his earlier *The Ideal Real: Beckett's Fiction and Imagination* (1994), Davies focuses on Beckett's creative imagination by engaging with poetic and mystic traditions and by plumbing Buddhist parallels that illuminate his writing.[17] In her *Iconic Spaces: The Dark Theology of Samuel Beckett's Drama* (2007), Sandra Wynands analyzes Beckett's *Film* and several of his late plays in a sophisticated blend of Buddhist thought on emptiness, negative theology, and modern/postmodern philosophy.

Even if Schopenhauer as the source of Beckett's knowledge of Buddhism is being increasingly acknowledged, without the awareness of the recent archival and other investigations of Schopenhauer's knowledge

---

above. His book having appeared too late for substantial engagement with it in this study, discussion is limited to a number of notes drawing attention to the Buddhist elements Wimbush reviews in Beckett's prose fictions.

[16] See also Matoba 2000.   [17] See also Davies 2001.

of Eastern thought, some Beckett exegetes continue to accept the earlier tendency to question Schopenhauer as a viable source of Buddhist philosophy. My first chapter addresses this doubt in detailing the recent archival findings and in drawing attention to the judgment of scholars of Buddhism on this question. In the same chapter, a section on Schopenhauer's understanding of Upanishadic and Buddhist concepts should set aside doubts about his ability to distinguish between the two. The brief survey of what these two systems of Indian thought share and where they part ways is intended to lessen the chance of mistaking one for the other or singling out one when it could be either. My example of such a mistaken identity at the end of the first chapter is intended as a cautionary tale.

The second chapter explores in more detail the Buddhist concepts, conveyed by Schopenhauer, infusing Western culture in the late nineteenth and early twentieth century. Focusing on the Beckett of the 1930s and writers and artists with whom he was conversant, this chapter chronicles the reverberations of the Buddha and Schopenhauer's teachings in their works. Subsequent sections consider the analogies that are evident for Schopenhauer between Eastern and Western mysticism, between the Buddha and Meister Eckhart's teachings in particular, resulting in Beckett's allusions throughout his oeuvre, over six decades, to both Buddhist and Christian Neoplatonic thought. The Buddha and Schopenhauer's two-world view of the empirical and the metaphysical serves to interrogate nihilistic interpretations of the Buddhist absolute and to focus closely on Schopenhauer's rescue of *nirvāṇa* from such misreadings. A short disquisition on the unknowable and silence, values Beckett shared with Eastern and Western thinkers, concludes this chapter.

Continuing the investigations of Beckett's first novel *Dream of Fair to Middling Women*, posthumously published in 1992, the third chapter probes in greater detail the family resemblances (in the Wittgensteinian sense) between *Dream*'s creative asylum and space of writing in the mind and Buddhist and Christian mystical thought. Further examined, beginning with his first novel, are the forerunners of Beckett's aesthetics of emptiness and creation from nothing. The chapter's discussion of the 1933 short story 'Echo's Bones', posthumously published in 2014 and the final story about the author's fictional persona Belacqua, uncovers the Buddhist allusions kept out of sight by the story's burlesque drift. In contrast, the chapter's reading of *Murphy* counters some commentators' Buddhist analysis of Beckett's second novel. This chapter concludes the investigation of Beckett's fiction of the 1930s in relation to Schopenhauer's relay of Eastern thought.

With the fourth chapter, the focus pivots from the introductory investigation of the major Buddhist and mystic concepts Beckett secreted into his early fictions, to engage with the paradoxical, aporetic (insoluble), and apophatic (negative) procedures of his writing and their disorienting effects on audiences. The chapter begins by examining Beckett's involvement with what he himself qualified as the Buddha's *folle sagesse* (mad wisdom) (*Dis* 146). Further, interrogating Mādhyamika philosopher Nāgārjuna's paradoxical logic serves to examine Beckett's similar challenges to the principles of noncontradiction. Introducing the Mādhyamika view of language as a veil that keeps us from experiencing *śūnyatā*, or emptiness, the chapter's second section reexamines Beckett's proposed 'literature of the unword' and the controversy raging about the influence of Fritz Mauthner's Indian-tinged nominalism on Beckett's critique of language. Beckett's commonalities with the French literature of silence of the 1940s and an exploration of Beckett's paradoxical ethics of emptiness bring this chapter to an end.

The second half of the book launches into the heady task of reading Beckett's postwar and late texts from the perspective of the Buddhist concepts and interrelated domains of thought probed in the first half. Certain recurring topics such as the no-self and dissociative voices in Beckett's fiction and drama are further examined by calling on the insights of contemporary philosophers of mind and cognitive scientists in their affinity with Buddhist thought. Chapters 5 through 8 thus investigate some of the most elusive aspects of Beckett's oeuvre by attending to the occluded transtextual strands twined into his texts and his inventive techniques to reposition his audiences from the known to the unknown.

Extending the previous chapter's exploration of Beckett's embrace of contradiction, Chapter 5 investigates the dynamic blend of contraries, among which are laughter and weeping and, most insistently, birth and death. Further examined is Beckett's adoption of the posthumous voice in his four postwar *nouvelles* of 1946 and his subsequent fictions and dramas. The chapter argues that the life-in-death ghostliness of Beckett's spectral voices and the harrowing tales they tell to attain peace in the mind are analogous to the Buddhist purgatorial dramas of Japanese dream noh. This art form, it is claimed, provided a channel for Beckett's indirect postwar witnessing. Beginning with the *nouvelles*, this chapter introduces Beckett's visions of an 'elsewhere' or 'a way out', further pursued in the 1961 radio play *Cascando*, staging the author's mind fashioning the play and distilling the postwar fiction's explorations of an 'elsewhere', a topos taken up in the imaginative cylinder-world of *Le Dépeupleur / The Lost Ones* of 1970.

In Chapter 6, the parallels with the Buddhist no-self and dream noh's purgatorial telling of traumatic life stories are pursued in an in-depth analysis of Beckett's 1972 play *Not I*. Explored is the startling dramatic situation of a spotlit Mouth converging with the 'mouth on fire' of the old woman telling the tale of woe that is echoing through her. Analyzed in detail are the two conflicting voices ventriloquizing the onstage Mouth and the role of the Auditor listening to the ghostly speaker's tale and the need for forgiveness pouring out of Mouth. Of the two conflicting voices, the inner storytelling voice is linked to earlier scenes of the dispossession of Beckett's narrators by voices whose dissociative nature is investigated in light of the findings by cognitive scientists that counter claims identifying such voices as 'schizoid'. The second interfering voice is tied to the social scripts that, for postmodern thinkers, serve to ventriloquize and eclipse subjects and authors, an eclipse resonating with the Buddhist no-self doctrine. The chapter concludes with the discussion of two of Beckett's late plays situated in the liminal space between life and death – *That Time* and *Ohio Impromptu* – in which the emptying out of memories results in resignation and the solace of going into timelessness and mindlessness congruent with Buddhist *śūnyatā* (emptiness) and Zen 'no-mind'.

The three sections of Chapter 7 explore (1) the collapse of the birth and death contraries, (2) the rebirth topos, and (3) the Buddhist doctrine of the *unborn*. The first section concentrates on *A Piece of Monologue* of the late 1970s, noting its allusions to cycles of rebirth and scenes of wall gazing and repeated evocations of a 'beyond' that resonate with Schopenhaueriran will-lessness and Buddhist scriptures. In the second section, which reflects on the drama of rebirth throughout Beckett's writings, allusions to a Schopenhauerian hellish existence are linked to parallels between Dantean and Buddhist conceptions of hell and purgatory. In contrast, the last pages of the 1981 *Mal vu mal dit / Ill Seen Ill Said* are seen to allude to an end to rebirth in a coming home to the void via detachment from illusion. This chapter's third and longest section concerns the family resemblances between the Beckettian theme of unbornness and the Buddhist doctrine of an original and immanent state of mind beyond birth and death.

Chapter 8 takes up Beckett's poetics of elsewhere in which, as intimated in two of his late poems, the impression of going 'where never before' is contradicted by the feeling of having always been there. Because Beckett's texts dating from the last decade of his life allude to his entire writing career in the manner of the life reviews he lends many of his creatures, a close scrutiny of three of Beckett's works dating from this period – his penultimate play (for television) *Nacht und Träume* (Night and Dreams), his final prose piece *Stirrings Still*, and his last poem 'Comment dire' / 'What Is the Word' – permits the appraisal of many of the elements investigated in the previous chapters. Finally, this concluding chapter, reiterating his engagement with the philosophical, religious, and mystic traditions on which he drew throughout his career, argues for Beckett's strong consonance with the Buddha's teachings that he first learned from Schopenhauer. Hence the persona of *Stirrings Still*, immersed in meditative mindlessness beyond thought, hears the whispered call for going into an elsewhere, where he has always been, beyond grasping, beyond 'time and grief and self so-called' (*CSP* 265). The chapter explores Beckett's clearest and final homage to the Buddha's teachings.

CHAPTER I

Schopenhauer's Buddhism Revisited: Recent Archival Evidence

What the Archives Tell Us about Schopenhauer's Knowledge of Buddhism

Schopenhauer's interest in Buddhism was aroused when translations of ancient Brahmanic and Buddhist texts became available at the end of the eighteenth century, causing considerable intellectual excitement among European thinkers, who hailed the event as the coming of a new Renaissance based on Eastern wisdom.[1] They were not far off the mark. An astonishing number of philosophers, writers, musicians, artists, psychologists and analysts were influenced by or took up the relay of this rediscovery of Eastern thought and, what is more, by Schopenhauer's transmission of it. However, by the time Beckett came to the attention of the wider scholarly community in the early 1950s, the early enthusiasm for the Eastern Renaissance had waned without disappearing, awaiting its revival toward the end of the twentieth century.[2]

At the time, Schopenhauer had this to say in the 1844 second edition of *The World as Will and Representation*, published twenty-six years after the first edition of 1818:

> If I wished to take the results of my philosophy as the standard of truth, I would have to privilege Buddhism above all other religions. I am pleased in any case to see that my doctrines are in such profound agreement with a

---

[1] The term 'Brahmanism', used by Schopenhauer in his works, was coined in the early nineteenth century to refer to a stage following Vedism and preceding Hinduism, which dates to roughly the first half of the first millennium BCE. The term is thought to derive from the belief in the ultimate reality *brahman* and from the status of the priestly Brahman class. The term is still in use today.

[2] By the 1940s in France, Hegel, as theorized in Alexandre Kojève's lectures, Nietzsche, and Heidegger captivated the imagination of the Parisian intelligentsia, resulting in an eclipse of Schopenhauerian influence. Exegetes have traced the presence of the newly influential philosophers in Beckett's writing, whether in a mocking mode (Kojève) or not, as he remained up to date with intellectual trends in the French capital throughout his writing life. As evident in this study, his engagement with Schopenhauer and Eastern thought nevertheless continued unabated to the end.

religion followed by the majority of people on earth . . .. This agreement is all the more satisfying because I was certainly not influenced by it in my philosophizing. Until 1818, when my work appeared, there was very little information in Europe about Buddhism, and that little was itself very incomplete and problematic. (*WWR II* ch. 17, 178)

Most later commentators took Schopenhauer at his word, but not Urs App, a Swiss scholar of Buddhism, who, beginning in the 1990s, set out to document Schopenhauer's early access to Buddhism by studying the philosopher's unpublished manuscript notebooks, lists of publications he borrowed from lending libraries, and his annotated texts and books on Eastern thought in the Schopenhauer-Archive in Frankfurt.

How do the archival findings about Schopenhauer's knowledge of Buddhism call into question Beckett's claim of knowing nothing about Buddhism? While still in Paris in July and August 1930, on completing his two years as *lecteur* at the École Normale Supérieure, Beckett read *The World as Will and Representation* and essays in the later collection of Schopenhauer's philosophical writings *Parerga and Paralipomena* before getting down to writing his *Proust* monograph, with its partly Schopenhauerian reading and quotations derived from the above two works. On returning to Dublin to teach at Trinity College that fall, he began to write his first novel *Dream of Fair to Middling Women* (*Dream*) shortly thereafter. My claim is that in this early Beckett fiction and in the jettisoned story 'Echo's Bones', we find the first of the Beckettian figural mindscapes, the oxymoronic tomblike womb and womblike tomb, which is imaginatively modeled on the timeless before- and afterlife that Schopenhauer borrowed from Indian thought. Other writers and artists had equally come under the spell of this metaphysical space containing the unborn and the dead, which, they identified, as did Beckett, with the wellspring of their art.

We know that Beckett was never to lose interest in Schopenhauer. His six-volume German edition of the philosopher's works remained in his personal library until his death (Van Hulle and Nixon 2013, 144). He must have dipped into it as late as 1979 or 1980, judging by the eight Schopenhauer quotations in German he entered into his 'Sottisier' note-book at the time.[3] And a few months before his death, he advised the Spanish Beckett scholar Antonia Rodríguez-Gago to tell her daughter, who was studying philosophy, to read Schopenhauer (Rodríguez-Gago 2017,

---

[3] My citations of the 'Sottisier' notebook – UoR MS 2901 – give the dates of the entries as noted on consulting the notebook in Reading.

24). Finally, throughout his writing career spanning six decades, there are allusions to Schopenhauerian concepts in his fiction and drama.

Tracing Beckett's allusions to Buddhism in his early fiction, following closely on his reading of Schopenhauer, helps to extend our understanding of his later writings. If most of the early excursions into Beckett and Buddhism cautiously favored establishing affinities without claiming influence, recent research permits balancing congruence with evidence of contact with Buddhism, especially in Beckett's reading and rereading of Schopenhauer. The Buddhism Beckett and other writers and artists found in Schopenhauer thus becomes of particular significance to understanding their works in new ways.

App's archival discoveries, which are putting the philosopher's disavowal of Buddhist influence in doubt, help us to ascertain the extent of the Buddhist teachings Beckett and other modernists found in Schopenhauer.[4] App discovered that Arthur Hübscher's 1966 publication in five volumes of Schopenhauer's manuscript remains mostly omits his manuscript notes on Buddhism. In studying the philosopher's notebooks directly in the Frankfurt archive, App uncovered almost fifty pages of notes on Asian religions and cultures taken as early as 1811 in the ethnography course Arnold Heeren taught at Göttingen University, where the then twenty-three-year-old Schopenhauer was studying medicine before switching to philosophy. Schopenhauer in these notes refers to the religions of the Buddha in India, Tibet, China, Burma, and Japan, the Western neologism 'Buddhism' not yet having been coined at the time. Additionally, App found forty-five pages of notes Schopenhauer took on his 1815 readings on Indian thought in the scholarly British journal *Asiatick Researches*. In these notes, Schopenhauer refers to the major Buddhist concepts that were to interest him for the rest of his life and to which he compares his own thought throughout his writings:

(1) Life is suffering (the Buddha's first principle of the four noble truths);
(2) karma (in Buddha's interpretation of this Indian concept, the effects of intentional actions, which result in the cycle of birth, death, and rebirth); .
(3) transmigration;
(4) *nirvāṇa* (the release from suffering and rebirth).

---

[4] The information in this paragraph is taken from App 1998, 37–9, and confirmed in Cross 2013, 37–40.

In addition, in these notes, Schopenhauer underscores the atheism of the followers of the Buddha and emphasizes their impressive ethics, which, in the absence of belief in a creator god, has as its highest ideal an enlightened human being.

If we compare the Buddha's four noble truths at which, in part, Schopenhauer's early notes hint, then astonishing correspondences appear with the 'system' Schopenhauer was in the process of developing:

(1)   Life is suffering.

       With this first truth, Schopenhauer, as is well known, is in full agreement.

(2)   The cause of suffering is the craving thirst that leads to rebirth.

       For Schopenhauer, the craving will to life is the cause of the unhappiness of the world as well as of rebirth.

(3)   The solution is the emancipation from craving.

       In Schopenhauer's philosophy, freedom from suffering follows the denial of the will that gives access to an ineffable existence analogous, for him, to Buddhist *nirvāṇa*.

(4)   An eightfold path leads to a higher wisdom and *nirvāṇa*: right understanding, right intentions, right speech, right action, right livelihood, right effort, right mindfulness, right contemplation.

       Akin to the Buddha's path, Schopenhauer combines the ethics of good conduct with the understanding of the unreality of self and world, while privileging ascetic and artistic contemplation and the compassionate concern for others, the ethical priority of Mahāyāna Buddhism.

Although Mahāyāna, one of the two major schools of Buddhism, dating to around the beginning of the common era, is the school with which Schopenhauer was primarily concerned, he also knew of the older Theravāda tradition.

App's discovery of these early Schopenhauer notes brings to light that several years before Schopenhauer began the composition of his major work in 1816, he knew more about Buddhism than he recalled a quarter of a century later.

Of the two works by Schopenhauer we know Beckett to have read before writing his first novel, *The World as Will and Representation* was first published in one volume in 1818 divided into four books. By its second edition in 1844, it had grown to two volumes, Schopenhauer having added a volume of supplements to the 1818 edition. A third slightly expanded edition appeared in 1859, the year before his death. At the time of each later edition, Schopenhauer added material, clarifications, and notes into both volumes of his major work, a practice resulting in additional insights about the confluence of his and Indian philosophy, and especially Buddhism, as he became increasingly emerged in it, even calling himself a Buddhist at the end of his life (Cross 2013, 47). As App points out, Schopenhauer studied a large part of the major publications on Buddhism of his time in several languages over five decades (App 1998, 36, n. 5). The philosopher's other major work, the 1851 two-volume collection of philosophical essays *Parerga and Paralipomena* consists of further elaborations and additions to his major work, including updated references to Buddhist literature.

As early as 1816, as he began to compose his magnum opus, Schopenhauer confides to his manuscript notebook: 'I admit, moreover, that I do not believe that my teaching could ever have come into being before the Upanishads, Plato and Kant simultaneously cast their rays into one person's mind'.[5] Schopenhauer repeated this claim in so many words in his preface to the first edition of *The World as Will and Representation* (*WWR 1*, 8–9). In assembling the three forerunners to his philosophical idealism, Schopenhauer intimates that their teachings parallel his view of one ultimate metaphysical reality that lies behind the world of appearances. In Schopenhauer's system, the empirical world, as we experience it through our senses and understand it through the concepts of time, space, and causality, is but a construct of our minds – a representation – that appears real to us but is an illusion, a dream, or a shadow world.

The Upanishads, of course, are not Buddhist texts. The Buddha's reform dating from the fifth century BCE overlapped, in part, with an increasing influence of the Upanishads whose composition began roughly two hundred years before the Buddhist era. Important for our topic is that Buddhism shares some of the ideas developed in these religious and philosophical texts commenting on the Vedas of the previous millennium, concepts such as karma, transmigration, and liberation by renouncing the world and calming the mind through deep meditation. The Buddha, in the view of his disciples, however, did not simply accept ideas as he knew them to be in the Upanishads but transformed them in light of his own experience and insights (Kalupahana 1976, 44–5). There are, of course,

---

[5] 'Ich gestehe übrigens, daß ich nicht glaube, daß meine Lehre je hätte entstehn können ehe die Upanischaden, Plato und Kant ihre Strahlen zugleich in eines Menschen Geist werfen konnten.' This remark from Schopenhauer's manuscript remains #623 is quoted in both German and in App's English translation in App 2014, 246. His translation has been slightly amended.

also major differences. Buddhism developed as a corrective to the Vedic emphasis on rituals, sacrifice, and mythology. Specifically, through his teaching of the eightfold path and the middle way, the Buddha enjoined his followers to abstain from the extreme self-mortification practiced by certain Hindu ascetics of his time, a path Gautama had tried and rejected, as well as to avoid the other extreme of sensual self-indulgence.

The difficulty, especially for Western commentators, in recognizing what belongs to Brahmanic and what to Buddhist teachings has led some of them to accuse Schopenhauer of failing to keep Hindu and Buddhist teachings apart, an uncertainty also troubling critical evaluations of Indian thought in Beckett's and other modernist writing. The question is related to how much Buddhism pervades Schopenhauer's thought, a subject of some controversy, and the answer to which the philosopher himself and his commentators and readers were partly unaware. The explanation for this unawareness is to be found in App's archival study of the particular translation of the Upanishads Schopenhauer explored over the four years preceding the publication of *The World as Will and Representation*. It is an amazing tale of crosscultural transmission and the polyphonic or transtextual nature of sources.

Much of Schopenhauer's fascination with Indian thought is based on his over forty-year-long study of the *Oupnek'hat*, a two-volume translation of fifty Upanishads (over one hundred are recognized). Having begun his reading of the *Oupnek'hat* in 1814 (at the age of twenty-six; he was only thirty when the first volume of his major book appeared), he was to write at age sixty-three that it was the consolation of his life and will be of his death (*PP II* § 184, 357). See Figures 1.1 and 1.2.

Why the Upanishads when at this point Schopenhauer had extensively studied books on Buddhism and Buddhist texts and proclaimed himself a Buddhist? App made some astounding discoveries in the Frankfurt archive by paying close attention to Schopenhauer's annotated copy of his favorite book and the notebook he kept on his reading. Its importance, of course, for our topic is that Schopenhauer was in thrall to the *Oupnek'hat* from 1814, a point when he was working out his system of thought. Even though it is not difficult to trace debts to Schopenhauer, my concern is to establish how much of the debt includes Buddhism.

The *Oupnek'hat* (a Persian corruption of the Sanskrit word 'Upanishad') is from all points of view an astonishing book, doubly translated from the original Sanskrit: first into Persian by the seventeenth-century crown

Figure 1.1 Portrait of Arthur Schopenhauer by Ludwig Sigismund Ruhl, 1815, oil on canvas. Schopenhauer Archiv der Stadt- und Universitätsbibliothek Frankfurt am Main.

Figure 1.2 Daguerreotype of Arthur Schopenhauer, 1852. Schopenhauer Archiv der Stadt- und Universitätsbibliothek Frankfurt am Main.

prince Dārā Shikūh, the son of the powerful Mughal emperor Shah Jahan, the builder of the Taj Mahal, and then, a century later, rendered from the prince's Persian first into French and then Latin (at the time, the lingua franca of Europe) by the French scholar A. H. Anquetil-Duperron. His translation into Latin, the first published translation of the Upanishads into a European language, appeared in 1801–2. It is this translation that was in Schopenhauer's possession.

The Muslim Sufi prince Dārā, who celebrated the belief in the all-oneness he found in the world's major religions, had gathered around him a number of Hindu Sanskrit scholars who not only assisted him in his translation but who provided commentary on the Upanishads, commentary that App found to be inflected by the idealism of Mahāyāna Buddhism. How did Buddhist interpretations slip into Hindu commentary? Two Mahāyāna philosophical schools in the second and fourth centuries – the Mādhyamika and the Yogācāra – developed the influential doctrine of a single ultimate reality, holding the phenomenal world as empty or illusory. The latter view influenced Hindu Advaita Vedānta philosophers in later centuries, and in particular Shankara, the eighth-century renowned interpreter of the Upanishads, who subsequently faced accusations of being a crypto-Buddhist.[6] It was Shankara's interpretation that slipped into the *Oupnek'hat* by means of the commentary of Dārā's Hindu collaborators (Cross 2013, 82–6, 88; App 2014, 145). App realized that the *Oupnek'hat* consists of a collage of Sufi-Advaita-Buddhist commentary enmeshed with the Upanishad translations, a Buddhist connection of which Schopenhauer or his commentators could not have been aware. Only about 40 per cent of the *Oupnek'hat* consists of translation, the rest is commentary by Dārā, the Hindu scholars that assisted him, and Anquetil-Duperron, which, because of its interpolated nature, is not always recognizable as a gloss but appears to be part of the translation (App 2014, 289–90). It is, then, the Advaita-Buddhist-inflected gloss that explains Schopenhauer's preference for the *Oupnek'hat* to later translations of the Upanishads directly from the Sanskrit. It is the book he had in mind in pointing to the agreement between his philosophy and the wisdom of the Upanishads. Indeed, it was in 1858, reiterating the consonance between his and Buddhist thought two years before his death, that Schopenhauer jotted into a notebook (as previously noted): 'Buddha, Eckhart and I teach essentially the same thing' (qtd. in App 2014, 25).

App's archival research, then, uncovered the flow of Buddhist teachings into Schopenhauer's notes at the time he was working out his system. The extent of Schopenhauer's knowledge of Buddhism has become increasingly clear from such archival research and scholarly studies, although it should be apparent to any reader paying attention to Schopenhauer's writing, in which his references to Buddhism are documented in the text and in footnotes, including page numbers, and in which he gives at one point an annotated bibliography of Buddhist texts and scholarly books on the subject in German, English, and French, stating that these are in his possession and would be useful to readers interested in a closer acquaintance with Buddhism.[7] Although throughout the literature on Schopenhauer and Buddhism there are repeated claims of his making superficial or faulty use of Buddhist thought, serious scholars of both Indian philosophy and Schopenhauer, from the second half of the twentieth century onward, on the basis of archival research and the growing

---

[6] Advaita Vedānta is the Hindu school of philosophy recognized for its interpretation of Upanishadic thought, especially as taught by Shankara (Cross 2013, 5). The term *advaita* refers to the nonduality, or oneness, of all with the supreme principle *brahman*, which, for Shankara, is the unknowable 'ground of the universe' (qtd. in Cross 2013, 95).

[7] See the long note Schopenhauer destined for the 'Sinology' section of the posthumous third edition of his *On the Will in Nature* (1889 [1867], 361–3).

scholarship on Mahāyāna Buddhism, have expressed appreciation for Schopenhauer's knowledge of Eastern thought. Dorothea Dauer, in her excellent study of his dissemination of Mahāyāna Buddhist thought, concludes that 'Schopenhauer's knowledge of Buddhism and Brahmanism was much more accurate than is usually believed' (Dauer 1969, 8). For Edward Conze, one of the most respected Buddhologists and translators of Buddhist texts of the last century, Schopenhauer's thought 'exhibits numerous, and almost miraculous, coincidences with the basic tenets of Buddhist philosophy', and in the view of British philosopher Bryan Magee, 'Schopenhauer remains the only great Western philosopher to have been genuinely well-versed in Eastern thought, and to have related it to his own work'.[8]

Schopenhauer's Affinity with Upanishadic and Buddhist Thought

A closer look at several important Upanishadic and Buddhist concepts and their parallels in Schopenhauer's own thought will help us disentangle which Indian teachings relayed by Schopenhauer are Upanishadic and which are Buddhist and which could be either.

The Illusory Real: Māyā *and* Śūnyatā

Scholars of Indian thought who have been exploring the intersection of Brahmanic and Buddhist philosophy have concluded that the debts continuously go both ways. As Stephen Cross maintains, 'the idea that the empirical world is *māyā*, illusion or magic, and has only an apparent reality is deeply rooted in Indian thought' (2013, 83). In fact, Schopenhauer attributes this view of *māyā* to the Brahmanic Vedas and the Purāṇas, the latter a popular, quasi-encyclopedic collection of information, myths, and stories (*WWR I* § 5, 38–9). As a result, Cross postulates, the concept of the ultimate unreality of the world was absorbed both into Upanishadic and Buddhist thought. The strong philosophical development this concept received in Mahāyāna Buddhism in the doctrine of *śūnyatā* (emptiness) resulted in its being reclaimed by Shankara and other Advaitins to clarify

---

[8] There are more quotations along these lines in Cross 2013, 19, from which the last two are taken. The Conze quote dates from his *Thirty Years of Buddhist Studies* (Oxford: Bruno Casirer, 1967), 222; the Magee one from his revised edition of *The Philosophy of Schopenhauer* (Oxford: Clarendon Press, 1997), 15.

their own tradition (Cross 2013, 84). Whose concept can it be said to be or not to be?

Cross affirms that the concept of the veil of *māyā*, to which Schopenhauer frequently alludes in his works, came to be identified in Europe and America with Indian thought largely through the philosopher's writings (Cross 2013, 243, n. 11). Of the many possible meanings of the term, dating back to the Vedas, Purāṇas, and the Upanishads, Schopenhauer adopted the Buddhist meaning of illusion. In his 1896 lectures on Vedānta, influential Swami Vivekananda (1863–1902) regrets that the idealist interpretation of *māyā* by Buddhist philosophers has more or less prevailed (Vivekananda 1958 [1896], 89).

Citing the poetic expression of life as a dream by Pindar and Sophocles, Shakespeare and Calderón, Schopenhauer draws attention to the wide acceptance of this view beyond ancient Indian thought (*WWR I* § 5, 39). Similarly, his philosophical idealism, as he himself points out, has numerous forerunners, foremost Plato and Kant, but he also pays tribute to Berkeley and Descartes (*WWR I* § 1, 24), among others. But when he adds the Upanishads to these forerunners, then he, without being aware of it, is following Shankara's Mahāyāna-inflected interpretation of the metaphysical real versus the illusory real that weaseled its way into the *Oupnek'hat*.

Beckett's many variations on this theme, beginning with the early fiction of the 1930s, are among the family resemblances that crisscross between his work and Buddhist teaching.

Tat Twam Asi *and Buddhist Compassion*

Schopenhauer frequently alludes to the Upanishadic identity of the microcosmic soul or self (*ātman*) with the macrocosmic soul of the universe (*brahman/Ātman*) and the Sanskrit phrase *tat twam asi* from the Chāndogya Upanishad, meaning, 'you are that', referring to the identity of self with other beings and all things that are *brahman*. (*Brahman*, in this sense, is not a god but a neuter-gendered universal principle.) Similar to the term *māyā*, readers of Schopenhauer adopted the *tat twam asi*, as did Beckett, who cites it in a 1936 letter, for instance, referring to his recognition of himself in Murphy, the anti-hero of his second novel (*LSB I* 350), and, as Dirk Van Hulle tells us, writing it out in 1938 for Joyce in reporting on Heinrich Zimmer's 1936 book *Maya: Der indische Mythos*, a retelling of mythic tales from the Purāṇas (Van Hulle and Nixon 2013, 146). For the atheist Schopenhauer, however, a blind will displaces the *brahman* of the Upanishads as 'the inner essence of the world' (*WWR I* § 29, 187). Still, aware of the homology of his view with the Upanishadic *tat twam asi*, Schopenhauer draws on the identity of all with the inner will to ground his doctrine of compassion (*WWR I* § 66, 400–1). This Upanishadic-inspired view, however, cannot be attributed to Buddhism.

At the same time, Schopenhauer's emphasis on compassion finds a parallel in the Buddhist ethical path, modeled on the Buddha's life and his preaching of the eightfold path and further emphasized by the primordial importance Mahāyāna teachings attach to compassion. In Mahāyāna, compassion is tied to the wisdom of attaining renunciation and selflessness by recognizing the unreality of the world, a wisdom that does away with separateness and which, in the ideal of the *bodhisattvas* is to be shared with all on the path to liberation (Hamilton 1950, 149; Keown 2001 [1992], 163). Compassion as an ethical obligation emphasizing connectedness is based in Vedānta on the oneness of all with *brahman*, whereas, in Mahāyāna, it follows from the interrelatedness that is the basis of the doctrine of the empty nature of the self: the interdependency of all beings precludes an inherent separate existence. In the words of one scholar of Buddhism, 'If all beings are inextricably connected, then the most meaningful thing to do is to dedicate oneself to the benefit of all beings. For this reason, the arising of unconditioned compassion is said to be the mark of a true realization of emptiness' (Simmer-Brown 2001, xix). Combining the Mahāyāna path highlighting compassion and insight, Schopenhauer maintains that 'to be cured of this delusion and deception of *māyā* and to perform works of love are one and the same' (*WWR I* § 66, 400).[9]

The 'I' and the 'Not I': Ātman *and* Anātman

On the matter of the existence of the self, there is a clear difference of views between Brahmanism and Buddhism. As succinctly put by scholar of Indian thought Tirupattur R. V. Murti, 'For the Upaniṣads, the self is a reality; for the Buddha it is a primordial wrong notion' (Murti 1955, 19). In Shankara's teaching of nonduality (*advaita*), absolute reality is *brahman/Ātman*, the ultimate world principle and true self in which individual selves (*ātmans*) participate (Cross 2013, 79–81). An individual *ātman* (Sanskrit for 'self' or 'breath') is the timeless life-force in each personality that is indivisible from *brahman/Ātman*. The similarity to Schopenhauer's timeless will and its manifestation in each personality is striking. But whereas,

---

[9] See also *WWR I* § 51, 280, and *PP II* § 156, 273–4.

in Vedānta, *ātman* and *brahman/Ātman* are positive principles, in Schopenhauer, the will and its manifestations, including the self, are, as in Buddhism, to be denied to achieve liberation from suffering and the cycle of rebirth. In powerful pages on the tragedy of human existence and the guilt of birth, Schopenhauer affirms that when we become conscious of the appearance – 'the veil of *māyā*' – of self, time, and space, then this consciousness of the illusory nature of the world 'acts as a tranquillizer' of the will and leads to the fading away of egoism and ultimately resignation and the end of willing (*WWR I* § 51, 280–1).

Schopenhauer's view of the self as appearance is congruent with Mahāyāna's concept of a no-self (*anātman*). The Buddha is said to have dispersed the concept of a unified subject into an ever-changing series of five psychophysical aggregates, or *skandhas*, that condition our personality: form (material elements and the five senses), feelings, perceptions, dispositions (impulses, mental habits, volitions, and so on), and consciousness. 'Thus there is dissolved away', writes Buddhologist Paul Williams, 'any real Self, any essence or unchanging referent for the name, the word "I"' (P. Williams 2009, 2).[10] Further, in Mahāyāna, the I's ultimate nature is *śūnyatā* (emptiness) in that it has no intrinsic existence but exists only in relation to other phenomena. And it is this insight, which, akin to Schopenhauer's consciousness of the illusory nature of the self, prepares the path to liberation. To what extent Beckett's 'I' and 'not I' paradoxes chime with the Mahāyāna no-self is investigated throughout this study.

Metempsychosis, Palingenesis, and Karma

To metempsychosis, or the transmigration of souls, Schopenhauer prefers the Buddhist esoteric, or learned, doctrine of palingenesis (rebirth). According to this doctrine, rebirth consists in the transmission from one personality to another of 'karmic seeds', accumulated over a lifetime or many lifetimes and stored in an unconscious mindstream or store-container. Holding that karmic effects result from intentional actions, Buddhists teach the means of inner purification. In Hinduism, karmic impressions, on the other hand, result from emotional attachment to the actions performed, whereas purification involves detachment by means of devotional practices and rituals, such as physical asceticism.[11]

[10] On the five *skandhas*, see Edward Conze's commentary on the Heart Sūtra in Conze 2001 [1958], 87–8.
[11] See Williams and Tribe 2000, 69, 73, 159–60; Cross 2013, 139–40, 154–64.

Schopenhauer emphasizes that Buddhist palingenesis 'rests on moral grounds' (*WWR II* ch. 41, 519), a view shared by Buddhologist Richard Gombrich, who contends that the Buddha's teaching of karma 'ethicised the universe' (qtd. in Williams and Tribe 2000, 73). Schopenhauer's agreement with the intricate Buddhist doctrine of rebirth will be examined in Chapter 2.

Mokṣa *and* Nirvāṇa

Both the Upanishadic and Buddhist concept of liberation from *saṃsāra*, the cycle of rebirths, includes detachment from the world and deep meditation. But whereas the Upanishadic *mokṣa* consists in realizing the full identity of *ātman* and *brahman* (the nondual view) or a return of *ātman* to the metaphysical reality of *brahman* (the dual view), Buddhist *nirvāṇa* is beyond words, and its meaning of extinction of craving and separate selfhood, compared to the extinction of a flame, is not the same as the nothingness that it has been mistaken to mean.

Schopenhauer alludes to *mokṣa* only rarely (two times in his major work), whereas he compares *nirvāṇa* frequently to the existence that follows his denial of the will (ten times alone in the second volume). Of his concept of the negation of the will and salvation from rebirth, Schopenhauer writes: 'These constant rebirths would then make up the succession of life dreams of a will that is in itself indestructible until, informed and improved by traversing so many and various successive cognitions, always in a new form, it abolished itself ('abolished itself' in the sense of no longer willing). And he adds that esoteric Buddhism's teaching of palingenesis agrees with this view (*WWR II* ch. 41, 519). The abolishment of the will through cycles of rebirth, for Schopenhauer, is analogous to the extinction of *saṃsāra* in *nirvāṇa* (*WWR II* ch. 44, 576). Schopenhauer's lucid understanding of Buddhist *nirvāṇa,* in contrast to the unfounded view of his contemporaries and followers in the nineteenth century who identified it with nothingness, are explored in Chapter 2.

Beckett, then, we can now claim, could glean a considerable knowledge of both Hindu and Buddhist thought from Schopenhauer's writings. In this, he was joined by many other modernists. Just to mention a few besides Beckett so influenced: the writers W. B. Yeats, T. S. Eliot, André Gide, Marcel Proust, Thomas Mann, Robert Musil, Italo Svevo, Jorge Luis Borges, and Thomas Bernhard; the philosophers Eduard von Hartmann, Friedrich Nietzsche, Henri Bergson, Fritz Mauthner, and Ludwig Wittgenstein; the psychoanalysts Freud, Jung, and Otto Rank;

the composers Wagner, Mahler, Stravinsky, and Schoenberg, and the painters Wassily Kandinsky and Paul Klee. App tells us that readers of Schopenhauer even today, including in Japan, China, and Korea, become scholars of Buddhism via Schopenhauer (App 2010, 207).

What the Critics Say about Beckett, Schopenhauer, and Buddhism

Some essays written at the beginning of the new millennium briefly and tangentially trace Beckett's Buddhist allusions to Schopenhauer. The difficulty of identifying what is Buddhist and what is Hindu or what could be either one or the other is apparent in some of these investigations. The following mini-saga of misreadings involving the sacred bo tree in Beckett's *Comment c'est* / *How It Is* (French, 1961; English, 1964) will serve as an example. In this work of fiction, a first-person speaker, claiming he is murmuring a text as he hears it, tells in the work's three parts of crawling through the mud, before, with, and after Pim.[12] The second part with Pim stages cruel scenes of torture the speaker is said to administer to Pim, mimicking the enforced imposition of individualization by way of speech, naming, and indoctrination into belief systems, a torture in which victims become tormentors and tormentors victims, stretching into an unending chain of tormenting couples, until all is denied at the end.

Three Beckett critics have advanced a Buddhist interpretation of a tableau in the work's second part involving a self-mutilating 'extreme eastern sage' and of another passage a few pages later about the already mentioned 'oriental' who has renounced (*How* 53, 56). In his essay on the possible Buddhist significance of Beckett's topos of excremental 'muck', Edouard Magessa O'Reilly briefly identifies Schopenhauer as the source of Beckett's knowledge of Buddhism. Devaluing, however, Beckett's source as well as the use made of it, he claims that, 'Beckett's (like Schopenhauer's) use of Buddhist themes remains quite superficial' (Magessa O'Reilly 2006, n.p.). Agreeing with an earlier piece by Paul Davies, Magessa O'Reilly mistakenly conflates the 'oriental my dream he has renounced' (*How* 56) with the 'extreme eastern sage', squatting in the shade of a tomb or a bo, whose nails punctured his palm after having clenched his fist throughout his life (*How* 53). For Davies, the sage and oriental are one figure, who 'is almost certainly to be associated with

---

[12] Although the designation *roman* (novel) appears on the cover of *Comment c'est*, there is no indication of genre in Beckett's 1964 translation. It has aspects of a mock-epic (Abbott 1996, 72) or an anti-narrative prose poem.

Figure 1.3   *The Buddha* [under a bodhi tree] *and Worshippers*, second–third century CE, Gandhāra, Northern Indus Valley, stone. Metropolitan Museum of Art, New York

Gautama Buddha' (Davies 1994, 235); for Magessa O'Reilly, he 'can be no one but Gotama Buddha' (2006, n.p.), both basing their claim on the mention of the bo, or bodhi, tree under which Gautama is said to have attained enlightenment. And yet the middle way the Buddha preached specifically warns against extreme self-mutilating ascetic practices. Nor does the image of the sage's 'turbaned head bowed over the fists' (*How* 53) evoke depictions of the Buddha. See Figure 1.3.

Nevertheless, a third critic, referring to Magessa O'Reilly's claim, but aware of the Buddha's rejection of self-mortification, asserts that the sage with the pierced palm is 'a blend of Buddhism and Hinduism' (Wimbush 2013, 123, 128). In his article on the influence of Ernst Haeckel and

Schopenhauer on *How It Is*, Andy Wimbush, although tracing Beckett's knowledge of Buddhism largely to Schopenhauer, nevertheless speculates that Beckett could have found his information on Buddhism in the articles by Thomas W. Rhys Davids on the Buddha and Buddhism in the eleventh edition of *The Encyclopaedia Britannica* (Wimbush 2013, 127). This is the edition of which Beckett received a copy as a gift in 1958 at the time he was beginning the composition of *Comment c'est*. Although he is known to have drawn on the eleventh edition as early as the 1930s for the notes on Greek mythological figures he entered into his 'Whoroscope' notebook (Van Hulle and Nixon 2013, 118), Beckett does not appear to have turned to the *Britannica* for the knowledge of Buddhism apparent in his fictions of the early 1930s nor for his allusions to Indian figures and to renouncing, karma, *māyā*, and rebirth in *How It Is*. As impressive as are Rhys Davids's discussion of the Buddha's four noble truths and the early Buddhist commentaries on them, a discussion based on his knowledge and translations of the Pāli *suttas*,[13] he has little to say about karma, rebirth, and ecstatic meditation in the eleventh edition of the *Britannica*. There is then no way of determining whether Beckett consulted Rhys Davids's articles either before or after receiving his own set in 1958. There appears to be no trace of such a reading at the time he was writing *Comment c'est* in the set that remained in his library at his death (Van Hulle and Nixon 2013, 7, 192–3).

Wimbush helpfully uncovered Beckett's source for the self-mutilating sadhu with the pierced palm in German naturalist and artist Ernst Haeckel's 1882 book *Indische Reisebriefe* (Indian Travel Correspondence), published in English under the title *A Visit to Ceylon* (Wimbush 2013, 127). As is his practice, Beckett hinted at his source for this scene by including the name of Haeckel in *How It Is* in the narrator's description of himself as 'mad or worse transformed à la Haeckel born in Potsdam' (*How* 42), referring no doubt to Haeckel's evolutionist law of recapitulation. A look at the Haeckel intertext will help us decide whether Beckett could have had the Buddha in mind in introducing the sage and the oriental into *How It Is* as suggested by three critics.

Haeckel's 1882 travelogue, popular enough to be translated and undergo several editions, situates the sadhu with the pierced palm in what Haeckel terms the 'sacred Brahmin settlement of Valukeshwar', which he visited in Bombay before traveling on to Ceylon (Haeckel 1911 [1882],

---

[13] *Sutta*, the equivalent of the Sanskrit *sūtra*, refers to a canonical text of Theravāda Buddhism written in the Pāli language.

Figure 1.4   Bodhi tree (*Ficus religiosa*) and the great stūpa Ruvanvāli, Anurādhapura,
Sri Lanka.
Photo courtesy of Dr. Peter Schmidt-Breitung

60). Wimbush, in fact, points out the Brahmin origin of the sage's extreme
asceticism (2013, 128). He spent many hours in this Brahmin village,
Haeckel recalls, 'under the shade of a sacred banyan tree' (a tree sacred to
Hindus), sketching a group of fakirs, 'accomplished hypocrites' in his
disdainful view, whose only virtue, he maintains, consists in self-
mutilation. Among the fakirs, he focuses on 'one [who] has held his fist
convulsively clenched for a number of years, so that his nails have grown
deep into the palm of his hand' (Haeckel 1911, 61). Later in the travelogue, as Wimbush notes, Haeckel speaks of a 'bo-gaha', which he describes
as 'a banyan or sacred fig (*Ficus religiosa*)', adding that these 'Buddha-trees,
with their huge trunks, fantastically twisted roots, and enormous expanse
of leafy top', ornament the Buddhist temple precincts in Ceylon (Haeckel
1911, 123). See Figure 1.4.

The bodhi or bo, however, is sacred to both Hindus – who have their
own beliefs attached to it – and Buddhists, who venerate the bo because of
the tradition that Gautama attained enlightenment under this tree. For
Hindus, the *Ficus religiosa* (variously named *bodhi* – Sanskrit for

'awakening' – or *aśvattha*) is the eternal tree of life with its roots in *brahman*. Further, in the Bhagavadgītā (10.26), the god Krishna identifies with this sacred fig tree (Stutley and Stutley 1977, 27). It follows that in Beckett's tableau identifying the sage squatting in the shade of a tomb or a bo does not warrant associating the self-mutilating Brahmin sadhu with Gautama Buddha. Recalling that Haeckel depicts himself 'under the shade of a sacred banyan tree' while sketching the sadhu with the pierced palm, Beckett most likely took the unspecified species of sacred fig tree in the Brahmin village to be a *Ficus religiosa*, as it may well have been, and situated his squatting sage in its shade or that of a tomb.

Whether the later passage about the renouncing 'oriental' is an allusion to the Buddha's path, we cannot say for certain, as renouncing is a solution shared by Hindus and Buddhists. A passage from the Bṛhadāraṇyaka Upanishad (4.4.7) is apropos: 'When all the desires that dwell in his heart are gone, then he, having been mortal, becomes immortal, and attains Brahman [*brahman*] in this very body' (qtd. in Cross 2013, 213). However, that the 'oriental' does not pertain as such to Gautama is further evident from a close reading of the surrounding text. The narrator is puzzled by the identity of Pim, the character he is about to torment (or is it rather self-torture?), whose words he cannot make out, and surmising, therefore, that he may be speaking or singing in a 'foreign tongue', he concludes that he is 'perhaps a foreigner'. His conjecture leads into the next verse's 'an oriental my dream he has renounced I too will renounce I will have no more desires' (*How* 56). No doubt this could be an allusion to the path of the Buddha that would put an end to the mutual or self-torture, but renunciation is also the path to liberation of Hindu sadhus, so that when the narrating voice imagines the foreigner to be 'an oriental', it is best to leave it at that.

The mini-saga of the bo tree is meant to highlight the care it takes to establish whether Beckett's allusions to Indian thought or traditions are to Buddhist or Hindu concepts or whether they could be to either. At times, however, as evident from the sage with the pierced palm, there is no ambiguity, as the Haeckel intertext further confirms.[14]

To continue a little longer with Haeckel: while in Ceylon, he witnessed the brutal branding of oxen and breaking of colts (Haeckel 1911, 159–60), some of which, for Wimbush, appears to have influenced Beckett's

---

[14] In the fourth chapter of his 2020 study, Wimbush revisits and expands his discussion of the two Eastern figures in *How It Is*. He continues, however, to identify the 'eastern sage' with both Hinduism and Buddhism and the 'oriental' who renounces with Buddhism (2020, 188, 189).

description of the cruel marking and training of Pim. In quoting Haeckel's taunting accusations against the Buddha for not preaching against the torture of animals, Wimbush, however, is aware that both the Buddha and Schopenhauer taught compassion toward all sentient beings, including animals (Wimbush 2013, 132, 136, 161). Haeckel's glaring lack of knowledge about the Buddha in this travelogue, which his admonishments addressed to the preacher of universal compassion display, and his contemptuous presentation of the followers of both Hinduism and Buddhism is a counterexample to Schopenhauer's respectful and knowledgeable presentation of Eastern thought, both Buddhist and Brahmanic, with which Beckett was familiar.

The next two chapters probe what Beckett, joining other modernist writers and artists, adopted and transformed, in his early fiction, from Schopenhauer's relay of Buddhist philosophy and from the sermons of Meister Eckhart, which, in Schopenhauer's view, parallel the teachings of Gautama Buddha and his own thought. In addition to reading Schopenhauer, Beckett, as we know, took notes on Christian mystical thought, including Eckhart's, before composing his first novel *Dream of Fair to Middling Women*.

CHAPTER 2

East–West Dialogue via Schopenhauer

To trace the Buddhist concepts circling through the cultural productions of the early twentieth century, this chapter investigates more closely the most influential of these transmitted by Schopenhauer to the West: the timelessness beyond birth and death, the doctrine of the *unborn*, karma and rebirth, and *nirvāṇa*. The latter concept in particular has been charged with nihilism, a charge often made against not only the teachings of the Buddha but also the writings of Schopenhauer and Beckett in their affinity with them. As such, it requires special investigation. The second part of the chapter introduces Meister Eckhart's influential negative path, which for Schopenhauer and Zen Buddhist scholars overlaps, except for its Christian theology, with the Buddha's teachings.

Immanent Timelessness and the Buddhist *Unborn*

When in his first novel Beckett lingers over his persona Belacqua Shuah's limbo of dead and unborn shades in his 'darkened mind gone wombtomb' (*Dream* 44, 45) and conflates this prenatal and posthumous space into an inner crypt of generativity, he is combining Schopenhauer's influential concept of artistic creation with the philosopher's exploration of an existence outside of time in Indian thinking. Throughout his writing life, Beckett was to associate the trope of a limbo in the mind to the space of writing, situating his ghostly speakers in this limbic or purgatorial space. The mind imagined as a place is a figure Beckett knowingly adopted throughout his oeuvre.[1]

Because other writers and artists of the period similarly sought to yoke creativity to a realm of the dead and unborn, a closer look at its origin in

---

[1] While translating *Molloy* with Patrick Bowles in the early 1950s, Beckett commented about the novel's eponymous personage: 'It's a habit he has of thinking of his mind as a place, he always thinks of it as a place' (qtd. in Bowles 1994, 26). Beckett's other creatures do the same.

Schopenhauer's writings will help elucidate their and Beckett's adoption of this space for creative work. Beckett's limbo corresponds to the existence Schopenhauer ascribed to both Brahmanic and Buddhist thinking: 'Brahmanism and Buddhism', he writes, 'are very consistent in having an existence prior to birth along with a continuation after death, so that this life exists to atone for the guilt of that previous existence' (*WWR II* ch. 41, 504). For Schopenhauer, the belief that birth is the beginning and death the end of our existence is tied to a conception of empirical time, whereas from the metaphysical perspective outside of time there is no such beginning or ending. In Schopenhauer's influential view, artistic production and contemplation enable a temporary experience of such a timelessness. In words that were to resonate with Beckett and other modernists, Schopenhauer describes the experience of art involving 'liberation of cognition from service to the will, forgetting oneself as an individual, and the elevation of consciousness to the pure, will-less, timeless subject of cognition, independent of all [subject-object] relations' (*WWR I* § 38, 223). As such, it is an entry into an existence devoid of the suffering and agitation of the phenomenal world, a foretaste, as it were, of release from the cycles of birth, death, and rebirth. The parallels with Buddhist *nirvāṇa* are unmistakable, a family resemblance that Schopenhauer recognized (*WWR II* ch. 44, 576).

Many artists and writers who adopted Schopenhauer's conception of art saw in his metaphysical, but resolutely secular, view an alternate refuge to religion. During Beckett's literary apprenticeship involving modernist writers in the late 1920s and early 1930s, he was no doubt largely indebted, after James Joyce, to Marcel Proust and André Gide, both having come under the influence of Schopenhauer's diffusion of Buddhism. Proust was the subject of Beckett's 1931 essay, and both French novelists were featured in his lectures the same year on the modern French novel at Trinity College Dublin. He owes his adoption of the 'ideal real' to both.

At the time he was composing *Dream*, the concept of the 'ideal real' helps to explain Beckett's double viewpoint in his first novel, in which grotesque scenes of an empirical 'real' intermingle with musings on a metaphysical space of creativity in the mind. In a letter of 21 November 1960 to Matti Megged, Beckett suggests that the Israeli writer's difficulties may be owing to his assimilating life to writing, which, as Beckett declares, must be kept apart: 'the material of experience is not the material of expression'. He then explains the difference in Proustian terms: 'The distinction he [Proust] makes between the "real" of the human predicament and the artist's "ideal real" remains certainly valid for me and indeed badly in need of revival' (*LSB III* 377). Not only in his early work but throughout his writing, Beckett kept the Proustian distinction in mind, on the one hand, 'the mock reality of experience' – as he put it in his 1931 essay – and, on the other hand, the 'ideal real', which in the same essay he defined as a 'mystical experience' (*P* 20, 56). In defining the ideal real in terms of a 'participation between the ideal and the real', that is, 'at once imaginative and empirical', limited neither to the 'abstract' nor the 'actual' (*P* 55, 56), Beckett is largely drawing on Proust's vocabulary in *Le Temps retrouvé* (*Time Regained*),[2] but the term 'ideal real' ('la réalité idéale') is Gide's in *Les Faux-monnayeurs* (*The Counterfeiters*). In the second part of this 1925 novel, Édouard, Gide's novelist within the novel, conceives of his writing in terms of 'la lutte entre les faits proposés par la réalité, et la réalité idéale' (the contest between the facts proposed by the real and the ideal real) (Gide 1968 [1925], 234). The two French writers' double viewpoint of the empirical and the metaphysical is also Schopenhauer's and goes further back in time to the Buddha's two-truths and Plato's two-worlds doctrines. For Schopenhauer, the reconciliation of these opposite viewpoints is 'the real theme of philosophy' (*PP II* § 140, 251) as it was for Buddhist philosophers. (See Chapter 4.)

Beckett alluded to the ideal real in Proust and Gide's novels in his lectures at Trinity, and drew attention to its 'extratemporal' nature in Proust's *À la recherche du temps perdu* (*In Search of Lost Time*).[3] Such a timeless existence is further described by Schopenhauer in the second volume of his *Parerga and Paralipomena*, asserting that if we consider life as a dream and death an awakening, then 'from this point of view it [death] is not to be regarded as the transition to a state that is entirely new and foreign to us, but on the contrary only as the retreat to one that is originally ours, of which life was only a brief episode' (*PP II* § 139, 245, 246). Accordingly, he writes, 'every human being can be regarded from two opposed points of view', on the one hand, as a transitory being, 'the dream of a shadow' in a 'world of finitude, of suffering and of death', and on the other hand, as 'indestructible', knowing 'neither time nor death' (*PP II* § 140, 250–1). For him, everyone carries infinite time within themselves (*PP II* § 139, 245).

---

[2] On the ideal real in *Le Temps retrouvé* (*Time Regained*), see Proust 1989 [1927], 450–1.

[3] This information is found in the final pages of Rachel Burrows's unpaginated 1931 lecture notes (TCD MIC60). The young Beckett was keeping himself impressively up to date, the final volume of Proust's novel having appeared only four years and Gide's novel six years earlier. Beckett refers to Proust's *extra-temporel* in *Le Temps retrouvé* (Proust 1989 [1927], 450).

Schopenhauer's view has a family resemblance to the Buddha's doctrine of an ultimate and original reality beyond birth and death – known as the *unborn* – which is immanent in all sentient beings. In declaring that 'we can only think of ourselves as *immortal* to the extent that we think of ourselves as *unborn*', Schopenhauer was aware of this convergence (*WWR II* ch. 41, 503–4; emphasis in the original). Consequently, from the double perspective of the empirical and metaphysical, 'born and unborn' is, for him, 'an apt expression' (*WWR II* ch. 41, 511). Meditation, in Buddhist thinking, renders this immanent timelessness accessible in this life by inducing a temporary relief from the turmoil of *saṃsāra* and a foretaste of *nirvāṇa* with which, as we have seen, Schopenhauer's artistic asceticism is in consonance, assigning to art the temporary liberation realized by Buddhist meditation (Dauer 1969, 23).

Described by the Buddha in terms of 'an unborn, an unbecome, an unmade, an unconditioned' (qtd. in Loy 1996, 23), the ultimate reality of the *unborn* is envisioned in terms of the creative potential of emptiness, which, as explored in the next chapter, is echoed by *Dream*'s aesthetic of the hyphen and silence (*Dream* 138). Five decades later, the beginning lines of one of Beckett's last poems 'go where never before / no sooner there than there always' (*CP* 223) vouch for his repeated musings during his writing life on the Buddhist/Schopenhauerian immanent timelessness, from which one comes and to which one returns. This overlapping or crisscrossing between Beckett's early imagined timeless refuge in the mind and his late poem, Schopenhauer's 'retreat' to an original timelessness, and the Buddha's concept of the immanent *unborn* strengthens the intertwining strands of family resemblances among the three to be explored in detail throughout this study.

Analyzed particularly in Beckett's essay and lectures on Proust, the earlier writer's association of the *extra-temporel* with writing was similarly adopted for *Dream*'s asylum in the mind, in which *Dream*'s narrator or, rather, the fictionalized author in the text 'Mr Beckett', is said to attain 'creation' (*Dream* 16).[4] In *Proust*, the young Beckett renders the inner timelessness in the aphoristic terms of, 'Death is dead because Time is dead' (*P* 56). Proust, in his condolence letter of 10 November 1910 to Robert Dreyfus on the loss of his mother, uses similar terms to encourage

---

[4] It could be the example of Proust's teasing allusions to the identity of the author, narrator, and main character in *A la recherche du temps perdu* that led Beckett to adopt in *Dream* the role of textual author/narrator commenting ironically on his alter ego. Both Proust and Beckett's novels, without being autofictions, are based on their own lives, with their personas taking on many of their own traits, and with their characters fashioned into fictionalized composites of people they knew.

his friend to continue writing, adding that 'in thus continuing to live you will live in a region of yourself, where the barriers of flesh and time no longer exist, where there is no death because there is no time, nor body' (Proust 1983, 208; my translation).[5] Proust reiterates this view on the pages celebrating the *extra-temporel* in *Le Temps Retrouvé*, where he maintains that, from the timeless standpoint of the ideal real, the word *mort* (death) holds no meaning (Proust 1989 [1927], 451). Some twelve years after his letter, continuing to make insertions into his novel shortly before his own death, Proust added the musings of his narrator about our being burdened at birth with obligations contracted in a previous life into the famous episode of *La Prisonnière*, in which the writer Bergotte dies while contemplating Jan Vermeer's *View of Delft*. In answer to the question 'mort à jamais?' (dead forever?), Proust's narrator imagines a world from which we are born and to which we most likely return, deciding that for this reason the answer is probably not dead forever (Proust 1988 [1923], 693). Although there are also Platonic elements in these passages, they converge with Schopenhauer's views of artistic production and contemplation – these also intersecting with Platonism – and its will-less experience of timelessness beyond birth and death. In addition to the temporary or possibly final salvation from time, there are hints in these Proustian passages of Schopenhauer's Indian-related views of karma and rebirth. Belacqua's psychic retreat in *Dream*, recalling Proust's timeless region linked to writing, will follow a decade later.[6] (See the next chapter.)

In artistic circles, perhaps the most striking adoption of the Buddhist *unborn* in its Schopenhauerian version in the decade before Beckett's *Dream* is the 1920 credo and eventual epitaph composed by Swiss-born German artist and poet Paul Klee:

> I cannot be grasped in the here and now.
> For I reside just as much with the dead
> as with the unborn.
> Somewhat closer to the heart of creation than usual.
> And not nearly close enough. (Klee 1996, 7; my translation)

The affinity of 'Mr Beckett's' creative retreat, envisioned as a limbo containing the dead and the unborn with Klee's artistic manifesto is

---

[5] 'En continuant à vivre ainsi tu vivras en une région de toi-même où les barrières de la chair et du temps n'existent plus, où il n'y a pas de mort, parce qu'il n'y a pas de temps, ni de corps.'

[6] Because Beckett is unlikely to have seen Proust's 1910 letter, the similarity of his imagined space of writing with Proust's is most likely owing to its source in Schopenhauer and his reading Proust's novel (more than once). Beckett apparently was the first to point out Schopenhauer's influence on Proust (*P* 70). Careful checking of the earlier (unacknowledged) critics of Proust's novel, on whom Beckett drew for his essay, has shown that none had remarked it.

Figure 2.1   Paul Klee, *Felsengrab* (*Rock Tomb*), 1932, 255, indelible pencil and chalk on primed paper on cardboard, 31.5 × 47.7 cm. Private collection, Switzerland, deposit, Zentrum Paul Klee, Bern

further apparent from Klee's astonishing 1932 pencil and chalk drawing *Felsengrab* (*Rock Tomb*) depicting what could be a newly dead human or a human embryo in a crystalline tomb in the shape of a uterus. See Figure 2.1. For art critic Richard Verdi, the tomb unmistakably takes on the form of a uterus in a landscape doubling as the placenta (Verdi 1985, 210). Klee's fascination with 'the heart of creation', condensed in his *Rock Tomb* into the trope of a both unborn and dead phantom in a uterine grave is dated the same year as Beckett completed *Dream* with its conception of an enwombed and entombed mind as the wellspring of writing.[7]

---

[7] In an interesting parallel to Klee's *Rock Grave*, in Beckett's second notebook of *Watt*, dating from the early 1940s, the character Arsene urges the novel's narrators to dig deeper into the uterine and the 'pre-uterine'. The narrators decline the suggestion by stating that the pre-uterine reminds them of the 'rocks at Greystones', the latter referring to the location of the tomb of Beckett's father (qtd. in Nixon 2011, 53).

Clearly, artists of the early twentieth century participated in the fascination for the Buddha and Buddhism that pervaded the period's zeitgeist,
largely via Schopenhauer. In addition to Schopenhauer's influence, relay is
then no doubt at work in the interweaving of Indian thought into
modernist writings and art. The author of *Dream* became acquainted with
Klee's art early on, through the reproductions of the artist's works in
transition at the time Eugene Jolas's literary magazine published some of
Beckett's early short fiction, criticism, and poetry from 1929 to the mid-
1930s. And Klee's credo was much cited as his renown spread. Beckett
later took pains to view Klee's paintings during his museum tour through
Germany in 1936–7, before these were removed by the Nazi regime from
public collections as degenerate art. In a 1945 review, Beckett counts Klee
among 'the great' of his time (*Dis* 97).

There is little doubt from Klee's credo that he is to be counted among
the artists whose interest in Buddhism was in part derived from
Schopenhauer. In an article about Klee's attentiveness to Buddhism,
Japanese scholar Yubii Noda tells of the artist adding books on Eastern
art to his private library from 1919 onward.[8] In 1920, Klee fashioned a
hand puppet in his likeness – *Untitled* (*Buddhist Monk*) – for his son and,
as Noda suggests, he seemingly portrayed himself as a Buddhist monk in
his 1923 painting *Chinese Picture*. Although not mentioned in Noda's
article, Klee's 1919 self-portrait *Versunkenheit* (*Absorption*) similarly evokes
a Buddhist model. No ears to hear and eyes pressed closed, the meditating
figure of Klee's drawing and then lithograph shares some of the features of
the images of the Buddha in meditation. See Figures 2.2 and 3.1. Klee's
interest in Eastern art was shared by his colleagues at the Weimar Bauhaus,
where he began to teach in 1921: they and his students dubbed Klee
affectionately 'the Buddha'.

Klee's continued interest in Buddhism is apparent in his 1926 ink
drawing, perhaps a tribute to Zen art, depicting a garden containing ray-
leaved plants above which he drew the gate to a Japanese Zen temple and
garden. As is well known, Klee composed the poetic titles of his works only
after having completed them. For this drawing, he chose the descriptive
title *Botanischer Garten. Abteilung der Strahlenblattpflanzen* (*Botanical
Garden. Division of the Ray-Leaved Plants*). In writing the title at bottom

---

[8] The information about Klee's attraction to Buddhism in this paragraph is based on Noda 2016,
80–1, 86.

   Noda attributes the appeal Buddhism and Daoism held for German intellectuals at the time to
their search for new values during and after World War I (2016, 81). A similar interest in especially
Zen Buddhism occurred in the Western art world after World War II.

Figure 2.2   Paul Klee, *nach der Zeichnung* [*Versunkenheit*] (*After the Drawing* [*Absorption*]), 1919, 75/113, watercolored lithograph, 22.2 × 16 cm. Zentrum Paul Klee, Bern, donation of Livia Klee

right of the drawing, Klee, however, playfully 'divided' the last syllable of *Strahlenblattpflanzen* from the rest of the word to place *zen* on the next line by itself. My eyes on seeing this work fell first on the *zen* and only subsequently noticed the Zen temple gate on taking a close look at the drawing.[9] Klee's involvement with Buddhism is particularly attractive in his simultaneous serious and playful allusions to it in his art. Clearly, Beckett had company in his references to Buddhism a decade later. (More such parallels follow in this chapter and the next.)

[9] Unfortunately, no illustration is available for this privately owned work lent to the Phillips Collection in Washington DC for its 2018 exhibition 'Ten Americans after Paul Klee'.

In returning to Beckett's writing of the early 1930s, the saga featuring Belacqua comprises, in addition to *Dream*, *More Pricks than Kicks*, the story collection published in 1934 and partly derived from *Dream*, and 'Echo's Bones', the story solicited and then refused for the collection and unpublished until 2014. (An earlier story 'Sedendo et Quiescendo' [Sitting and Quietening], most likely written in 1930–1, is part of *Dream*). Asked by his publisher to round up the collection of stories with one more, Beckett imagined the adventures of a reborn Belacqua whose death and burial he had chronicled previously, interweaving, more often than not in parodic mode, among the story's multiple literary reverberations, a string of allusions to Buddhist and Schopenhauerian concepts including rebirth and karma, the no-self, life as a dream, the wish to undo birth, compassion, and *nirvāṇa*. A closer look at some of these concepts will shed light on the story (analyzed in detail in the next chapter) and the allusions in Beckett and other modernists' works to cyclical existence.

Karma and Rebirth

Schopenhauer envisions the process of a new genesis after death in both physical and metaphysical terms. In his view, on the physical plane, the fall into nature's womb at death is followed by the transformation of our dust or ashes via crystallization into new life. A living being, he thus asserts, 'does not suffer an absolute annihilation through death but persists in and with the whole of nature' (*WWR II* ch. 41, 490).[10] This return to the womb of nature and the new genesis that follows, however, is for him only a shadow of the continuance in new individuals of the metaphysical will, our unknowable and timeless metaphysical core (489), a view that leads Schopenhauer to assert that his teaching agrees with esoteric Buddhism's palingenesis, or rebirth (519). Death is the end of the individual, but in each one there is the seed of a new being, he contends, so that in death not everything dies away forever, and nothing that is born receives a totally new being (*PP II* § 140, 248). On the metaphysical plane, a human being, he maintains, 'is something different than an animated nothing' (*PP II* § 137, 244).

To the more easily understood doctrine of the transmigration of souls, Schopenhauer prefers Buddhism's palingenesis, adopting this rare

---

[10] If this view appears to contradict Schopenhauer's notion of life as an 'intermezzo' between two nothings in the same chapter, it appears that the nothings refer to the lack of consciousness before and after life, but not to the physical return to nature.

philosophical term from the Greek *palin* ('again') and *genesis* ('birth'), to accommodate his and the Buddhist doctrine that we have no permanent soul or self to be reborn (*WWR II* ch. 41, 519; *PP II* § 140, 249). Continuing from one individual to another in the Buddhist doctrine of palingenesis are karmic traces or imprints (also referred to metaphorically as 'seeds') in a newly embodied individual. These karmic traces, which are stored in a 'container consciousness' or substratum 'mindstream' (*ālayavijñāna*), to which Schopenhauer compares his immanent will (*WWR II* ch. 41, 516–17), are the results of actions (karma) performed in a past life or in previous lives theoretically going back to infinity. Such karmic influences also function at the different stages of one life (Williams and Tribe 2000, 69; Waldron 2003, 130).

Detailing the karmic effects as theorized by the fourth-century CE Yogācāra school of Mahāyāna, Williams and Tribe explain: 'While changing from moment to moment it [the *ālayavijñāna*] serves to provide a necessary substratum for individual experience and also individual identity not just throughout one life but over the infinite series of lifetimes', adding, however, that such an identity does not correspond to a self. 'One of the main functions of the substratum consciousness', they continue, 'is to serve as the "seedbed", the repository for seeds (*bīja*) which result from karmicly determinative deeds and which therefore issue in future experiences' (Williams and Tribe 2000, 159–60). Schopenhauer concurs that out of these traces, or seeds, which are left behind at the end of life, a new being is born: 'What dies perishes, but a seed is left over from which a new being proceeds ... without knowing whence it comes and why it is precisely such as it is' (*PP II* § 140, 248). This view, however, is not borne out by the Buddhist belief that knowledge of one's past lives is possible (Kalupahana 1976, 52) and by the tradition that the Buddha remembered many of them. Indeed, in the second volume of his major work, Schopenhauer refers to the Buddha as an exception to this lack of remembrance of previous births, whereas for others, recognition of people known in previous lives is limited to an 'obscure presentiment' (*WWR II* ch. 41, 520), The question of memory is of importance to our reading of the 'Echo's Bones' story in the next chapter.

Buddhist Enlightenment and the end of the cycle of rebirths follows upon the purification of the substratum consciousness (Williams and Tribe 2000, 160) and, as we have seen, upon abolishing the craving for existence. Similarly, for Schopenhauer, liberation from the cycle of rebirths, or the 'succession of the life dreams of a will that is in itself indestructible', is attainable when the will, improved by the knowledge obtained from its many rebirths, abolishes itself by ceasing to will (*WWR II* ch. 41, 519).[11]

On the subject of karma, Schopenhauer insightfully contrasts the Hindu and Buddhist doctrine with the Christian belief in original sin (*WWR II* ch. 41, 504). For him, the guilt of having been born, about which he cites the seventeenth-century Spanish dramatist and poet Calderón de la Barca more than once (a quotation Beckett famously used in his *Proust* after finding it in Schopenhauer), expresses the Christian dogma of original sin, whereas the Indian doctrine of transmigration matches the misdeeds in a previous life with the torments endured in the present (*WWR I* § 63, 381–3). In both views, the only way of eluding guilt is not to be born. In the Belacqua saga, Beckett alludes to both, first, in *Dream*, by tying his anti-hero's sufferings to his being a 'son of Adam' (*Dream* 5), whereas, in the story 'Echo's Bones', the reborn Belacqua is trailed in his new existence by his karma. Later characters fare no better. 'It's my fault' Molloy writes at the beginning of his narrative, 'Fault? . . . But what fault?' (*Mo* 8).

Nirvāṇa Controversies

Nihilistic interpretations of *nirvāṇa* have a long history before and after Schopenhauer. Among the readily available sources, at the beginning of the twentieth century, identifying *nirvāṇa* with nothing, was William R. Inge's *Christian Mysticism*, a collection of eight lectures the Anglican theologian and influential writer on Platonism and religion delivered at Oxford in 1899.[12] This is the book from which Beckett absorbed much of his early acquaintance with Neoplatonic mysticism at the time he was working on his first novel. (Further details on Inge's influence follow in the next two sections.)

The parallels between medieval apophatic mysticism and Indian think-ing were noted by both Schopenhauer in *The World as Will and*

---

[11] How is one to reconcile that something that is imperishable annihilates itself? One possible way of understanding this conundrum is that the timeless will that knows neither beginning nor ending can negate itself as the will to life in the life span of the individual. Because the individual's birth and death corresponds, for Schopenhauer, to the constant renewal of the will's manifestation in the world, each such moment 'offers a new possibility for negation of the will to life' (*WWR II* ch. 41, 516). See also Cross 2013, 186–7, on two different aspects of the will, one a relative manifestation in the world and the other absolute.

[12] Inge (1860–1954) was later Professor of Divinity at Cambridge from 1911 to 1934. His *Christian Mysticism* has gone through thirteen editions since publication in 1899 and is still being reprinted and read.

Representation and Inge in his *Christian Mysticism*. Whereas both of these sources for Beckett's *Dream* postulate a family resemblance between the two forms of spiritual deliberations, Schopenhauer does so approvingly, Inge disapprovingly. In contrast to the esteem in which Schopenhauer and many thinkers and artists in the West after him held Indian philosophical reflections, Inge bitterly condemns their influence. To explain his disapproval of the Neoplatonic *via negativa*, Inge argues that the doctrine holding that God can only be negatively described is neither Greek nor Christian but belongs to 'the old religion of India', adding that 'nearly all that repels us in mediæval religious life . . . springs from this one root' (Inge 1899, 111–12).[13] Inge does not doubt the early Neoplatonists' awareness of Persian and Indian thought, but he denounces 'Indian nihilism', including the concept of *nirvāṇa*, and its pernicious influence on Neoplatonist writings (Inge 1899, 101, 106, 112).

In later works, Inge was to moderate his view and come to see in Platonism a parallel development to Buddhism. Drawing attention to the 'new spiritual enlightenment' in the first millennium BCE that came first to Asia and then to Greece and southern Italy, he offers a perceptive summary of this new outlook, describing it as 'the recognition of . . . a spiritual universe compared with which the world of appearance grew pale and unsubstantial and became only a symbol or even an illusion' (Inge 1926, 7–8). He finds Buddhism to be the most characteristic representative of this new conception, which in its renunciation of the phenomenal world sought deliverance by means of the extinction of desire and 'the negation of the will to separate existence', while resolving to live on earth as strangers and pilgrims (8). Inge's new appreciation of Buddhism, however, was accompanied by a change of mind about Indian influence on the West. In his view, the Platonic conception of the sensory world as a dim copy of an eternal world is a parallel development to Indian thought. For him, the Platonic conception and its revival in the Neoplatonism of the third century CE account for its foothold in the West, and especially in Christian theology and mysticism (9). Was Beckett's inspiration, then,

[13] In the West, the *via negativa*, the path of apophatic, or negative, theology, goes back to fifth-century Neoplatonists, including Dionysius, who, holding that the divine is inconceivable and ineffable, speak of it and mystic union in negative and paradoxical terms. ('Apophatic' is derived from Greek *apophasis*, meaning 'other than to speak' or to deny or negate.) The parallel with Indian philosophy's unknowable absolute and particularly with the Buddhist insistence on the unknowability of *nirvāṇa* is generally recognized. Dionysius (who lived in the fifth to sixth centuries) is considered one of the most important Neoplatonists, whose influence on subsequent mystical philosophers, including Eckhart, cannot be overestimated (Inge 1899, 110). See also Bryden 1998, 181–3.

Platonic or Buddhist, was he 'reapplying' Neoplatonic mysticism or the
Buddhism relayed by Schopenhauer? Surely, the answer is both, especially
given the commonality between the two cited by Inge. Which one came to
predominate will continue to be explored in this study, most extensively in
the last two chapters.

In his condemnation of Indian nihilism, the early Inge of 1899 was no
doubt aware of the influential nineteenth-century philosophers who identified Buddhism with nihilism, among whom famously Hegel (in his 1827
Lectures on the Philosophy of Religion), Nietzsche, and Eduard von
Hartmann. In his late polemical tract *The Genealogy of Morality*, for
instance, Nietzsche scoffs at Schopenhauerian compassion and the tendency of the Europe of his time to give in to the self-effacement of the type
of Geulincx's *despectio sui* (contempt for oneself) (Nietzsche 1994 [1887],
106) and to 'a nihilistic turning-away from existence' (67), all of which he
suspects are but detours to a new European Buddhism or nihilism (7).
Nirvāṇa, in Nietzsche's view, is the Buddhist 'yearning for nothingness'
replacing the mystical union with the divine (17).

Nietzsche was versed in Brahmanic and Buddhist thought via
Schopenhauer and subsequent readings, and his own thought, such as
the fictionality of the 'I' and the falsification of the unconscious when
uttered in words, has affinities with both Buddhism and Schopenhauer.[14]
But he also resisted what he viewed to be the nihilism of Buddhist *nirvāṇa*
as well as Schopenhauer's turning of the will.

Further evidence of the shared philosophical conviction – erroneous as it
is – reducing Buddhism to a both pessimistic and nihilistic religion and
nirvāṇa to an ultimate nothingness, was captured in a popular 1883 book by
Olga Plümacher (1839–95) on the history of pessimism, a controversial
topic at the time. Entitled *Der Pessimismus in Vergangenheit und Gegenwart:
Geschichtliches und Kritisches* (Pessimism in the Past and Present: History
and Critique), Plümacher's critique can serve as a reminder of the conflicted
attitude toward Buddhism during the nineteenth century.[15]

---

[14] On this reading of Nietzsche's thought, see Pierre Klossowski's influential *Nietzsche et le cercle
vicieux* (1969). Klossowski explains that, for Nietzsche, language prevents us from seeing ourselves
as a succession of discontinuous states and our 'I' as a fiction. Nietzsche, Klossowski further
contends, ponders the paradoxical play of language that traps us into thinking in words of 'notre
fond' (our 'ground'), which is beyond the thought, the said, and the willed (Klossowski 1969,
68–9). There are several books probing the resonances as well as the parting of ways between
Nietzsche and Buddhism. See Davis 2004.

[15] Beckett acquired or received a copy of Plümacher's book shortly after traveling through Germany in
1936–7 and kept it in his library to the end (Van Hulle and Nixon 2013, 153). It is discussed at this
point for the insight it brings to the controversial reception of Buddhist philosophy at the time, not

Plümacher derived her definition of modern pessimism from Schopenhauer, which she later applies to Buddhism: the amount of pain in the world exceeding the amount of pleasure, nonexistence is preferable to existence (Plümacher 1888, 1, 27). Although Plümacher accurately cites Schopenhauer's preference for nonexistence over existence, he did not refer to himself as a pessimist, nor do Buddhists think of the doctrine of liberation from the sufferings of *saṃsāra* as a pessimistic philosophy. As a matter of fact, Nietzsche was to see in Schopenhauer a failed pessimist, claiming that, in spite of wanting to be one, Schopenhauer's possible redemption from the will through aesthetic contemplation failed to make him one, adding, humorously, that Schopenhauer's anger at sexuality and praise of the ascetic are signs of happiness (Nietzsche 1994 [1887], 80–1).

In the brief section on Buddhism in her historical study, Plümacher adopts Eduard von Hartmann's view of the metaphysical nihilism of Buddhist thought (Plümacher 1888 [1883], 24–7.) She draws attention to the 'the pure nothingness' ('das reine Nichts') behind existence, and *nirvāṇa* as 'deliverance into blissful nothingness' ('Erlösung im seligen Nichts'). Agreeing with her predecessors, Plümacher is convinced of Buddhism's embrace of philosophical nihilism – as Inge was to be a decade later – a misconception that later Buddhologists have taken pains to correct, although admitting that even within Buddhism there is some controversy on this subject.

Reducing *nirvāṇa* to nothingness is not a mistake Schopenhauer makes. In the second volume of his major work, Schopenhauer has this to say about the Buddhist definition of *nirvāṇa*: 'If *nirvana* is defined as the nothing, this is intended only to mean that *samsara* does not contain a single element that could serve to define or construct *nirvana*' (*WWR II* ch. 48, 623). The *via negativa*, whether Mahāyāna Buddhism's, apophatic theology's, or his own is not an approach Schopenhauer would deny. Contrary to the many readers of Schopenhauer – both admirers and detractors – who claim he identifies *nirvāṇa* with an ultimate nothing, there is no evidence for this claim in Schopenhauer's works. Instead, he clearly distinguishes between the two. Teasing out the difference between nothingness and *nirvāṇa* will serve to clarify the problematical manipulation of these concepts by Beckett, his exegetes, and all intent on understanding the distinction between them.

as a source for Beckett's early writings. It is uncertain what Beckett thought of Plümacher's views on Buddhism.

In the first volume of his magnum opus, Schopenhauer at one point describes *nirvāṇa* as the Buddhist promise of an end to the cycles of rebirth and therefore 'a state in which four things are lacking: birth, ageing, sickness and death' (*WWR I* § 63, 383). This view does not identify *nirvāṇa* with nothing. Could readers have been misled about Schopenhauer's view of *nirvāṇa*, when at the end of the same volume, he repeatedly insists that the negating of the will to life ends the illusion of self-existence and the phenomenal world, leaving nothing? 'No will, no representation, no world. Only nothing remains before us', he hammers away to ensure the reader doesn't miss the point (*WWR I* § 71, 438).[16] But more importantly for our argument, he adds 'we must not evade [the final goal of nothing] through myths and meaningless words as the Indians do, words such as "re-absorption into *Brahman*", or the *Nirvana* of the Buddhists' (*WWR I* § 71, 439). Here he is clearly distinguishing between the 'meaningless word' *nirvāṇa* and his own 'nothing' in referring to what remains after the abolition of the will.

Schopenhauer's sharp critique of the 'meaningless words' of the Indians to refer to the state following the negation of the will to life is puzzling. But the clarifications he provides in later writings help to counter his seemingly nihilistic 1818 view. In the 1844 second volume of supplements to the first, that is, twenty-six years later when he had considerably increased his knowledge of scholarship on Indian thought, Schopenhauer was to clarify that *mokṣa* and *nirvāṇa* refer to the salvation that follows the denial of the will to life (*WWR II* ch. 48, 623). Schopenhauer obviously had second thoughts about the avalanche of 'nothings' with which he concluded the first volume of his major work. In the second volume, he takes pains to explain the negativity of that ending: what he described as nothing, he asserts, is not an ultimate nothing but applies only to the phenomenal world and to what is given up, not to what is attained, at death (*WWR II* ch. 48, 627).

Schopenhauer inserted a long note at the end of his chapter on 'Death and Its Relation to the Indestructibility of Our Essence in Itself' listing the different etymologically derived interpretations of *nirvāṇa* in the scholarly literature on Buddhism of the time. Among these interpretations, only one refers to the annihilation (of life); the others allude to an extinguishing as

---

[16] Although Schopenhauer insists on the unknowability of the will as the thing-in-itself, he nevertheless intimates that we have an intuition of it. He further admits about the will, 'We can describe it only as that which is free to be or not to be the will to life', that is, the will is free not to will (*WWR II* ch. 44, 576).

of a fire, the negation of desire, the escape from sorrow, or the opposite of *saṃsāra*, 'which is the world of perpetual rebirths, of craving and longing, of the illusion of the senses and changeable forms, of being born, aging, sickening and dying' (*WWR II* ch. 41, 525).

When Schopenhauer in 1818 ends the first volume of his major work with the poetic pronouncement: 'For those in whom the will has turned and negated itself, this world of ours which is so very real with all its suns and galaxies is – nothing' (*WWR I* § 71, 439), he is writing about the nothingness of the phenomenal world. In adding a handwritten note to these words, in between the appearance of the third edition of 1859 and his death in 1860, stating that his view corresponds to the Buddhist Perfection of Wisdom, the *prajñā-pāramitā*, Schopenhauer shows his awareness of Mahāyāna's highest form of wisdom, that is, the 'beyond all knowledge' of metaphysical reality. Schopenhauer makes the same assertion in the 1859 edition of the second volume in relation to the *prajñā-pāramitā*: 'where the essence in itself of things begins, cognition falls away, and all cognition is fundamentally only cognition of appearances' (*WWR II* ch. 22, 288). About the denial of the will to life that Buddhists 'describe by the word *Nirvana*', he writes: 'It is the point forever inaccessible to all human cognition precisely as such' (*WWR II* ch. 44, 576).

The denial of the will to life, on which Schopenhauer bases liberation from suffering, corresponds to the Buddha's view that the craving for existence is abolished in the experience of awakening, whether in this life or after death (Kalupahana 1976, 52). Further, stating that there are no means of knowing what happens after the death of a liberated person, the Buddha is said to have explained: 'When all phenomena (*dhammā*) are removed, then all means of description are also removed' (qtd. in Kalupahana 1976, 81), a view with which Schopenhauer agreed in citing the Buddhist *prajñā-pāramitā* claim that 'all cognition is fundamentally only cognition of appearances'. The extent to which Schopenhauer's unknowable metaphysical beyond converges with *nirvāṇa* is evident, when he maintains, 'With the disappearance of the will from consciousness, individuality is in fact annulled, along with all its attendant sufferings and needs' (*WWR II* ch. 30, 388) and asserting that after the negation of the will, which, he adds, Buddhists describe by the word *nirvāṇa*, 'we have no concepts or even information what it [existence] then is' (*WWR II* ch. 44, 576).

Blending Buddhism and Christian Mysticism

At the time Beckett was composing *Dream*, he observed in André Gide's collection of essays on Dostoevsky the blending of Christianity and

Buddhism evident in his own early work. Not only did Beckett alert his students at Trinity College to Gide's views on Buddhism, but he 'pilfered' several of Gide's views on the aesthetics of the novel for *Dream*. For Gide, 'Dostoevsky's Russian comedy' originates 'in the contact between the Gospels and Buddhism, the Asian spirit', and he maintains, owing to the Russian author's emphasis on renunciation: 'Dostoevsky leads us to a kind of Buddhism, or at least a kind of quietism' (Gide 1981 [1923], 107, 151; my translation).[17] Among other writers intrigued by the analogy between Buddhism and Christianity after the former's influential reappearance in Western thought is T. S. Eliot, who combines Christianity, including mysticism, with Buddhism, particularly in *The Wasteland* (1922) and *The Four Quartets*, written between 1935 and 1942 (McLeod 1992, 3–16).[18]

We owe it to John Pilling's annotation of Beckett's 'Dream' notebook (so named later) that we know that soon after completing his *Proust* study, Beckett consigned the results of what he called his 'notesnatching' into this notebook largely destined for use in the Belacqua saga (Pilling 1999, xiii). There are some thirty-seven phrases taken from Inge in the notebook, many of which we find verbatim and unacknowledged in Beckett's early fictions of the 1930s. As we know, Beckett is here following the example of other modernists; Joyce famously termed it 'stolentelling' in *Finnegans Wake* (Joyce 1968 [1939], 424), whereas Geoffrey Hartman's 'self-exposing plagiarism' (Hartman 1977, 308) is even more a propos to describe the 'pilfering' confessed by *Dream*'s narrator: 'We stole that one. Guess where', he teases at one point about a favorite passage in Proust reverberating in the novel (*Dream* 191–2; Pilling 2003, 311). In another ploy displaying his unnamed sources, Beckett lists both Schopenhauer and Inge among other writers whose 'darkest passages' Belacqua comically spurns in his failure to find comfort for an attack of colic (*Dream* 61).

Besides the notes on *Christian Mysticism*, entries into Beckett's 'Dream' notebook from St. Augustine's *Confessions* and Thomas à Kempis's *The Imitation of Christ* attest to his interest at the time in religious thinkers and

---

[17] See Le Juez 2009, 38, on Beckett's 1931 lectures on Gide's *Dostoïevski*, in which the young lecturer included Gide's view on the contact between the Gospels and Buddhism.

[18] Because Eliot studied Sanskrit and Pāli as well as Eastern philosophical texts at Harvard during the years immediately before World War I, his knowledge of Buddhism was not uniquely indebted to Schopenhauer, of whom, moreover, he was critical, seemingly unaware of some of the Mahāyāna texts that were Schopenhauer's preferred source.

mystics.[19] In fact, many of the Christian mystics introduced by Inge are cited in Beckett's 'Dream' notebook and alluded to in *Dream*.[20] Given the emphasis on a timelessness beyond the here and now by writers, artists, and thinkers at the time Beckett was beginning his writing career, Beckett would no doubt have paid attention to Inge's Neoplatonic views on mysticism resonating with Schopenhauer's description of the Indian-inspired timelessness immanent in finite existence. For the Anglican clergyman and theologian, mysticism has its origin in 'that dim consciousness of the *beyond*' and corresponds to '*the attempt to realise, in thought and feeling, the immanence of the temporal in the eternal, and of the eternal in the temporal*' (Inge 1899, 5; emphasis in the original). Those following Schopenhauer, however, did not share the Neoplatonic theological visions of the 'beyond' reviewed by Inge in his lectures.

The kinship, then, of the retreat in his mind by *Dream*'s protagonist with the Buddha's teachings found in Schopenhauer is doubled by an affinity with Christian mysticism, the Neoplatonic strain of which is best represented by Meister Eckhart (1260–1328). In fact, Schopenhauer contends that not only Eastern religions and his own philosophy but 'true Christianity', and Christian mysticism in particular, teach asceticism, quietism, renunciation, self-denial, and 'mortification of the will' (*WWR II* ch. 48, 629–31).[21]

The reasons are several for privileging Eckhart in this study over the other mystics whose presence in Beckett's writings has been traced and analyzed by scholars. Foremost is Schopenhauer's claim about the parallels between the teachings of the Buddha and Eckhart – Dante's contemporary and one of the most renowned mystical philosophers of Christianity of all times – a claim seconded by twentieth-century Zen scholars who engaged

---

[19] See Pilling 1999, xvi–xvii, on Beckett's note taking in 1931. No notes, however, have been discovered on Beckett's 1930 reading of Schopenhauer and Proust, the latter begun earlier. His later reading notes on literature, history, philosophy, psychology, and psychoanalysis, on the other hand, are dated after the completion of his first novel.

[20] On the allusions in the Belacqua saga to St. Augustine's *Confessions* and the mystics cited in Beckett's 'Dream' notebook, see Bryden 1998, 84–101, 181–3; Pilling 1999; and Ackerley and Gontarski 2004, 30–31, 274–5, 573.

[21] Exegetes have identified Beckett's quietism with, among others, the late medieval German-Dutch mystic Thomas à Kempis's *Imitation of Christ* and more peripherally with Arnold Geulincx's *Ethica* (Ackerley 2000, 81–92). Thomas is cited several times in the Belacqua saga, whereas Beckett's notes on Geulincx date from 1936 while he was completing *Murphy*. On the importance of Geulincx for understanding Beckett's texts, see the impressive study by David Tucker, in which he, moreover, provides a cogent summary of views on Thomas à Kempis by Beckett scholars (Tucker 2012, 44–5). In his 2020 book on Beckett's quietism, Andy Wimbush discusses Geulincx on pages 68–73, and, in his second and third chapters, engages with Thomas's influence on *Murphy* and *Molloy*, further noting the influence of Schopenhauer, Inge, and Gide's views on quietism.

with Eckhart's thought. Further, Beckett's continuous interest in Eckhart's sermons, after first reading of their importance in Schopenhauer and Inge, is shared to an astonishing degree by twentieth-century thinkers, including several on whom Beckett drew, so that his Eckhartian echoes enhance our understanding of the elements of his writings attuned to Buddhist concepts. The 'Dream' notebook provides evidence of Beckett's engagement with Meister Eckhart's sermons beyond what he found in Schopenhauer. This and subsequent chapters will detail these interconnections.

One year before his death, in the 1859 edition of his major work, Schopenhauer, as already noted, came to identify his own system with that of the Buddha and the mystics but in philosophical terms, stopping short of the mystic 'beyond all knowledge' (*WWR II* ch. 48, 627). As you will recall, having declared in his 1858 entry in a notebook, 'Buddha, Eckhart and I teach essentially the same thing', he moderated this claim in the 1859 edition of his major work in writing that if one focuses on 'the root of things' and discounts cultural contexts, the Buddha and Meister Eckhart 'teach the same thing'. Still, he found it prudent to explain that 'except that the former was allowed to express his thoughts straightforwardly while the latter was required to clothe them in the garb of Christian mythology' (*WWR II* ch. 48, 629). Even though he omitted mention of himself when adding this declaration to the second volume of his magnum opus, Schopenhauer continued to see family resemblances between the teachings of the founder of Buddhism and of the medieval philosopher and his own.[22]

What is the 'same thing' that bridges the cultural and historical spans between the fifth-century BCE Buddha, the medieval Master of Christian theology, and the nineteenth-century idealist philosopher? In quoting the Buddha's words, 'my students reject the idea "I am this", or "this is mine"' (*WWR II* ch. 48, 629), Schopenhauer evidently had in mind that both the Buddha and Eckhart advocate renouncing the 'I' and 'mine' and the visible world in order to reach an ultimate reality. If for the Buddha, the ultimate *nirvāṇa* can be spoken of only in negatives, such is the case for Eckhart's innermost 'ground of the soul', where the unknowable *gotheit*, the divine

---

[22] This late addition to the second volume of *The World as Will and Representation* may be attributed to the availability of some of Eckhart's Middle High German sermons in the 1857 first edition of Franz Pfeiffer's second volume of *Deutsche Mystiker des vierzehnten Jahrhunderts* (German Mystics of the Fourteenth Century), to which Schopenhauer refers in *WWR II* ch. 48, 627. German philosophers of the nineteenth century were discovering ancient Indian texts at the same time as they were rediscovering Meister Eckhart's sermons so that the similarity Schopenhauer perceived between the two was facilitated by the newness of philosophical engagement with both.

nature beyond God (Latin *deitas*, translated as 'divinity' or 'Godhead'), can manifest itself. For Edward Conze, too, 'the Buddhist idea of ultimate reality is … not easily distinguished from the notion of God among the more mystical theologians, like Dionysius Areopagita and Eckhart' (Conze 1959a, 110–11).[23] It is to the Buddha and Eckhart's views of the absolute that Schopenhauer associated the unknowable reality that results from the negation of the will in his philosophy. Nevertheless, the Buddha and Schopenhauer's nontheistic vision of an unknowable beyond distinguishes their philosophy from Christian parallels, including Eckhart's mystical theology.

Independent of Schopenhauer's view on Eckhart and the Buddha's teachings, two Beckett exegetes have commented on the similarity between Eckhart's mystic philosophy and Zen Buddhism. Marius Buning, associating Eckhart's and Zen thought on emptiness, briefly compares Beckett's late plays with Eckhart's views on emptiness and detachment (Buning 1990, 135–40; 2000, 44–5). In her exploration of Zen *yohaku*, Junko Matoba similarly draws on Eckhart's likeness with Zen to probe Beckett's empty and darkened onstage spaces (Matoba 2003, 108–10, 116–19, 127–8, 131). She contends that 'Beckett's path is as strict and ascetic as that of the Zen Buddhist in contemplation of the non-self [no-self]' (128). To my knowledge, Buning and Matoba's are the most extensive previous engagements with Eckhart's thought in relation to Beckett's writing.

Reading Inge one year after he read Schopenhauer, Beckett would have found the Anglican theologian's appreciation of Eckhart more than a match for Schopenhauer's. In his fourth lecture on 'Christian Platonism and Speculative Mysticism' in the West, Inge devotes nearly half of the lecture to Eckhart, who is, for him, 'the greatest of all speculative mystics' (Inge 1899, 148).[24] These early introductions to Eckhart prompted

[23] In focusing on the parallels between the Buddha and Eckhart, first suggested by Schopenhauer, and the family resemblances between the concepts all three broadly share – leaving aside for the moment their different paths to salvation – it follows that conceiving of mystical, or spiritual, concepts as either a form of thought shared across cultures or as culturally constructed is not a matter of either/or. Rather, mystical thought has universally shared elements modulated by cultural and individual differences in the manner Gaston Bachelard conceptualizes imaginative constructs: derived from a common biological substratum, they are tempered by the cultural unconscious and further transformed by the poetic imagination (Bachelard 1973, 12, 14, 25–6). Similarly, the cognitive substratum that modern cognitive science is mapping can be seen to underlie (but not cause) mystical thought across cultures and millennia, undergoing further shaping in each of the contexts in which it emerges.

[24] The author of *Christian Mysticism* knows Eckhart's German sermons well, and, in the absence at the time of their availability in English, or so it seems, appears to have rendered some passages himself from Eckhart's Middle High German, citing the original at times but failing to indicate from which

Beckett's fondness for his sermons, reading them up to the last year of his life (Buning 2000, 49).

Eckhart's daring and often witty colloquial phrasing and rhetorical genius in his German sermons and his startling philosophical prowess and paradoxes make Eckhart exhilarating to read, especially in the original, traits that got this great medieval thinker into trouble with the Inquisition. His German sermons are considered among the most valuable and beautiful texts of medieval German literature (Flasch 2015, 195), and his influence on philosophers from Schopenhauer to Hegel, Mauthner to Wittgenstein, and Heidegger to Derrida attests the continuing importance of his thought.

Eckhart consistently preaches self-denial and the nothingness of all that is created and encumbered by time and space : 'There is something that transcends the created being of the soul, not in contact with created things, which are nothing', he asserts in one sermon (*DW* 28; *MEW I* 322; *CMW* 131), and in another he maintains, 'if a person [*mensche*] turns away from self and from all created things ... you will attain to oneness and blessedness in your soul's spark [*Funke*], which time and place never touched' (*DW* 48; *MEW I* 508; *CMW* 310; translation modified.)²⁵ The resemblance of Eckhart's sermon with the Buddhist doctrine of an immanent reality of the *unborn* and uncreated, a bliss to which everyone has access when they relinquish the illusion of self and worldly defilements, is remarkable. It is further evident in Eckhart's rendering of the divine in terms of 'uncreated beingness [*istikeit*]' and 'nameless nothingness [*nitheit*]' (*DW* 83; *MEW II* 193; *CMW* 463; translation amended), even if his teaching is theological, and the Buddha's is not.

Beckett would have found in Inge's pages on Eckhart in *Christian Mysticism* more highlights of the German preacher's sermons that corroborate the family likeness with the Buddha's teachings detected by Schopenhauer. At one point, Inge motivates his readers to pay close

---

sermons he is quoting. He most likely made use of Pfeiffer's 1857 edition of some of Eckhart's German sermons, which was not translated into English until 1924.

²⁵ Citing Eckhart's sermons is complicated by the fact that various editions and translations number them differently. The most commonly cited for the German sermons are volumes 1–5 of *Meister Eckhart. Deutsche Werke* (shortened to *DW*) (Stuttgart: Kohlhammer, 1958–2003.) The sermon numbers in this study cite this edition, and the citation – *MEW* – refers to two volumes edited and commented on by Niklaus Largier that use the *DW* text and sermon numbering, with facing Middle High German and translation into modern German by Josef Quint et al. The subsequent citation – *CMW* – refers to the English translation of Maurice O'C. Walshe who follows his own numbering system, but provides a helpful concordance at the back of his book. Walshe's translation has been modified in some instances to avoid his generic 'man' for Eckhart's *mensche* (human being, person) and to correct obvious errors of translation after checking Eckhart's original and the translation into modern German by Quint et al.

attention to a long passage in quotation marks, introduced as 'perhaps the most instructive passage' of the medieval philosopher's views (Inge 1899, 157). The 'quotation' is actually a patchwork – partly translation, partly summary – piecing together fragments from several of Eckhart's German sermons that give prominence to his key teachings. The first sentence of Inge's long 'quotation', 'There is in the soul something which is above the soul, Divine, simple, a pure nothing; rather nameless than named, rather unknown than known' (157), is a poetic abridgment of a number of lines from several sermons, including 'If God is neither goodness nor being nor truth nor one, what then is he? He is pure nothing [*nihtes niht*]: he is neither this nor that' (*DW* 23; *MEW I* 270; *CMW* 287). In his preaching the nothing of created things (as in the already quoted *DW* 28) and the unknowable nature of the divine, Eckhart teaches a *via negativa*, which has affinities with the Mahāyāna Perfection of Wisdom literature.[26]

The final lines of Inge's compilation, as Beckett would have read them, correspond to an abridged but otherwise faithful rendition of the conclusion of *DW* 48 (*MEW I* 509; *CMW* 311), one of Eckhart's most popular sermons:

> It [the *Fünkelein* (little spark)] is determined to enter into the simple Ground, the still Waste, the Unity where no man [*nieman* (no one)] dwelleth. Then it is satisfied in the light; then it is one: it is one in itself, as this Ground is a simple stillness, and in itself immovable; and yet by this immobility are all things moved (Inge 1899, 158).

Beckett was to echo this passage in his later works.[27]

On Silence and Unknowing, East and West

Before examining more closely, in the next chapter, Beckett's fiction of the 1930s to further elucidate its family resemblances with Buddhist and

---

[26] In *A History of Philosophy*, Wilhelm Windelband, whom Beckett will read only later, similarly clarifies that the 'nothing' of the divinity (of negative theology) means that as the 'original ground', the divinity is beyond being and knowledge. 'It has no determination or, quality', he explains, 'it is "Nothing"', whereas the God who is and knows and creates out of nothing is the divinity actualizing itself in the triune God (Windelband 1901, 335). Windelband uses the neuter pronoun to refer to the original ground, as does Eckhart. 'God', however, is conceived of as masculine in gender.

[27] See the last section, '"Those calm wastes" of *The Lost Ones*' in Chapter 5 and the discussion of *Stirrings Still* in Chapter 8. Beckett's fidelity to his early sources is extraordinary, including in addition to Schopenhauer, the Buddha, and Eckhart and other mystics' teachings, allusions from his earliest to the latest writings to the Bible, Dante, Descartes, Joyce, Proust, and Shakespeare among others, whether in a parodic vein or not. Readers who know these sources well, regularly come upon indirect citations of them.

mystic thought, the intertextual dialogue on silence needs to be explored between Beckett's *Dream* and the three philosophers whose commonality Schopenhauer celebrated – the Buddha, Eckhart, and himself. Eckhart's teachings on stillness and silence in the face of the unknowable have influenced generations of thinkers and writers. Drawing in his sermons on the Neoplatonic apophatic tradition, and Dionysius in particular, Eckhart admonishes his listeners to refrain from trying to understand the unknowable divinity (*gotheit*), inviting them to be silent instead of 'chattering' about what is beyond understanding (*DW* 83; *MEW II* 193; *CMW* 463). Here, too, Eckhart and the Buddha are in agreement. When posed metaphysical questions, the Buddha would meet them with a noble silence (Cross 2013, 73). Moreover, in his interpretation of the Buddha's teachings in his *Mūlamadhyamakakārikā* (The Philosophy of the Middle Way), Nāgārjuna, while holding words to be useful for seeing to our everyday affairs, denounces them when used to make claims about an ungraspable ultimate reality. For the latter, there is only silence (Nagao 1979, 32).

To explain to his listeners that the unknowingness he preaches is not a lack, Eckhart speaks of a 'transformed knowing, an unknowing which comes not from ignorance but from knowledge'.[28] Eckhart's knowing unknowing, which was to become the famous *docta ignorantia* (learned ignorance) of his disciple Nicholas of Cusa – both deriving their knowledge-based ignorance from Dionysius – corresponds, as we have already surmised, to the unknowing status Beckett was eventually to adopt for himself, affirming, for instance, about *Waiting for Godot*: 'The end is to give artistic expression to something hitherto almost ignored – the irrational state of unknowingness where we exist, this mental weightlessness which is beyond reason.'[29] Beckett's statement resonates with Wilhelm Windelband's explanation of Eckhart's 'not-knowing': 'As the deity [*gotheit*] is "Nothing," so it is apprehended only in this knowledge that is a not-knowing … ; and as that "Nothing" is the original ground of all

[28] This quotation from *DW* 101 is taken from the excellent Oliver Davies translation of selected sermons by Eckhart (Eckhart 1994, 220).

[29] It has been difficult to find an accurate reference for this remark. In his biography of Beckett, Anthony Cronin, listing Alec Reid's *All I Can Manage, More Than I Could* (Dublin: Dolmen, 1964) as his source, explains that Beckett made the comment to this Dublin acquaintance in 1956 to counter the tendency of critics and audiences to read symbolic meanings into *Waiting for Godot*, which sought instead to avoid definition (Cronin 1997, 457, 615). It is not, however, in Reid's book (first published in 1968), but rather in his 1962 article, where it is not directly attributed to Beckett, but introduced by 'it is argued' (Reid 1962, 136–7). One can only suppose that, shown the manuscript of the article, Beckett asked Reid to take out his comment fearing that it would lead to interpretations limiting him to 'the irrational state of unknowingness'.

reality, so this not-knowing is the highest, the most blessed contemplation' (Windelband 1901, 337). Windelband, too, on whose *History of Philosophy* Beckett took notes in the 1930s after completing the Belacqua saga, compares the exaltation of German mysticism, its ideals of self-denial and renunciation of the world, to the 'ancient Oriental view' (337).

Beckett's literature of silence as it is first conceived, if not practiced, in *Dream* thus has affinities with the Buddha's teachings, Eckhart's sermons, and Schopenhauer's resolve to keep quiet about the unknowable, which the latter may well have adopted under the tutelage of the Buddha and apophatic mysticism. Following the example of Joyce, Proust, and Gide, Beckett embeds a future writer into his first novel, sketching and comically demonstrating through his use of commas his own future poetics in having his persona declare: 'The experience of my reader shall be between the phrases, in the silence, communicated by intervals, not the terms, of the statement', although he also promises 'to state silences' (*Dream* 138). The gaps in Beckett's fiction and the stating of silences by unwriting the written, as well as the stage emptiness and moments of stillness and silence in Beckett's drama, are anticipated here.

Eckhart's praise of silence proved to be particularly influential at the beginning of the twentieth century. In fact, two scholars have separately hypothesized Eckhart's influence on Wittgenstein's *Tractatus Logico-Philosophicus* (1921), the one suggesting that it was mediated by Schopenhauer (Sebastian 2016, 42) and the other proposing that Fritz Mauthner brought Eckhart's teaching of silence to Wittgenstein's attention (Nájera 2007, n.p.). Early commentators repeatedly drew attention to the parallel between the import of silence in Beckett's writing and the final proposition of Wittgenstein's *Tractatus*, 'Whereof one cannot speak, thereof one must be silent'. It is not surprising that they would see such an influence, which, however, turned out to be a matter of consonance and shared sources.[30]

Since the 1970s, Beckett critics have switched from Wittgenstein to explore Fritz Mauthner's influence on Beckett, who is known to have read Mauthner in the 1930s, although exactly when remains debatable.[31]

---

[30] Beckett's repeated denials of having read Wittgenstein before the 1960s are corroborated by the books by and on Wittgenstein in his library with publication dates of 1960 and later. For an overview of Beckett's reading by and about Wittgenstein and the critical literature on Beckett's affinities with the author of the *Tractatus*, see Van Hulle and Nixon 2013, 163–7.

[31] Fritz Mauthner, a Czech-German writer and philosopher, was born in 1849 in Horice, Bohemia, in what is now the Czech Republic. Like the thirty-five-year younger Franz Kafka, he was born into an upper-middle-class German-speaking Jewish family during the time that Bohemia was part of the

Mauthner praises Eckhart's view on silence toward the beginning and end of his influential three-volume *Beiträge zu einer Kritik der Sprache* (Contributions to a Critique of Language).[32] In the *Beiträge*'s first volume, a brief subsection entitled '*Schweigen*' (Silence) quotes from Eckhart's German sermon *DW* 101 on an inner unknowing (*Unwissen*) involving a forgetfulness of self and all things of sense (*BKS I* 82–3).[33] Even though Mauthner praises Eckhart's profound and beautiful words on the 'greatness of silence' (*BKS I* 82), he finds the praise of silence in the Upanishads even more subtle, quoting the story about the sage Bāhva who met a request to define the world principle *brahman* with silence, finally explaining after being repeatedly solicited, that his silence is the explanation: '*Ātman* [another term for *brahman*] is silent' ('Âtman ist stille'). Mauthner adds that the sacred sound *Om* – considered a symbol for *brahman* – although still too much of a word, nevertheless points to the possibility of a silence beyond silence (*Überstille*) by way of a *Nichtwort* (nonword) (83). The implication of the *Nichtwort* as something that is not a word for Beckett's proposed 'Literatur des Unworts' (literature of the unword) in his 1937 letter to Axel Kaun is discussed in Chapter 4.[34]

The source Mauthner gives for the 'Âtman ist stille' story is Paul Deussen's 1898 *Die Philosophie der Upanishads*, in which the German Indologist and Upanishad translator and specialist explains that the story, seemingly based on a lost Upanishad, was retold by Shankara in his commentary on the Brahma Sūtra (Deussen 1907 [1898], 143).[35] In his explanation about the function of a *Nichtwort*, Mauthner is, then,

Austro-Hungarian Empire (as it was until 1918), making both writers Austro-Hungarian citizens at birth. For some reason, unlike Kafka, who is known as a Czech writer, Mauthner continues to be called an Austrian or Austro-Hungarian writer by some, even though, after studying law at the Charles University of Prague, as did Kafka, he spent most of his working life as a writer and journalist in Berlin. He died in 1923 in Meersburg, Germany.

[32] The sections on silence are found in *BKS I* 81–4, and *BKS III* 617–8. We do not know which of the three editions of the *Beiträge* Beckett used in the 1930s to collect notes for Joyce and to copy passages into his 'Whoroscope' notebook. Joyce's edition of the *Beiträge* is missing, and the third edition that remained in Beckett's library at his death was seemingly obtained after 1954, Beckett having mentioned not having a copy of the *Beiträge* in a letter of that year (Van Hulle and Nixon 2013, 162–3). My citations from the *Beiträge*'s first volume are taken from the third edition of 1921, whereas those from the second and third volumes refer to the second edition of 1912. However, since the page numbers are identical for the second and third editions, all my citations nevertheless correspond to the third edition.

[33] Translations from Mauthner's untranslated *Beiträge* are my own.

[34] For Dirk Van Hulle, Beckett's *Unwort* (unword) resembles the *Nichtwort* (nonword) cited in Mauthner's *Beiträge* (Van Hulle and Nixon 2013, 159).

[35] In another instance of the influence of Schopenhauer and Indian thought at the turn of the nineteenth century, Deussen (1845–1919), whose work on the Upanishads is still cited today, founded the Schopenhauer Society and edited Schopenhauer's works.

paraphrasing Deussen who seemingly chose this term to translate the passage of the Maitrāyaṇīya Upanishad (6.22) advocating going beyond *Oṃ* by means of something other than a word (Deussen 1907 [1898], 351). The *Nichtwort* (nonword) for the uncreated, impersonal, eternal principle *brahman* (neuter gender) that is beyond its three principle manifestations, the *trimūrti*, consisting in the masculine-gendered Brahma, the Creator; Vishnu, the Preserver; and Shiva, the Destroyer (Stutley and Stutley 1977, 31, 49–51), bears a striking resemblance to Eckhart's citation of Dionysius's 'unspoken word' for the unsayable divinity (*gotheit*) beyond the Trinitarian God (*DW* 53; *MEW I* 564; *CMW* 152). In their attentiveness to an uncreated ultimate reality, whether termed the *unborn*, *brahman*, *gotheit*, or simply an unknowable beyond, the Buddha, Shankara, Eckhart, and Schopenhauer concur on their insistence on silence in face of the unknowable. Beckett chimes in with his persona's proposed writing of silence in *Dream*, reiterated by his own 'literature of the unword' in his 1937 letter to Axel Kaun (*Dis* 173) and subsequent insistence on unknowingness and maneuvers of unwriting.

The Upanishadic nonword, then, is another instance of the common heritage of Indian thinking into which the various strands dip. Silence, as we know, is the proper response to the Buddhist absolute, as it is envisioned by the Buddha and Nāgārjuna. For one scholar of Indian thought, both the Upanishads and the Buddha speak of ultimate reality 'as incomparable to anything we know; silence is their most proper language' (Murti 1955, 19). There is, however, a major difference between the silence beyond silence associated with the *brahman* and *gotheit*, on the one hand, and, on the other, the Buddhist unknowable beyond envisioned in terms of emptiness, with which Schopenhauer and Beckett are attuned. Beckett's 'unword' and his association with the proponents of the 1940s French 'literature of silence' are discussed further in Chapter 4. Interesting to note here is that Maurice Blanchot, the major proponent of the 1940s French literature of silence, retold the Shankara story about the silence beyond silence in his *Faux Pas* (Blanchot 2001 [1943], 36).

The next chapter will discuss Beckett's *Dream* in more detail in relation to the sources plumbed so far and examine Beckett's subsequent fictions of the 1930s with regard to the Buddhist concepts elucidated in these first two introductory chapters.

CHAPTER 3

Buddhist and Mystic Threads in the Early Fiction

'Wild Thoughts' and 'Ecstatic Mind' in Beckett's First Novel

The Buddhist reverberations in Beckett's Belacqua saga of the early 1930s have long remained undetected, as *Dream of Fair to Middling Women* and the short story 'Echo's Bones' languished in the archives of Dartmouth College until posthumously resurrected. When, in the 1970s, Beckett discussed the unpublished *Dream* with Eoin O'Brien, who was eventually to coedit the novel for its first publication sixty years after having suffered repeated rejections by publishers, Beckett described it as '*the chest into which I threw all my wild thoughts*'. He, moreover, admitted to having 'pilfered' this hoard of his thoughts for his subsequent works (qtd. in O'Brien 1992, xiii–xiv; emphasis in the original). It may indeed be the 'wild thoughts' that kept him from authorizing the publication of his *Dream* until after his death. But exempt from the 'wildness' is the trope of the enwombed and entombed mind that was to have many imaginative reincarnations in Beckett's later works.

Beckett's projection of simultaneously prenatal and posthumous spaces into his fiction and drama in the form of psycho-objects and psycho-environments can be read as forms of 'distributed' or 'extended' cognition involving the externalization of thoughts and ideas into objects. Such 'epistemic mediators', philosopher of cognition Lorenzo Magnani contends, are a means of making otherwise unattainable knowledge available within a social community (Magnani 2009, xiv, xv, 11).[1] There is further some similarity between the Beckettian psycho-spaces and the 'occluded image' described by Anthony Uhlmann (after the French philosopher Michèle Le Dœuff): in hiding meanings and glossing over aporias and difficulties, such images carry the conceptual power to provoke reflection

---

[1] As Magnani points out, 'distributed cognition' is related to the hypothesis of 'extended mind' – mind extended into body and environment – that is of increasing interest to Beckett studies (Magnani 2009, 44–5).

on what cannot be otherwise expressed (Uhlmann 2006, 80–2).[2] But beyond reflection, such paradoxical writing can further give rise to the 'cognitive sublime', which, in H. Porter Abbott's definition, is the 'immersion in a state of bafflement' or 'a kind of textual transaction that conveys the felt quality of a real extratextual unknown', an apt term for the effects of the unknown/unknowable in discourse (Abbott 2009, 132, 139). It is an interaction whose effects were anticipated, among others, by the Buddha, writers of the *via negativa*, Schopenhauer, and Beckett.

The first part of this chapter takes a closer look at Belacqua's prenatal and postmortem space of creativity in terms of its family resemblance with the Buddhist and Christian mystical thought Beckett encountered in his readings shortly before composing the Belacqua saga. From these sources he 'pilfered' bits to incorporate into his early writing but not before imaginatively blending, reshaping, and, intermittently, parodying them. As we have seen, it is a procedure he is well known to have followed in his borrowings.[3] Thus, in 'Dante... Bruno. Vico.. Joyce', Beckett's 1929 defense of Joyce's 'Work in Progress', he terms Joyce's echoes of Giambattista Vico's philosophy, 'reverberations' and 'reapplications', adding that these, however, do not receive 'the faintest explicit illustration' (*Dis* 20). Beckett's adoption of this method from his first writings to his last adds to the 'occlusive' nature of his images, leaving it to scholars to detect the hidden sources and their unsuspected reverberations (Uhlmann 2006, 82). An outstanding example of Beckett's tendency to secrete intertexts into his works is found in his 'Whoroscope' notebook of the 1930s about his future novel *Murphy*. Noting, 'Purgatorial atmosphere sustained throughout', Beckett admonishes himself to keep the Dantean analogy out of sight (qtd. in Ackerley 1998, xxiii).

On the topic of plagiarism and the ubiquitous tendency of modernists to parody classical texts, Linda Hutcheon aptly associates modern parody with intertextuality or 'transtextuality' in their Bakhtinian dialogic, 'double-voiced', and 'double-directed' mode. Rightly drawing attention to pragmatic recontextualizing, which necessarily effects altered meanings for a text transferred into a new context, she further emphasizes that the parodic dialogue between texts more often than not, entails both critique and homage. Unlike other echoic textual maneuvers, parodic texts, she

---

[2] 'Aporia' is either an inextricable textual paradox or a feigned declaration of doubt. The latter meaning is humorously illustrated in *The Unnamable*, when the narrator declares at the outset of a work abundantly practicing aporia in the former sense: 'I say aporia without knowing what it means' (*Un* 291). On aporia, see Chapter 4 and Dennis 2015a, 180–97.

[3] See Daniela Caselli's invaluable *Beckett's Dantes* (2005).

further maintains, repeat previous texts while taking an ironic distance from them, an irony that 'can cut both ways' (Hutcheon 1985, 6–10, 31–7). For her, parody excludes plagiarism, the latter occurring when the intertext is not apparent because of the author or artist's pains to keep it out of sight (39), as in Beckett's 'pilfering' and occluding tendencies. Nevertheless, discerning audiences (and sleuthing scholars) are able to undercut this ploy in a shared cognitive environment.

The mental limbo of unborn shades and source of creativity attributed to Belacqua Shuah, functions as a leitmotif in *Dream*. Throughout, however, the withdrawal into this inner retreat by *Dream*'s 'dud mystic' (*Dream* 186) clashes with his antiheroic misadventures involving other characters. Burlesque and even caustic versions of people close to the author, they are condemned by his persona, with few exceptions, as a 'nuisance' (36, 51). As the novel's title predicts, depicted with particular verve is Belacqua's flagging pursuit of women, his Dantean *dolce stil nuovo* (sweet new style), or troubadour-inspired praise for an idealized love object, undone by his flight from women's lusty and injuriously portrayed bodies into masturbation and the brothel. Beatrice or the brothel is a stated alternative (102). In an instance of double-directed irony, Beckett parodically inverts the *dolce stil nuovo* and religious and mystical language to portray Belacqua's sexual practices. The conflicting tone – at times lyrical and mystic, at other times grotesque and offensive, with each drawing on a different set of sources – inflects the flight from the 'world's woes' (*W* 247) into an inner haven.[4] *Dream*'s clash between flesh and spirit coincides with Schopenhauer's two poles of, on the one hand, sexuality as the expression of the will and, on the other hand, the will-less peaceful contemplation outside of time (*WWR I* § 39, 227).[5] Because of this foregrounded conflict, Beckett's novel may be taken as a spoof on the young Beckett's earlier erotic mysticism in his first published short story 'Assumption' of 1929, whose poet, mediated by a 'Woman', 'hungered to be irretrievably engulfed in the light of eternity . . . in infinite fulfillment' (*CSP* 7).

Hiding or mocking the mystical pursuits of his persona, Beckett called his work in progress a 'German Comedy' in a letter of 27 May 1932 to his friend Thomas MacGreevy (*LSB I* 78). In the first half of the novel, the episodes involving the Smeraldina are situated in German-speaking locales and peppered with German colloquial phrases, including choice

---

[4] Beckett's 'Dream' notebook contains numerous entries on flagellation, masturbation, and other sexual topics taken from late nineteenth-century texts. See *DN* #s 335–486.

[5] The conflict between spirit and flesh is amply demonstrated in patriarchal culture's simultaneous overvaluing and undervaluing of women, themes which are treated throughout *Dream* with parodic brio.

scatological interjections. The Smeraldina – based on Beckett's cousin Peggy Sinclair – is one of Belacqua's three loves in this early fiction, each a fictionalized version of the author's own. In the willed 'incoherent continuum' of *Dream* (102), the grotesque undercuts the mystical, and the mystical the grotesque, resulting in the doubly ironic distance maintained by the fictionalized 'Mr Beckett' from the doings of his persona (69, 141, 186). Or, rather, the grotesque realism of the 'German comedy' and of the Dublin comedy that follows, peppered with social, political, and cultural critique, precipitates Belacqua's urge to retreat into his 'ecstatic mind'.[6]

In several further instances of double-voiced parody, there are a number of humorous examples involving Inge's comments in *Christian Mysticism* on Eckhart's wavering about the nature of the soul's *Fünkelein*, the diminutive of *Funke* (spark), a recurring Neoplatonic metaphor in Eckhart's sermons. The *Fünkelein*, or little spark, Inge explains at one point, is the divine immanent in the soul (Inge 1899, 156). Beckett duly 'pilfered' it, noting it in his 'Dream' notebook' (*DN* #s 690, 691) and bestowing it on Smeraldina, 'his dear little sweet little Fünkelein' (*Dream* 17). Belacqua's 'Fünkelein' thus occurs in a paragraph bristling with the parodic use of mystic terms 'snitched' from Inge and comically denatured in an allusion to the flame mystique of the medieval and Renaissance love lyric.

Later in the novel, 'the divine and fragile Fünkelein of curiosity' plays a role in the 'presticerebration' – coined from 'prestidigitation'– involving the mental sleight of hand of stripping away the layers of representation, or our mental construction, of the world, likened to 'so many tunics of so many onions', to reach an empty inner core, 'a bel niente' (*Dream* 160–1).[7] Here Beckett in this early work is in tune with the recurring lesson of the nothingness/emptiness of the empirical world in Schopenhauer's introduction to the Buddha and Eckhart's thought, to arrive at the inner void of Belacqua's aesthetic of emptiness or the interval.

In an instance of persiflage, the *Fünklein* (missing an 'e' this time) reappears in the 'Walking Out' story of *More Pricks than Kicks*. It stands

---

[6] Of the clashing viewpoints of the 'ideal real' represented in Beckett's first novel – the grotesque real and the mystical – commentators of the novel have focused largely on the former. For instance, Patrick Bixby's compelling reading of the novel as a postcolonial bildungsroman, or coming-of-age novel, in the context of the newly established Irish Free State, does not mention Belacqua's mystic tendencies or retreat to his 'ecstatic mind' (*Dream* 16). Yet, could these not be a response to Joycean 'epiphanies', given Bixby's focus on the novel's intertextual dialogue principally with Joyce's *Portrait of an Artist as a Young Man* and 'The Dead' (Bixby 2009, 40–83)?

[7] Beckett's 'bel niente' no doubt contracts the Italian motto 'il bel far niente' (the beauty of doing nothing) to turn it into Belacqua's 'beautiful nothing'. It is noteworthy that this praise of nothing precedes Beckett's adoption of the nothing of Democritus and Geulincx in *Murphy*.

for the 'private experiences' Belacqua prefers to the company of his fiancée
Lucy, further clarified by the pun on 'sursum corda' that transfers the
admonition of Christian worship to 'lift up your heart' to Belacqua's
voyeuristic sexual practices (*MPTK* 114–15). In the double-voiced parody,
apparent throughout the Belacqua saga, Eckhart's divine *Fünkelein* is
travestied to intimate Belacqua's erotic proclivities and adopted for serious
contemplation of the nothingness at the heart of existence.

First acquaintance with Belacqua's mental limbo comes in *Dream*'s long
second part, contrasting with the first, which, covering less than a page,
depicts, in a Joycean pastiche, the overfed child Belacqua engaged in self-
titillating acrobatics. The second part begins more sedately with the adult
Belacqua's ironically narrated attempt to direct his mind to grieve for the
departure of Smeraldina, a melancholy soon 'swallowed up', as we are told,
by 'the much greater affliction of being a son of Adam' (*Dream* 5). The
narrator takes pains to emphasize that Belacqua's psychic maneuvers to
enwomb and entomb his mind are in response to the world's woes. Not
only 'its own asylum' (*Dream* 44) and 'a real pleasure' (6), the entombed
mind, as already noted, is 'the ecstatic mind ... achieving creation', with
the narrator coyly pointing to his own mind as an example (16). Genesis is
conceived of in terms of exuberant cosmic imagery of the night sky and,
borrowing from Inge's portrayal of Dionysius, the mind's 'creative integ-
rity' is envisioned as a mystic circular ascent from darkness to an 'apex' of
the mind (*Dream* 16–17; Inge 1899, 7, 106–9). The inner asylum and
spectral space of 'creation' is repeatedly described in the novel:

> [Belacqua] lay lapped in a beatitude of indolence ... dead to the dark pangs
> of the sons of Adam .... He moved with the shades of the dead and the
> dead-born and the unborn and the never-to-be-born, in a Limbo purged of
> desire. (44)

> [Belacqua's retreat was] the dark gulf, when the glare of the will and the
> hammer-strokes of the brain ... were expunged, the Limbo and the
> wombtomb alive with the unanxious spirits of quiet cerebration, where
> there was no conflict of flight and flow .... The cities and forests and beings
> were without identity, they were shadows .... The emancipation ... from
> identity, his own and his neighbour's, suits his accursed complexion. (121)

> It was the descent and the enwombing, assumption upside down. (181)

In summary, Belacqua's mental haven is pictured in terms of

(1)   a womblike and tomblike space comparable to a limbo containing
      shades of the dead and unborn;
(2)   desire-lessness ('purged of desire');

(3)   an asylum, beyond desire, free from suffering and fluctuating attraction-repulsion ('dead to the dark pangs of the sons of Adam', 'no conflict of flight and flow');

(4)   will-lessness ('the glare of the will ... expunged');

(5)   and the liberation from will: no I, no you, no world, no subject-object relation ('The cities and forests and beings were shadows'; 'emancipation ... from identity, his own and his neighbour's');

(6)   quietude ('beatitude of indolence'. 'quiet cerebration');

(7)   a descent into inner darkness ('dark gulf', 'assumption upside down');

(8)   a place of contemplation ('spirits of quiet cerebration');

(9)   generativity ('ecstatic mind ... achieving creation');

(10) 'real pleasure'.

In this psychic refuge, Belacqua, liberated from desire, suffering, will, self, and the relation of self to non-self, or world, can contemplate and 'achieve creation' among the shades. The congruence with Schopenhauer's influential views on art and aesthetic contemplation is hard to miss: its timeless will-lessness, self-forgetting, independent of subject-object relations, resulting in the end of suffering, inner calm, and resignation (*WWR I* § 38, 219–23). As seen in the previous chapter, the Buddhist tenor of Belacqua's imagined space is indebted to Schopenhauer's envisioning artistic production in terms analogous to the Buddha's path to emancipation. That, along with the Buddha's thinking, Plato influenced Schopenhauer's view of aesthetic contemplation and Beckett's adoption of it can be traced to the common elements of Platonism and Buddhism pointed out by Inge. Eckhart's negative path calling for renunciation of self and world to reach an unknowable, unsayable absolute, is further remarkably consonant, as Schopenhauer claims, with his and the Buddha's teachings, absent his theistic vision. In fact, for Schopenhauer, the tranquilizing of willing in the contemplation of art results in the resignation, 'which is the innermost spirit of both Christianity as well as Indian wisdom' (*WWR I* § 48, 259). Negating the will (by means of aesthetic contemplation or asceticism), Schopenhauer writes, 'is the only possible redemption from the world and its miseries' (*WWR I* § 65, 394), accounting for the many times Beckett alludes to tranquilizing the will in his subsequent fictions and theatre.

The darkness of Belacqua's mental haven, however, has a different source, perhaps Dionysius's mystical darkness of unknowing about which Beckett would have read at the end of Inge's third lecture, darkness being a common metaphor for the unknowingness that is part of the *via negativa*.

In *The Mystical Theology*, Dionysius writes: 'I pray we could come to this darkness so far above light! If only we lacked sight and knowledge so as to see, so as to know, unseeing and unknowing, that which lies beyond all vision and knowledge' (qtd. in Kügler 2005, 95). In fact, when writer Charles Juliet told Beckett in the 1970s that reading the mystics reminded him of Beckett's writing, the latter conceded that 'peut-être y avait-il parfois une même façon de subir l'inintelligible' (perhaps there was at times an identical way of experiencing the unintelligible; qtd. in Juliet 1986, 38).[8]

Beckett's psychic limbo of dead and unborn shades further evokes the doctrine of rebirth. John Pilling, on the other hand, glosses Belacqua's limbo as the first circle of Dante's *Inferno* in Canto 4 (Pilling 2003, 86). More closely than Dante's Limbo, however, Belacqua's resembles the Limbo of Dante's guide Virgil in book 6 of the *Aeneid*, inhabited by the ancient dead and souls awaiting rebirth. Virgil's belief in reincarnation was shared not only by Hindus and Buddhists, but, as Schopenhauer tells us, by the ancient Egyptians, the Pythagoreans, Plato, the Gnostics, the Druids, and the indigenous populations of America and Australia, among others (*WWR II* ch. 41, 521–3). Beckett, for example, along with other modernists, including Joyce, who were fascinated by the *Egyptian Book of the Dead*, was to draw on several underworlds in his works, including the Egyptian. Nevertheless, in reading Belacqua's limbo in concert with the other facets of his mystic asylum that make of it a space of creativity and rebirth, Schopenhauer's adoption of Buddhist palingenesis (see Chapter 2) is the more compelling and one that concurs with the state of the reborn Belacqua in 'Echo's Bones' to be analyzed below.

Despite Belacqua's experiments with ascetic practices – breath control and restraint of the senses – 'Mr Beckett' admits that to linger in the 'ecstastic mind' is no easy matter. Flare-ups of desire and will check his persona's attempts 'to enwomb him[self], to exclude the bric-à-brac and expunge his consciousness' (*Dream* 123). Sporadic returns to his inner retreat and the 'spirits of his dead and his unborn' (44) are all he will be able to muster. It is a matter of 'waiting until the thing happens' (124).

Belacqua's limbo can be seen as an early attempt to imagine what Maurice Blanchot in his famous review was to describe as *L'Innommable*'s imaginary space of writing, a radical and timeless exteriority (*dehors*) of a no-self,

---

[8] Beckett's privileging darkness for the generative space in the mind further concurs with Proust's dictum, in *Le Temps retrouvé*, identifying genuine books with darkness and silence: 'Les vrais livres doivent être les enfants ... de l'obscurité et du silence' (1989 [1927], 476).

inhabited by phantoms, but in which quietude has given way to feelings of unease and anxiety and alienated voices murmuring through the silence (Blanchot 1979 [1953], 116–21; *Un* 293–303). For Beckett, Blanchot's 1953 review of *L'Innommable* was 'la chose capitale', the review that mattered most to him (*LSB II* 441). If in the work of the 1930s the inner space of creativity is an ideal asylum – 'Assumption upside down' – in the postwar work, it is shadowed by the entrapment and persecutory dimension of inner space – linked to the real of the 'human predicament' spun out of control in a catastrophic war .[9] More on this topic in later chapters.

In *Dream*, as previously noted, creativity fostered by the eclipse of self and world in consciousness resonates with Buddhist thinkers, Eckhart, and Schopenhauer. In the double viewpoint of the everyday 'real' and the mystic 'ideal real', Beckett's first novel's 'ecstatic mind' and embrace of the creative potential of emptiness – the hyphen or interval – is shadowed by its ending in a depraved physical equivalent, as Belacqua, sitting on a Dublin bridge, drenched in pouring rain, is looking at his hands in a drunken stupor until told to move on.

Throughout Beckett's first novel, the narrative scaffolding encompasses the homopseudonymous 'Mr Beckett' who, as the writer in the text, functions as the omniscient narrator of the inner and outer adventures of Belacqua, and conceives of the enwombing tomb or the entombing womb in his persona's mind where identity vanishes and ecstatic creation takes place. Preferring this inner asylum to the 'nuisance' of interactions with the world without, Belacqua, a budding poet and writer in the parodically deformed image of 'Mr Beckett', dreams of the void that remains when all illusions are peeled away, the 'bel niente', which is the ground that will generate a different kind of relation, the one of the 'interval'. And in the company of unborn phantoms, *Dream*'s writer in the text recognizes his own generative powers.

In his subsequent works, Beckett reshuffles this early narrative structure in his repeated attempts to reconceptualize the space of writing from which issue the ghostly voices that speak through his narrators and personages. Increasingly, though, as the early quietude of this self-dispossession and renunciation is displaced by scenarios of hellish imprisonment, reminiscent of the cyclical births, deaths, and rebirths of *saṃsāra*, the suffering of life dreams screens the always there but elusive horizon of timelessness and pregnant void.

[9] Of Beckett's trilogy of postwar novels, written from 1947 to 1950 in French, *L'Innommable* / *The Unnamable* (French, 1953; English, 1958) is the third, preceded by *Molloy* (French, 1951; English 1955) and *Malone meurt* / *Malone Dies* (French, 1951; English, 1956).

The Womb Metaphor and the Pregnant Void

The womb metaphor in Beckett's oeuvre bears some further investigation, especially its reverberations with this topos in theological and philosophical writings. In addition to the womb trope in *Dream* and later works, Beckett, in some of his letters, figuratively and wittily speaks of the uterine origin of his works (see *LSB I* 381 and *LSB II* 263). In fact, the womb metaphor holds a distinctive place in conceptions of male generativity. An embryonic life that matures outside of conscious control is no doubt one of the reasons for this fascination, although womb envy, the desire to appropriate maternal generative powers, is not easily dismissed. Beckett's adoption of the psychic womb-and-tomb metaphor in *Dream*, a motif that was to resurface throughout his writing, not only hearkens back to distant forerunners but is a figural translation of a concept shared, as we know, by his contemporaries who similarly imagined their artistic making welded to the Indian-inspired space of a before- and afterlife that Schopenhauer popularized in the West.

The womb metaphor to designate male creativity, however, is not Schopenhauer's. It functions, as it were, as a simulacrum,[10] which from the 1920s onward was encouraged by the writings of still another thinker under the influence of Schopenhauer's relay of Buddhist teachings. In his influential *Das Trauma der Geburt / The Trauma of Birth* (German, 1924; English, 1929), psychoanalyst Otto Rank conceived of death as the pleasurable return to the womb or the 'projection of the life before birth into the future after death' (Rank 2010 [1924], 61). Was Beckett, who took notes on *The Trauma of Birth* a few years after composing his first novel, startled by this convergence with his womb-and-tomb asylum? Or could he have read or heard about Rank's theories earlier? The affinity of their conceptions is less surprising when they can be traced to a common Schopenhauerian source: Rank refers specifically to Schopenhauer in describing *nirvāṇa* as 'the pleasurable Nothing, the womb situation, to which even Schopenhauer's half metaphysical "Will" yearned solely to return' (Rank 2010, 119).[11] Rank's view of *nirvāṇa*, however, diverges from Schopenhauer's, who contends, as we know, that *nirvāṇa* can be

---

[10] In Deleuze's Platonic definition, a simulacrum, unlike an iconic copy of the Idea, produces a perverted '*effect* of resemblance' only simulating similarity (Deleuze 1990 [1969], 256, 258; emphasis in the original). In a critique of representation, unlike Plato, Deleuze and other postmodern thinkers favor the simulacrum over the iconic copy.

[11] For Phil Baker (1997, 64, 65), Rank's *The Trauma of Birth* popularized the 'mythical womb' which contributed to making the 1930s 'the decade of the wombtomb'.

designated as 'nothing' only because there are no concepts or words to define it. Moreover, instead of identifying *nirvāṇa* with the 'womb situation', Schopenhauer cites the Buddhist view that it is an escape from *saṃsāra* and its cycles of birth, death, and rebirth. To what extent Beckett at times draws on Rank's view as contrasted with Schopenhauer's is probed in the discussion of *Murphy* at the end of this chapter.

A number of earlier visions of a pregnant nothing helps us to understand the philosophical underpinnings of Beckett's poetics of the 'interval' and of 'stating silences' at this early stage (*Dream* 138). Two variations on the male womb metaphor are the figure of a divine birth-giving creator and the notion of a 'pregnant void', the latter another commonality between Eckhart and Buddhist thought. The young Beckett is unlikely to have missed the Eckhartian motif of the divine birth in the soul that Inge mentions on several pages and nested into his patchwork of quotations (Inge 1899, 158). Eckhart compares the soul's fruitfulness to childbearing, and few are the sermons in which he fails to celebrate God giving birth to his son in the soul. 'He lies in childbed', Eckhart says of the Creator, 'like a woman who has given birth' (*DW* 75; *MEW II* 120; *CMW* 429).) In fact, imaginatively portraying the male-gendered God's generativity in the maternal terms of giving birth is a rhetorical device with a long biblical and Neoplatonic past. Feminist theologians refer to it as a 'transgendered metaphor' (D. Williams 2016, 283–5) and feminist scholars in the 1970s famously theorized in terms of *écriture féminine* and 'gynesis', the adoption of the matric metaphor by male thinkers, writers, and artists who marry their creative productions to the act of giving birth.[12] In enlarging our horizon, we find transgendered metaphors in many mythological and religious texts and artworks around the world, including the Upanishads, the Purāṇas, Mahāyāna scriptures, and Hindu and Buddhist Tantric sculptures and mandalas.[13]

Beckett's 'transgendered metaphor' of the mind-womb as the space of literary creation resonates with the maternal metaphors tentatively proposed by Plato, Eckhart, and the Buddhist doctrine of the womb of the Buddha, for the creation out of nothing. The womb functions as a trope for a process of creation from nothing that philosophers and religious

---

[12] On male pregnancy and 'text as child' metaphors that male writers and artists draw on, see Paul Lawley's 'Hedda's Children' (n.d.) in which he explores the 'text as child' metaphor of early and late modernists including Beckett.

[13] See Zimmer 1936, 89, 105, 486, 489; Moorjani 2000, 55–7.

thinkers, Eastern and Western, declare unsayable, while nevertheless, seemingly irresistibly, drawing on the womb trope of whose limitations they are aware. A startling variation on this motif is Eckhart's account of 'someone' who dreamed he was pregnant with nothing, 'like a woman with child', and in this nothing God was born (*DW* 71; *MEW II* 72; *CMW* 140).

Eckhart's dream of a birth-giving nothing is analogous to the Platonic dreamlike *khōra* in *Timaeus,* which Plato conceives of as both an empty space and a 'Receptacle – as it were, the nurse – of all Becoming' and 'a matrix for everything' (*Timaeus* 49 and 50c).[14] In fact, Eckhart knew of the kinship between the *khōra* and his conception of the divine birth from nothing. Aware of the abiding philosophical fascination with the second part of Plato's *Timaeus,* in which he introduces the concept of the *khōra,* a fascination stretching from the Neoplatonists to Jacques Derrida, philosopher Kurt Flasch maintains that Eckhart owes his conception of the divine as the archetypal ground of the world to *Timaeus* (Flasch 2015, 182). That Beckett may have had *Timaeus* in mind in conceiving of his enwombed space of creativity and aesthetic of the interval cannot be excluded, especially since Schopenhauer appended an epigraph, suggesting *Timaeus* as a source, to his third 'book', on art (*WWR I* 191).[15]

Plato uses a number of analogies which, he declares, may be misleading, to describe his all-receiving container, admittedly 'very hard to apprehend' (50 a–b and 51b). The most worked-out figure is its likeness to human childbearing, in which in the understanding of the times, the father sows the seed, the mother matures it in her womb (50c–d). Other figures involve the work of artistic and artisanal production, a piece of gold molded into various shapes, a neutral liquid into which scents are infused, and a smooth and level surface on which shapes can be inscribed (50a–b and e).

Derrida, in heeding Plato's warning about the possibly misleading metaphors he proposes for the *khōra,* qualifies this space as unknowable

---

[14] My quotations from *Timaeus* refer to the Cornford translation in Plato 1937.

[15] Although there appears to be no absolutely certain way of establishing when Beckett began his notes on philosophy (after reading Schopenhauer), Everett Frost and Jane Maxwell surmise, based on a number of indices, that he could have begun them during his time on the Trinity College faculty from autumn 1930 to the end of 1931 (Frost and Maxwell 2006, 70). He may accordingly have learned about *Timaeus* at the time of the composition of his first novel. Belacqua's aesthetics of the interval would make it seem so. In his *Beckett's Books,* Matthew Feldman, however, pointing out that Plato is mentioned on page 235 of *Dream,* adds the caution that this and other brief references to philosophers in the novel 'come from varied sources and are not evidence of any sustained study of philosophy before 1932' (Feldman 2006, 60).

and beyond all words and figurations. He is here following the Neoplatonic apophatic tradition of Dionysius and Eckhart, without, however, subscribing to their theological interpretations (Derrida 1989, 38–53). In arguing for the total 'otherness' of the *khōra,* whose apprehension, Plato writes, is dreamlike (52b), Derrida reads the *khōra* as 'a spatial interval [that] neither dies nor is born' (Derrida 1989, 35), 'the wholly other' (39), and 'something that is neither a being nor a nothingness' (36).

In envisioning a pregnant emptiness to speak of the unsayable, the *khōra,* about which Plato repeatedly insists that it has no characteristics of its own (50b–c), and Eckhart's birth-giving void derived from the *khōra* are consonant with the Mahāyāna concept of *śūnyatā* or emptiness. The analogous Platonic/Neopolatonic and Buddhist conceptions can be taken as another of the parallels that Inge found to exist between the Platonic and Buddhist 'spiritual enlightenment' around the fifth century BCE. In the Mahāyāna doctrine of the *unborn,* the ultimate reality beyond birth and death – the *tathāgatagarbha* – is an equivalent of *śūnyatā.* As previously noted, the *tathāgatagarbha* inheres in all sentient beings and enables the attainment of an unborn 'Buddha-nature' and *nirvāṇa* (Ruegg 1969, 262, 305, 501). The term is variously translated into a figural conception of emptiness, that is, the 'inner sanctum', 'womb', or 'embryo' (*gharba*) of the Buddha (the *Tathāgata*) (Williams and Tribe 2000, 162). The Dzogchen tradition of Tibetan esotericism – a later development of Mahāyāna – too, draws on the womb metaphor in describing *śūnyatā* in terms of the 'the womb of the great mother, emptiness' (qtd. in Davies 2000, 21). Beckett's transgendered metaphor follows an impressive number of forerunners, East and West, in imagining the ground of generativity.

Returning now to Eckhart's dream of a pregnant void and Beckett's variation on this topos, Eckhart's teachings of a generative void were bound to intrigue the Buddhist (mostly Zen) commentators who followed Schopenhauer's example of exploring the resemblances between Eckhart's thought and Mahāyāna Buddhism. Thus, beginning his study of Christian and Buddhist mysticism by comparing Eckhart's teachings with Buddhist thought, Daisetz T. Suzuki (1870–1966), clarifies that, for Buddhists, emptiness is not nihilism but 'a zero full of infinite possibilities, it is a void of inexhaustible contents' (Suzuki 1957, 28). The Mahāyāna reconciliation of opposites (to be discussed in the next two chapters) – here emptiness and fullness – is apparent in seeing fullness in the void and the void in fullness. In 1961, concurring with the generative potential of the void, Beckett explained to a group of students: 'I want to bring poetry into drama, a poetry which has been through the void and makes a new start in a new room-space. I think in new dimensions' (qtd. in Knowlson 1996, 427).[16] Japanese author Junto Matoba has taken up the challenge of defining this new 'room-space'. Explaining that *yohaku* is the empty space in Zen painting that makes possible the creative act of giving 'form to what had no form' (Matoba 2003, 85), she provides, as already noted, a compelling Zen interpretation of the empty space in Beckett's theatre. Beckett's affinity with the Zen view of the creative act is further apparent in his comment to Charles Juliet that 'giving form to the formless' ('[donner] forme à l'informe') is the only affirmation available to artists (qtd. in Juliet 1986, 28).

There are more Beckett exegetes who explore the role of emptiness in Beckett's oeuvre. In her *Iconic Spaces*, Sandra Wynands draws on Mahāyāna *śūnyatā* to analyze Beckett's late drama in fascinating ways, claiming that emptiness can be made most evident visually on stage (Wynands 2007, 14). In a further instance of the consonance between emptiness and negative mysticism's apophasis and 'apotropism' – the turning away from figures – Shira Wolosky (without reference to Buddhism) aptly maintains that the stripping away of figures does not lead to a true self, but a no-self (Wolosky 1989, 182). In her view, Beckett converts nothingness into 'a fertile source of continuous imaginative effort' (184). In fact, in a 1978 entry into his 'Sottisier' notebook, Beckett transforms Parmenides' cosmological argument 'ex nihilo nihil fit' (nothing comes from nothing), by substituting *omne* for *nihil*, so that turning the argument around, it reads, 'everything comes from nothing' (UoR MS 2901).[17]

A charge of nihilism nevertheless continues to be a temptation for commentators on the writers and thinkers who embrace the 'infinite possibilities' of emptiness. Thus in his impressive study *A Taste for the Negative: Beckett and Nihilism*, in which he cites a formidable cast of philosophers who refute the charge of nihilism against Beckett – Adorno, Badiou, Blanchot, Cavell, Cixous, Critchley, Deleuze, Derrida – Shane Weller nevertheless suggests that *Dream*'s 'wombtomb fantasy' can be read (although he does not do so) as 'a classic case of what Nietzsche diagnoses as "passive nihilism" or "European Buddhism", Schopenhauerian through and through' (Weller 2005, 5). Schopenhauerian Buddhism, yes, but 'passive nihilism', Nietzsche

---

[16] Beckett made this comment in a bookstore in Bielefeld, Germany, during a discussion with a group of students in their final years of higher secondary school. As Knowlson explains, someone must have taken down his words, which subsequently appeared in print (Knowlson 1996, 427).

[17] For commentators who have explored the resonances in Beckett's texts with Christian apophatic thought, in addition to the ones mentioned in this chapter, see Abbott 2013, 33, n. 7.

notwithstanding, is a misreading of both Schopenhauer and the early Beckett's 'ecstatic mind ... achieving creation' in consonance with Mahāyāna Buddhist and Eckhartian claims of the creative potential of emptiness, an emptiness not to be confused with nihilism.

Concluding the Belacqua Saga: Buddhist Reverberations in 'Echo's Bones'

In the Belacqua stories, which Beckett added or transferred from his unpublished first novel to the collection of stories *More Pricks than Kicks*, he diminished the autobiographical, writerly, and mystical elements of *Dream* and its meditations on generativity, concentrating instead on a social and political satire of Dublin society alternating with the farcical portrayals of Belacqua's sexual escapades in the city's pastoral surroundings. The Dublin comedy, begun in the second half of *Dream*, takes the place of the 'German comedy'. The entombed and enwombed mind gets barely a nod. Instead, in 'Fingal', the collection's second story, the indolent Belacqua declares, 'I want very much to be back in the caul, on my back in the dark for ever', foreshadowing the 'one on his back in the dark' of *Company* some forty years later (*MPTK* 31; *Co* 7) and the many reiterations in subsequent Beckett texts of a re-enwombing as a means of undoing birth. And in 'Draff', the collection's final story, the preparation of Belacqua's grave, following fast on his demise in the previous story, suggests an 'upholstered' grave resembling the cushioned walls of the womb, from which Belacqua will be reborn (*MPTK* 195–6). This uterine grave is perhaps the first of a long series of externalized objects or simulacra of *Dream*'s imaginary space of writing.

The request from Beckett's publisher to add another story to increase the bulk of the collection of ten stories resulted in 'Echo's Bones', in which Belacqua is reborn from the 'wombtomb' in what could be described as a Buddhist fantasy, this one as well interwoven with multiple threads. Rejected by Chatto & Windus as 'a nightmare' that would depress sales of the book (qtd. in Nixon 2014, xii), the story remained unpublished until some eighty years later.

Dream's wombtomb, then, makes a come-back in 'Echo's Bones', the story written in 1933, which, after languishing in manuscript form was given a new existence in Mark Nixon's annotated edition of 2014. The story was written quickly between September and November, while Beckett was in mourning for his father and his cousin Peggy Sinclair, the model of the Smeraldina, and shortly before beginning psychotherapy with

Wilfred R. Bion in London. In tracing the story's Buddhist themes, I agree
with Richard N. Coe who, among the earliest of the scholars discovering
Buddhist allusions in Beckett's texts, asserts that Beckett's major themes
'lie hidden away behind a smoke-screen of parody . . . and the clues to their
existence are often no more than half-quotations, passing allusions or the
intrusion of an unexpected name' (Coe 1970 [1964], 27). Peripheral
elements screening major motifs are, of course, a well known displacement
tactic. The hints that serve as clues to the story's Buddhist/
Schopenhauerian themes of rebirth, karma, and *nirvāṇa* are easily missed,
especially concealed as they are in the story's exuberant Joycean style and
Belacqua's long ebullient dialogues with three outlandish characters, the
Russian prostitute Zaborovna, the folk giant Lord Gall of Wormwood,
and the tippling graveyard keeper Doyle. Both the participants and readers
of the story have considerable difficulty making heads or tails of these
bizarre dialogues overloaded with learned echoes. Dante, Boccaccio,
Rabelais, and Shakespeare are among the literary greats whose visions of
the here and hereafter figure among the tale's literary intertexts.

At the story's beginning, Belacqua is nodding among the wombtomb's
'grey shoals of angels' (*EB* 4) imported from the at-the-time unpublished
Dream, in the interworld between death and a new life, until he, 'a human,
dead and buried', finds himself 'restored to the jungle' with 'all the old
pains and aches of [his] soul-junk return[ing]' (4–5). So, this is not the
Dantean Antepurgatory, where Belacqua's namesake wiles away the time,
but the rebirth into a new existence in which the 'soul-junk' of his former
life – a cheeky translation of bad karma – continues in a new state.
Nevertheless, if the allusions to karma and rebirth correspond to an
Indian intertext, the name that Belacqua keeps in his new life and his
memories of his former textual life suggest that Beckett is blending Indian
and Dantean views of the afterlife. As we know, in his imaginary journey
through hell and purgatory, Dante – in his role of narrator-pilgrim – tells
of meetings with souls he recognizes by name who recount to him their
past sins and crimes. They are embodied souls with the language to lament
past actions and present torments. In this story, Beckett's Belacqua is
similarly a spook or a ghost, lacking a shadow and an image in the mirror,
while at the same time presenting himself as a human come back to the
world, one, moreover, indulging in the bodily pleasures of cigars, drink,
and sex. He is on the fence, where we first meet him in this story,
straddling life and death.

For Belacqua, his present spooklike existence, is as dreamlike as his
former life, so that he wonders whether he was deader then or now (*EB* 3),

the Beckettian blurring of life and death at this early juncture. The necessity of inventing a posthumous existence for the character whose death and burial had taken place in the final two stories of *More Pricks than Kicks* gives rise to Belacqua's simultaneous deadness and aliveness in the form of a ghost. Such spectral doubleness, going beyond the portrayals of the souls in Dante's *Commedia*, was to become a trait of the characters of Beckett's later fiction and plays, if in a less ironic mode that in this early story.

My reading of 'Echo's Bones' is based on the intertwined Buddhist threads that Beckett spun in engrossing ways into this final story of the Belacqua saga. The 'double-directed' effects of his intertextual dialogue with the Buddhist concepts evoked by Schopenhauer shade into both irony and homage. Thus, Belacqua's dreamlike existence, echoing Schopenhauer's 'succession of life dreams', takes the form of 'back into the muck' and 'dust of the world' (*EB* 3) – metaphors with an enduring life in Beckett's oeuvre – and the need for atonement. Atonement for what? The narrator tells us: for 'the injustice' of his 'definite individual existence' (3), which, as we know, from the Presocratics and the Buddha to Eckhart and Schopenhauer, is an illusion, sin, and error. For Mark Nixon, rightly so, the particular term of 'injustice' points to the Presocratic Anaximander (Nixon 2014, 55–6), but the condemnation of a separate individual existence is also found in the Buddha and Eckhart's indictment of the 'I' and 'mine', in Mahāyāna Buddhism's definition of *śūnyatā*, or emptiness, precluding the individual existence of anything, and, finally, Schopenhauer's reiterated critique of the principle of individuation.

Belacqua's present round of existence is portrayed as only one 'dose of expiation' of many, from which he is 'caught up each time a trifle better' (*EB* 4). This claim echoes Schopenhauer's previously cited explanation of his agreement with Buddhist palingenesis: 'These constant rebirths would then make up the succession of life dreams of a will that is in itself indestructible until, informed and improved by traversing so many and various successive cognitions, always in a new form, it abolished itself' (*WWII* ch. 41, 519). As Belacqua declares to the Zaborovna, 'I am Belacqua ... restored for a time by a lousy fate [read 'bad karma'] to the nuts and balls and sparrows of the low stature of animation' (6). The allusion to the doctrine of palingenesis is hard to miss, especially echoing as it does Schopenhauer's description of it.

As the story winds down in the graveyard setting (with allusions to *Hamlet* and *Macbeth*), it becomes clear that Belacqua would have preferred not to have been born and thereby avoid the atonements and trials of individual existence: 'Scarcely', he admits 'had my cord been clumsily severed than I struggled to reintegrate the matrix [another word for 'womb'], nor did I relax those newborn efforts until death came and undid me' (*EB* 46).[18] His unabated struggle with the will to life dates from birth. *Nirvāṇa*, which, as Beckett would have read in Schopenhauer and elsewhere, is referred to as 'extinction', is evoked when Belacqua is said to be 'at last on the threshold of total extinction' (36). Was it then his negation of the will to life along with the compassion and good words and good deeds of the proper path that brought him to this threshold? He had, in effect, been shown at one point, in the narrator's outrageously burlesque mode, to be 'crazed with compassion' on listening to the troubles of the giant Lord Gall and not only to '[feel] it incumbent upon him to hazard a kind word' (21) but to follow through on the giant's request to assure him of an heir by impregnating his syphilic wife, even if it goes awry. True to the Buddhist reinterpretation of the dogma of karma, intention determines the nature of the action.

Thus, at the very end of the story, Belacqua having placed a lantern in the coffin containing his mortal remains, his bones turned to stone, the candle in the toppled lantern is snuffed out, the Buddhist trope for *nirvāṇa*. This too Beckett would have found in Schopenhauer, who, as we have seen, devotes a long note to the etymology of the word (*WWR II* ch. 41, 525). And the stones in Belacqua's coffin, which refer to the myth of Echo of the story's title, can be taken to suggest, akin to Klee's *Rock Grave*, Schopenhauer's view of the eventual transformation of the dust or ashes of the defunct via crystallization into new life.[19] But instead, in the story, the 'snuff of candle' 'kills' off the 'sweet smell of the tubers' the new life sprouting inside Belacqua's grave (51). His last birth as a fictional character has come to an end.

The snuffed-out flame was to reappear in the 1979 *A Piece of Monologue*, a meditation on birth, death, birth again, death again in the guise of a flame extinguished, relit, extinguished, and relit seemingly endlessly, until at the end it is 'gone' and, as the stage directions state, 'Lamp out. Silence' (*CSPL* 265), in what can be taken to be a reprise of the *nirvāṇic* 'total extinction' of Beckett's 1933 story. (More on this play and other texts, both dramatic and fictional, featuring rebirth scenarios, in Chapters 7 and 8.)

---

[18] The word 'matrix' resonates with the *Timaeus*.

[19] Or possibly the stones suggest that Beckett at this early juncture was aware of *Beyond the Pleasure Principle*, in which Freud writes about the 'instinct' of organic life to return to the inorganic (Freud 1955 [1920], 36–9).

There is one more detail to consider: What is one to make of the cushioned basket into which Belacqua is repeatedly tossed, also called a 'cauldron' (*EB* 20, 21, 23, 31) – two figures of generativity – and which, reappearing in the graveyard scene, is labeled 'a coffin in its own way' (50)? Could this be another early instance, admittedly a bizarre one, of the many containers in Beckett's texts that objectify the imaginary womb and tomb in the mind by turning it into externalized 'psycho-objects', as they are known in art?

Murphy's End: Buddhist *Nirvāṇa* or Freudian Nirvana?

In Beckett's second novel, *Murphy*, the rocking chair is the next 'fatal' psycho-object, its containing embrace suggesting the rocking motion of existence in the womb and the rocking off into death, the first of several in Beckett's fiction, plays, and *Film*.

If Belacqua is described as a failed mystic who would prefer to turn his back on a troubled and farcical world, Beckett's second antihero is rather a would-be ascetic whose repeated failures to renounce the world are narrated with considerable ironic distance. And unlike Belacqua, Murphy is not a budding writer and mouthpiece for the author's views on aesthetics. Rather, Beckett tried to avoid the 'Aliosha mistake' of identifying too closely with his character. In a letter to Thomas MacGreevy of 7 July 1936, after having just finished *Murphy*, Beckett writes that he treated his protagonist with a 'mixture of compassion, patience, mockery and "tat twam asi"', but admits to losing patience at times. About the risk of taking his character too seriously, he adds, 'As it is I do not think the mistake (Aliosha mistake) has been altogether avoided' (*LSB I* 350). The 'Aliosha mistake' no doubt refers to Gide's claim that Dostoevksy loses himself in each of his characters, but that in *The Brothers Karamazov*, Aliosha (and Father Zosima) best embody the author's views (Gide 1981 [1923], 70, 151). Intriguingly, Beckett avoids the 'Aliosha mistake' in his subsequent novels by introducing several narrators, beginning a career, with his third novel *Watt*, of what Bion was to term 'non-pathological splitting' depending on several vantage points (Bion 1989 [1977], 46).

Murphy's refrain, 'I am not of the big world, I am of the little world' (*Mu* 178) is a reprise of Belacqua's preference for his asylum in the mind. The wish to escape the woes of the world and both the conflictual and erotic relations of 'flight and flow' plays a similar role in Beckett's first two novels, even if the locale changes from mostly Dublin to primarily London, the city in which Beckett penned the first part of *Murphy* – from

August to December 1935 – while in psychotherapy with Bion, subsequently completing the manuscript in Dublin by June 1936. The cast of five characters, including the likable prostitute Celia, in pursuit of the illusive Murphy, the witty allusions and dialogue, and twists and turns of the plot make the novel another comedy.

Murphy seeks to facilitate his retreat into his mind by tying himself naked into his rocking chair to quiet his body and induce it to set him free to enjoy 'pleasure' in his mind, 'where he could love himself' (*Mu* 2, 7). The motif of the self-love of Narcissus with its fatal outcome is reinforced by Celia's desperate attempt to convince Murphy to find useful employment instead of 'apperceiving himself into a glorious grave' (21). Later, on finding work in a mental asylum, Murphy is said to be drawn to the psychosis of the schizophrenic Mr. Endon 'as Narcissus to his fountain' (186). His self-love makes Murphy's rocking a different exercise from the partly Indian-inspired meditation and the renunciation of self and world and desire that we find in Belacqua's inner retreat.[20]

Still, an interweaving of Schopenhauerian and Indian threads is particularly evident in Murphy's famous chess game with Mr. Endon and the notorious chapter 6 describing Murphy's mind as it pictures itself: a 'large hollow sphere, hermetically closed to the universe without' and 'full of light fading into dark' (*Mu* 107, 110). This psychic container has been interpreted from multiple points of view based on Beckett's readings in the 1930s in literature, philosophy, mysticism, psychoanalysis, and, not to forget, science.[21]

Of Murphy's tripartite mind, the third zone is a version of Belacqua's mental haven, extended by Beckett's readings since *Dream*, but minus the shades of the dead and the unborn and the emergence of generativity. The two versions share the same 'will-lessness' (*Mu* 113), which in Schopenhauerian (and Buddhist) terms necessarily precedes the liberation from desire, self, and world by abolishing the craving for existence. In Gide's collection of articles on Dostoevsky that Beckett discussed with his students in 1931, in which the French author asserts the Russian writer's 'sort of' Buddhism or quietism (Gide 1981 [1923], 151), he further alludes to Schopenhauer in his analysis of the three psychic regions Dostoevsky envisioned for his characters. In a reversal of the mind's ascending journey

---

[20] Intriguingly, for Richard Begam, the scarves that tie Murphy to his chair correspond to an infusion of self-eroticism and Sadean self-mortification into meditation (Begam 2007, 53–4).

[21] For an overview of the interpretations of Murphy's mind, see Ackerley and Gontarski 2004, 388–9, and for a descriptive catalogue of Beckett's reading notes of the 1930s, archived at Trinity College Dublin, see Frost and Maxwell 2006.

to the divine, found in Neoplatonic and medieval mysticism and the *Divine Comedy*, Dostoevsky, Gide maintains, situates hell on top (the intelligence), the passions in between, and heaven deep down, which Gide explains is the region, spoken of by Schopenhauer, in which the loss of individuality results in a blissful state out of time (Gide 1981 [1923], 144–6). Such a topsy-turvy construction is also Murphy's view of his mind. The first zone's light of consciousness consists in the devilish pleasure of reprisals; the second, twilight, zone corresponds to the Dantean Belacqua's purgatorial bliss; whereas the third zone is the dark of Schopenhauer's metaphysical and timeless will-lessness beyond understanding (*Mu* 112–13).[22]

The will-lessness of Murphy's third zone, however, is checkmated by his narcissistic self-love and erotic desire for Celia – the two in conflict and both irreconcilable with his ascetic pretentions – and finally undone by the fatal pleasure principle. Although Richard Coe identifies Murphy's rocking with *zazen* meditation (Coe 1970 [1964], 25), it ends not in Buddhist but in Freudian 'Nirvana'. When, in *The Trauma of Birth*, Otto Rank describes *nirvāṇa* as 'the pleasurable Nothing' (Rank 2010 [1924], 119), he appears to be citing the Freudian 'Nirvana principle', which, in *Beyond the Pleasure Principle*, Freud assimilates to the Pleasure principle's reduction of outer and inner excitations to zero, in which he sees an expression of the death drive (Freud 1955 [1920], 55–6). The Nirvana principle was most likely so named because of Schopenhauer's popularization of *nirvāṇa* in the West (Laplanche and Pontalis 1973, 331–2), even if it misconstrues Schopenhauer's view of it. Freud himself states his debt to Schopenhauer in *Beyond the Pleasure Principle*: 'We have unwittingly steered our course into the harbour of Schopenhauer's philosophy. For him death is the "true result and to that extent the purpose of life", while the sexual instinct is the embodiment of the will to live' (Freud 1955 [1920], 49–50). In *Molloy*, Beckett was to put the 'fatal pleasure principle' into Moran's report (*Mo* 99), but that he was aware of it earlier seems borne out by his emphasis on 'pleasure' to characterize the third zone of Murphy's mind. That this zone is twice described as 'such pleasure that pleasure was not the word' (*Mu* 2, 113), as contrasted with the simple 'pleasure' attributed to the other two

---

[22] For Ulrich Pothast (2008, 150), Murphy's view of himself as 'a mote in the dark of absolute freedom' (*Mu* 112), corresponds to Schopenhauer's will-less existence beyond identity, time, space, and causality. For a discussion of the similarity between Murphy's three mental zones and Gide's description of Dostoevksy's three psychic regions, as well as of other Gidean elements in the construction of *Murphy*, see Moorjani 2009, 216–21.

zones, strengthens the surmise that Beckett is obliquely alluding to the fatal 'pleasure' that finds expression in the Freudian Nirvana principle.

If the mental asylum in which Murphy finds work, the first of several such asylums in Beckett's fiction, is analogous to Belacqua and Murphy's mental refuge, it is only so if one ignores its painful aspects, as Murphy tends to do. Despite the attempt to avoid the Aliosha mistake, Beckett's recognition, at the time, of the pathology of his own 'morbid' (his word) tendency to isolate himself and feel superior flows into his ironic treatment of Murphy.[23] Not unexpectedly, then, womb-and-tomb spaces make their appearance in the novel on Murphy's move to the Magdalen Mental Mercyseat: the confining space of Murphy's small garret, also termed a 'remote aery', or bird's nest – a term familiar from 'Echo's Bones', in which Lord Gall whisks Belacqua to a tree-top 'aerie' (*EB* 19, 27) – is rendered even more womblike by Murphy's efforts to assure its warmth (*Mu* 162–3). It was to become the site of his demise in his rocking chair. Further, a building on the grounds Murphy takes to be a nursery turns out to be the mortuary (165) in a commingling of birth and death as it reappears in work after work. Murphy's rocking into death in a womblike enclosure is echoed in *Film* (1964), in which the character is rocking in his mother's room until the 'rocking dies down' (*Film* 52), to be followed, in *Rockaby* (1981), by the condensed 'mother rocker' (*CSPL* 280). Consonant with Schopenhauer, the movement toward death is simultaneously a retreat to a time before birth to result in another turning of the wheel of rebirth or to a final liberation from it, a topic to be taken up in Chapters 5 and 7.

But it is the chess game with Mr. Endon that is finally the occasion of the fateful pleasure of nothing for Murphy. The schizophrenic and suicidal Mr. Endon is an adept of inner ruminations as his name suggests (*Mu* 186–7). His black and scarlet finery, ring-bedecked hands, and pose evoke a half serious, half ludic amalgam of a flamboyant Eastern guru and world-renouncing sage. Seated on his bed in his flowing scarlet robe in the propitious lotus – or yogic meditation – posture, described as 'tailor-fashion . . . , holding his left foot in his right hand and in his left hand his right foot' (241)[24], Endon plays a game of chess with Murphy oblivious to his opponent's moves. Rather, negating the game's strategies of attack

---

[23] See Beckett's revealing letter to Thomas MacGreevy of 10 March 1935 (*LSB I* 258–9). For a discussion of a psychoanalytically imbued critique of Murphy's fatal narcissism, see Moorjani 1982, 70–80.

[24] Beckett obviously was familiar with images of Indian gurus as evident from the ironically named 'Ramaswami Krishnaswami Narayanaswami Suk', who casts Murphy's horoscope (*Mu* 32). Andy

and defense, he moves his pieces in symmetric patterns with the intent of returning them to their original position, suggesting the Indian and Schopenhauerian retreat to where one has always been.[25]

At the conclusion of the game, Murphy sees himself unseen in Mr. Endon's unseeing eyes, reminiscent of meditating figures such as representations of the Buddha, with gaze turned inward, shutting out the world. See Figure 3.1. If the effect of witnessing a figure immersed in meditation can result in a liberating release of one's own ties to self and world, such is not Murphy's response. Rather, in the sense of Berkeley's perceivedness tied to being, his being unperceived in Endon's unperceiving eyes results not in the positive void of Buddhist meditation, but rather, in the 'rare postnatal treat', echoing Otto Rank, of the 'Nothing, than which . . . naught is more real', ascribed to Democritus (*Mu* 246). Murphy, however, is shattered, not calmed, by his nothingness in the idealized mirror (or fountain) of Mr. Endon's eyes so that he succumbs to the fatal pleasure of the Freudian Nirvana principle. The excitations in his mind reduced to zero – 'He could not get a picture in his mind of any creature he had met, animal or human (251–2) – he contemplates returning to Celia whom he fled in his ascetic, or rather narcissistic, attempts to accede to the pleasure in his mind. This last-minute reaffirmation of the will to life, however, comes too late, as Murphy rocks himself into a fiery death. His rocking into death in a womblike space, aligns it with Rank's 'Nirvana', the 'pleasurable Nothing, the womb situation', which corresponds to the Freudian Nirvana principle rather than to the Buddha's unknowable, unsayable *nirvāṇa* beyond the cycles of birth, death, and rebirth, transmitted by Schopenhauer.[26]

For Richard Coe, the strong temptation to interpret Murphy's encounter with nothingness in terms of Taoist or Buddhist teaching is not entirely misleading (Coe 1970 [1964], 24). Yet he devalues such interpretations,

---

Wimbush, too, recognizes in Mr. Endon 'an Asian holy man' and, tracing his flowing scarlet robe and position to that of a Tibetan Buddhist monk, he cites evidence of Beckett's knowledge of the lotus position in an entry in his 'Whoroscope' notebook, possibly, Wimbush surmises, from having read Alexandra David-Neel's *With Mystics and Magicians in Tibet* (London: Penguin, 1931) (Wimbush 2020, 106–7).

[25] For a detailed analysis of the chess game, see Moorjani 1982, 70, 75–83.

[26] Of interest is Beckett's preference in *Murphy* for the maxim of Arnold Geulincx – 'ubi nihi vales ibi nihi velis' (where you are worth nothing you should want nothing) – and the 'Naught is more real than nothing', attributed to Democritus (*Mu* 178, 246), his involvement with both philosophers dating to after writing *Dream*. To my mind, the punning word and sound play of their aphorisms – Geulincx's being, moreover, a perfect alexandrine – explains in part Beckett's partiality for them. Beckett's peculiar phrasing of the Democritean nothing in *Murphy* has its source in his 1932 note taking from philosophical texts (Weller 2008, 323–5.)

Figure 3.1 *Samādhi Buddha* (The Buddha in Meditation), ca. fourth–sixth century CE,
Mahamevnāwa Park, Anurādhapura, Sri Lanka, marble.
Photo courtesy of Dr. Peter Schmidt-Breitung

even as he suggests them, contending that the author of *Murphy* is
foremost a rationalist who only 'toy[s] with Oriental thought' (20, 26).[27]
Distinguishing *nirvāṇa* from nothingness and mere annihilation, Coe
agrees with Taoists who envisage *nirvāṇa* as a positive reality, a 'plenum
Void' (25). He suggests that Murphy may be using Eastern meditation
techniques – 'Yoga, Zen, and Za-Zen' – in his rocking chair maneuvers to
free himself of desire and attachment to the world (25), a view that
Murphy's self-love puts in doubt. In suggesting that Murphy's death by
fire in the throes of his final meditative rocking 'might *almost* be a parody

[27] Writing in the early 1960s, Coe had no access to the Belacqua saga. Even the previously published
collection of Belacqua stories was out of print. Nor could he have been aware of the texts of the
1970s and 1980s. The early critical tendency to consider Beckett a Cartesian, and *Murphy* a
Cartesian novel, continued until roughly the 1970s.

of the death of the Buddha' (23; emphasis in the original), Coe intimates that Beckett playfully stages his character's final liberation. But even as a parody, in my view, *nirvāṇa* is not Murphy's lot.

Unlike the Belacqua of 'Echo's Bones', this is not the last we hear of Murphy. No *nirvāṇa* for Murphy, but cycles of incarnation into new fictional characters, with each new existence one in a series of life dreams carrying the traces of previous existences. As the reborn characters take up the obligation to write or to utter, they exist as so many specters in the enwombed and entombed mind from which they recount their former lives in the phenomenal hell of their worldly existence; the paradoxes of this situation will be explored in the following chapters. In the meanwhile, the next chapter provides a respite from metaphoric revels by examining the paradoxical logic that Beckett shares with the Buddha and Mahāyāna thinkers, a commonality of which he was aware, and by probing the silence and ineffability topos that assimilates his writing to thinkers of the East and West.

CHAPTER 4

Beckett's Paradoxical Logic through Buddhist and Western Lenses

Challenging the Principle of Noncontradiction 1: Neither Being nor Nonbeing

Mahāyāna Buddhism is renowned for its celebration of paradoxical logic and its challenges to the classical laws of noncontradiction that were formulated off and on by Indian logicians and, in the West, decreed by Aristotle (Horn 1989, 18–19, 79–84). We know that Beckett was familiar with Mahāyāna's paradoxical patterns of argumentation from his piece 'Henri Hayden, homme-peintre', written in 1952 and frequently cited as proof that he had, at a minimum, an interest in the Buddha's thought.[1] Displaying more than a passing interest, Beckett in this brief text engages with the founder's teaching denying the validity of assertions about the self and the no-self: 'Gautama', Beckett writes, 'avant qu'ils [les mots] vinssent à lui manquer, disait qu'on se trompe en affirmant que le moi existe, mais qu'en affirmant qu'il n'existe pas on se trompe pas moins' (Gautama, before [words] began to fail him, used to say that one is mistaken in affirming that the self exists, but in affirming that it does not exist, one is just as mistaken; *Dis* 146). And Beckett goes on to find an intimation of what he qualifies as the Buddha's *folle sagesse* (mad wisdom) – an oxymoron par excellence – in the silence of Hayden's canvases and in the double erasure of the painter's 'impersonal and unreal oeuvre', adding the corollary that Gautama's words apply not only to the self but also to the rest (146).

---

[1] See, for instance, Foster 1989, 27–8.

Henri Hayden (1883–1970) was one of several of Beckett's artist friends on whom he wrote articles and shorter tributes. Born and educated in Warsaw, Hayden had moved to Paris in 1907, where, after an early Cubist period, he turned to landscapes as the subject of his paintings, for which he began to be recognized in 1952. His friendship with Beckett dates from their meeting in Roussillon where both were in hiding during World War II. Beckett's piece was written at a time of considerable interest by artists in the Buddha's thought in the wake of a horrendous war. On this interest, see Spretnak 2014, ch. 4.

Beckett's minimalist Mahāyāna Buddhist manifesto tellingly involves the work of an artist, but surely, as is usually the case, what Beckett took in from Hayden's canvases is given back in a form that tells us more about the writer of the piece than about the painter. Indeed, in *The Unnamable* did he not have Mahood exclaim, 'It's a lot to expect of one creature ... that he should first behave as if he were not, then as if he were, before being admitted to that peace where he neither is, nor is not, and where the language dies that permits of such expressions. Two falsehoods, two trappings, to be borne to the end' (*Un* 334–5)? Did Beckett not make the Buddha's *folle sagesse* here his fictional speaker's own?

Gautama's and Mahood's 'two falsehoods' of the neither 'I' nor 'not I' involve two contradictory statements that are paradoxically both false, instead of following the classical laws of logic holding that two contradictory statements can neither both be true nor both be false. The Buddha's teaching 'that neither self nor nonself [no-self] is the case' is cited in the sixth verse of chapter 18 'An Analysis of the Self' in Nāgārjuna's *Mūlamadhyamakakārikā* (The Philosophy of the Middle Way).[2] In effect, philosophers of the Mādhyamika (the Mahāyāna philosophical school of the 'Middle Path' founded by Nāgārjuna in the second or third century CE) define *śūnya* (empty) as 'lacking both being and non-being' (Cross 2013, 101). Whether it is a matter of disputing classical logic's 'either being or nonbeing' by declaring both true (being and nonbeing at the same time), or by asserting both mistaken (neither being nor nonbeing), both dialectical moves confirm Mahāyāna Buddhism's rejection of dualities. 'The Buddhist philosophers differ from philosophers bred in the Aristotelean tradition', Edward Conze explains, 'in that they are not frightened but delighted by contradiction' (Conze 1959a, 129).[3]

The Indian principle of fourfold negation is perhaps the most extreme form of negative argumentation. This principle, also known as the 'tetralemma', which was adopted by the Buddha and his followers, is traced to the classical Indian logician and skeptic Sañjaya (prior to the sixth century BCE) and is known to have been practiced particularly by Nāgārjuna (Horn 1989, 80). The tetralemma consists in four exhaustive logical alternatives that are all four rejected because of their deficiency (Westerhoff 2009, 89), for example:

---

[2] This work is cited as *MMK*, using the translation in the Siderits and Katsura edition listed in the bibliography as Nāgārjuna 2013.

[3] Conze obviously made this observation before poststructuralist philosophers adopted paradoxical logic.

(a)   The self exists.
(b)   The self does not exist.
(c)   The self both exists and does not exist.
(d)   The self neither exists nor does not exist.

If we compare the above cited words by Mahood in *The Unnamable*, the same four logical alternatives apply, if not in the same order:

(a)   I am not.
(b)   I am.
(c)   I both am and am not.
(d)   I neither am nor am not.

Beckett's awareness that the Buddha's negation of the self and the no-self also applies to the rest of the world is borne out by the Buddha's fourfold negation cited by Nāgārjuna: 'All is real, or all is unreal, all is both real and unreal, all is neither unreal nor real' (*MMK* 18.8).[4]

For the Buddha, as interpreted by Nāgārjuna, the tetralemma serves primarily to guide his followers on the path to the ultimate reality of *śūnyatā*. As a consequence, the ontological propositions about the existence and nonexistence of the self are discounted owing to the term 'self', which refers to something lacking an independent existence, so that anything said about it is mistaken (see Westerhoff 2009, 56–9). It is in this sense only a linguistic not an ontological entity, and in the absence of a referent for the term 'self', classical Indian logic held that such terms cannot be affirmed or negated, the latter presupposing its existence somewhere else. Bertrand Russell famously was to make the same argument more than two thousand years later in raising the question of the baldness of the present king of France (Westerhoff 2009, 70). Or, in terms of epistemology, when none of a tetralemma's alternatives are knowable, none can be asserted (Horn 1989, 82). In the case of Mahood's first-person pronoun, a similar argument can be made. As a deictic (or shifter), the pronoun 'I' refers to the person who says 'I' in a given context of saying it. But, as I have written elsewhere about Beckett's fictional trilogy of the 1940s, the narrative 'I' keeps shifting among personas, each a fragment of a 'not I' (Moorjani 1992, 177).

In his commentary on the Perfection of Wisdom Diamond Sūtra,[5] Red Pine (Bill Porter) offers the following explanation for this puzzling

---

[4] On the controversy about this tetralemma that some read as a 'positive tetralemma', see Westerhoff 2009, 89–90.

[5] The Mahāyāna Perfection of Wisdom (*prajñā-pāramitā*) literature comprises thirty-eight different *sūtras* (canonical texts) written in India between 100 BCE and 800 CE. The most revered are the Diamond Sūtra (between 100 BCE and 100 CE) and the Heart Sūtra (300s CE).

dialectic. In his view, the dialectical technique of affirming the reality of something while emptying it of any self-nature – which was adopted by the Buddha, some of his followers, Nāgārjuna and later Mādhyamika philosophers – corresponds to the concept of *śūnyatā* (emptiness). The advantage of using the dialectic, however, is that 'every concept, even the concept of emptiness, is likely to become another delusion and an obstacle to enlightenment, whereas the dialectic tends to remind those who use it of the futility of attachment to anything' (Red Pine 2001, 146).

In general, the Buddha used fourfold negation not only to point out the 'emptiness' of concepts or words, such as 'self', about which nothing can be stated, but also to refuse answering metaphysical questions without utility for the path to emancipation. Thus, he would answer the question about what happens to the *Tathāgata* after death – the *Tathāgata* being another word for the Buddha and one he used in referring to himself – in the form of a tetralemma (Viévard 2002, 37).

To account for the Buddha's *folle sagesse* of negating both the existence and nonexistence of self and world, Mādhyamika Buddhism draws on the two-truths doctrine. The two truths comprise, on the one hand, the conventional view of empirical phenomena in the everyday world and, on the other, the ultimate awareness of the conventional view's illusionary nature from which one awakens as if from a dream. For Cross, the doctrine, which has its roots in ancient Indian thought and was later adopted by both Mādhyamika and Advaita Vedānta, has affinities in the West with the Kantian distinction between phenomenon and noumenon, or appearance and the thing-in-itself, and Schopenhauer's between the provisional empirical reality of the world as our representation and 'transcendental ideality' (Cross 2013, 72–5, 100). Beckett's Proustian 'real' and 'ideal real' viewpoints, as expressed in his 1960 letter to Megged, too, bear a family resemblance to the doctrine of two truths.

In *MMK* (24.8–9), Nāgārjuna insists on the importance of the two truths: 'The Dharma teaching of the Buddha rests on two truths: conventional truth and ultimate truth'.[6] Accordingly, that there is a self is conventionally true, but ultimately untrue. And conversely, that there is no self is ultimately true, but conventionally untrue. The two truths seen from distinct standpoints, one empirical, the other ultimate, render the existence of the self and no-self either simultaneously true or simultaneously untrue (Westerhoff 2009, 90; Cross 2013, 101).

---

[6] 'Dharma' refers to the Buddha's teachings on the nature of reality and the code of conduct that derives from his teachings.

Commentators have wrestled with what to make of Nāgārjuna's para-doxes.[7] Their various surmises resonate with the possible impulses under-lying Beckett's taste for paradoxical negation and aporia. Are the purveyors of paradox primarily challenging classical logic or logic as such? In affirm-ing to Charles Juliet (1986, 51) that he likes the mystics' 'illogisme brûlant' (burning illogicality), 'cette flamme... qui consume cette saloperie de logique' (the flame... that burns up our foul logic), Beckett would appear to argue for the value of flouting logic as such. Or, on the other hand, is such paradoxical negation intended to puzzle the mind in the manner of Zen koans to the point of impelling us to see beyond conceptual reality? This view, as we have seen, is defended by Kundert-Gibbs. Or are paradoxical thinkers rather intent on having us give up all possible attach-ments to conceptual views dependent on the limits of language? Is it finally a form of nominalism?

For Mādhyamika, in fact, language is a veil that prevents experiencing *śūnyatā* (Viévard 2002, 67, 81). Fourfold negation, then, is a tool that serves to tear down the veil of words and deny language's relation to ontological and metaphysical truth. Similarly, in the already quoted words, Beckett's Mahood imagines a 'peace where he neither is, nor is not, and where the language dies that permits of such expressions'.

We do not know when Beckett first came to know of the Buddha's paradoxical wisdom, but it would appear to be by 1949, given its traces in the 'Three Dialogues' and the use of fourfold negation in *L'Innommable* begun the same year. Before then, Beckett would have encountered Schopenhauer's silence in the face of the unknowable, the mystics' apo-phatic discourse, and Fritz Mauthner's nominalist critique of language, which akin to the Buddha's tetralemmas respond to questions of being and nonbeing with answers that are no-answers, the equivalent of nonwords or silence.

Beckett's 'Unword' and Mauthner's Indian-tinged Nominalist Critique

Mauthner's extreme nominalist critique, denying the possibility of words to refer to the self or the phenomenal world, corresponds to the Buddha's challenges to logic, as transmitted by Nāgārjuna. Although Beckett's epistemological skepticism and the influence of Mauthner's language critique have been extensively interrogated by Beckett exegetes, another

---

[7] See Carpenter 2014, 80–2, for interpretations of Nāgārjuna's use of the tetralemma.

look at the Mauthner controversy will help elucidate the strains of Indian thought in Mauthner's philosophy. The question remains open on whether Mauthner's Indian-tinged nominalism served as an intertext in Beckett's famous letter to Axel Kaun of 9 July 1937, in which he advocates a 'literature of the unword' (*Dis* 173).

Beckett was not keen to have his letter to Kaun reprinted. At the time Ruby Cohn was putting together *Disjecta*, he asked her in his letter of 22 February 1982, to 'think seriously about omitting Kaun letter'. He no doubt could foresee the number of scholarly investigations and ruminations that would be based on it and, as usual, preferred not to be tied down to one view. Implying to Cohn that the letter to Kaun is a red herring, which can be taken rather as an admission of its importance, Beckett condemned his letter as 'embarrassing kitchen German bilge' (*LSB IV* 578). Despite grammatical errors in the original draft, 'kitchen German' it is not. Fortunately, Ruby Cohn knew how to take Beckett's disclaimer.[8]

There can be little doubt of the influence of Mauthner's self-defined skepticism and 'reine und konsequente Nominalismus' (pure and resolute nominalism) on Beckett's writing (*BKS III* 615). Given Mauthner's references to ancient Indian thought, the parallels between his and Mādhyamika's critiques of language and logic are of particular salience for the investigations in this chapter. In Mauthner's view, for example, Aristotle's principles of logic are but a 'shadowy web' ('schattenhaftes Netzwerk'), without any relation to reality (*BKS III* 269).

Although there is critical agreement that Beckett could not have transcribed passages from Mauthner's *Beiträge zu einer Kritik der Sprache* into his 'Whoroscope' notebook before 1938 (Pilling 2006, 164), this date for his notes does not preclude his reading parts of Mauthner's three-volume critique earlier, without taking notes or taking notes that have been lost. In a 2 August 1979 letter to Linda Ben-Zvi, Beckett recalled 'skimm[ing] through Mauthner for Joyce in 1929 or 30' (*LSB IV* 509). The earlier date Beckett remembered has proven difficult to verify, but, based on textual similarities, many scholars nevertheless argue for an earlier acquaintance with Mauthner.

---

[8] In *LSB* IV 579, n. 1, the editors explain that, as published in *Disjecta*, the transcription and translation of the draft of Beckett's 1937 letter in German (deposited at Dartmouth College) was silently corrected and translated by Martin Esslin. Because Esslin's minimal editing of grammatical errors – a common editorial practice – and his translation are excellent, his translation in *Disjecta* is referred to in this study. The draft of Beckett's letter without corrections and with a new translation is found in *LSB I* 512–21.

In a letter of 4 August 1978, Beckett famously asked Ruby Cohn to advise Linda Ben-Zvi that her attempt to establish Mauthner's influence on him was a 'wild goose or red herring', adding: 'My contact with his [Mauthner's] work was of the slightest & I have nothing to offer on the subject . . . . I am sorry to disappoint her' (qtd. in Frost and Maxwell 2006, 138).[9] Beckett did, however, send 'something' rather than 'nothing' on the subject to Ben-Zvi a year after his letter to Cohn. 'For me' he writes in his 1979 letter to Ben-Zvi, 'it came down to: Thoughts words / Words inane / Thoughts inane [.] Such was my levity'. – an impressive abstract not only of Mauthner's critique but also of his own – and he mentions that he had recently run across the commonplace book into which he copied passages from Mauthner (*LSB IV* 509).

The denial of influence in the letter to Cohn a year earlier was most likely an instance of conscious amnesia. In the early 1970s Beckett told John Pilling that he was 'particularly impressed' by Mauthner's *Beiträge*, while emphasizing that Joyce had first brought the work to his attention (Pilling 1976, 127). Two decades earlier he had acknowledged his interest in Mauthner in a 1954 letter to German translator Hans Neumann, admitting to having been 'fortement impressionné' ('greatly impressed') by the *Beiträge*, and of having often wanted to reread them, but, adding, that they seem impossible to find (*LSB II* 462, 465). In the same letter to Neumann, Beckett writes that he is not trying to appear recalcitrant to influences ('Je n'essaie pas d'avoir l'air réfractaire aux influences') (*LSB II* 462). Could this perhaps be a way of disavowing a trait (or at least an appearance thereof) he recognized in himself, which would help explain the 'wild goose or red herring' attempt to dissuade Linda Ben-Zvi? He was subsequently able to indulge his wish on obtaining a third edition of the *Beiträge* that remained in his library to the end (Van Hulle and Nixon 2013, 163).[10]

Whether or not Beckett did his 'skimming' earlier than 1938 or knew of Mauthner's thought secondhand, the parallels between Beckett's pre-1938 work and Mauthner have continued to intrigue commentators. Beckett scholars remain divided on the issue, some holding to the view that Mauthner's repute in the first decades of the twentieth century speaks in favor of a relay of his critique of language before 1938, whereas others

---

[9] In *LSB IV*, a note refers to this letter (509, n. 2); the letter itself is omitted.
[10] Beckett's Mauthner notes in his 'Whoroscope' notebook and his letter about dissuading Ben-Zvi are housed at the Beckett International Foundation, University of Reading (UoR MS 3000 and UoR MS 5100).

conclude that the evident similarity of Mauthner's and Beckett's views in the letter to Kaun is because they draw on the same sources: Eckhart on silence, Schopenhauer on the 'veil of *māyā*', and accounts of medieval nominalism.[11] What appears uncontested is evidence of Mauthner's influence beginning with *Watt*, written in the early 1940s.

In 1938, Beckett's first Mauthner entry into his 'Whoroscope' notebook – a successor since 1932 of the 'Dream' notebook – comprises a long paragraph stating Mauthner's view of nominalism in the final pages of his monumental critique of language.[12] In this paragraph Mauthner asserts that, for true nominalists, the human brain can neither know the world nor its own consciousness, and especially not by means of words. The same view is succinctly expressed in another passage Beckett transcribed into his notebook: 'Was die Menschen sprechen, das kann niemals zur Welterkenntnis beitragen' (What people say can in no way contribute to knowledge of the world; *BKS II* 310.) As a result of his extreme nominalism, Mauthner came to the same conclusion as Nāgārjuna when the latter extended the classical Indian and Buddhist critique of empty terms to all words. For Mauthner, too, there are only contentless words without reference to the extra-linguistic world (*BKS III* 634–5). He specifically refers to 'I' as an 'empty word' ('leeres Wort') (*BKS I* 667). For Mauthner, words are *nebelhaftig* (nebulous, or figuratively, like veils), as they are for Mādhyamika, and selfhood is only *Schein* (illusion) (*BKS III* 608–9, 616).

Furthermore, a typescript of passages Beckett transcribed from the second volume of Mauthner's *Beiträge* (TCD MS 10971/5, 1r) pertains to Mauthner's summary of the philosophical critique of metaphorical thinking.[13] In a passage Beckett transcribed, Mauthner asserts that in ancient Indian philosophy, the illusory view of reality was considered the 'Blendwerk der Maya' (the deception of Māyā) based on false analogies or

---

[11] On Beckett's notes on the *Beiträge* and a list of essays on the vexed question of dating, see Van Hulle and Nixon 2013, 6–7, 144, 157–63. On page 161, they list the 'Whoroscope' notebook pages (46r to 58v) of Beckett's Mauthner notes and the corresponding pages in the *Beiträge*. See especially Ben-Zvi 1980 and her extensive discussion of the *Beiträge* in relation to Beckett's works. Several Beckett scholars assert, or more cautiously suggest, Mauthner's influence on Beckett's assault on language in his letter to Kaun. It is stated as a fact in Ackerley and Gontarski 2004, 359. Garforth 2004, 55–6, is more circumspect, and Pilling 2006, 165, leaves the question undecided. On the conclusion or possibility that he did not require knowledge of Mauthner to compose his 1937 letter, see Feldman 2009, 192–5; Nixon 2011, 166–70; Van Hulle 2012, 221–8; Van Hulle and Nixon 2013, 145.

[12] The paragraph in question, beginning with 'Der reine und konsequente Nominalismus', is found in *BKS III* 615–16. There is an English translation of this passage in Ben-Zvi 1984, 65–6. See also Van Hulle and Nixon 2013, 155, 158–61.

[13] See Frost and Maxwell 2006, 137–8. The section on metaphor is found in *BKS II* 473–9.

metaphors (*BKS II* 473). Another passage in this section has affinities with Buddhist language critique and *śūnyatā* (emptiness): Speaking of the 'gates of truth' ('Pforten der Wahrheit'), Mauthner contends: 'Language critique alone is able to open these gates and show with smiling resignation that they lead beyond the world and thought into emptiness [*Leere*]' (*BKS II* 478). The Mādhyamika ring to Mauthner's statement is unmistakable.

In their impressive genetic study *The Making of Samuel Beckett's L'Innommable / The Unnamable*, Dirk Van Hulle and Shane Weller cite Mauthner's statement on the 'gates of truth' in relating Mauthner's critique of metaphor to the rejection by Beckett's narrator of both his past metaphorical avatars from Murphy to Malone and the new ones imagined in the novel – Basil, Mahood, Worm – adding that, as Mauthner suggests, such undoing of the metaphorical will lead to emptiness beyond world and thought. Van Hulle and Weller subsequently argue that Beckett's aporias serve to avoid making another metaphor of emptiness (Van Hulle and Weller 2014, 190). From the viewpoint of this chapter, *The Unnamable*'s unwording in the interest of silence and emptiness resonates with the critique of metaphor going back to ancient Indian thought.

In summary, for Mauthner, words, logic, and metaphor are a shadowy and nebulous illusion, comparable to the veil of *māyā*. Mauthner perhaps owes this view to Schopenhauer, on whom he published a study and to whom he frequently refers in the *Beiträge*. Schopenhauer, as we know, adopted the Mahāyāna interpretation of the veil of *māyā* in comparing our illusory mental representation of the world to it.[14] The extent to which Mauthner draws on ancient Indian thought is apparent from his allusions to it in the *Beiträge* and his periodic citation of Indologist Paul Deussen's work on ancient Indian philosophy. Mauthner's allusions, in addition to language and metaphor compared to the delusion of *māyā*, include *Oṃ* as a step toward the Upanishadic *Nichtwort* that leads to a transcendent silence, *tat twam asi* (*BKS I* 668), and his claim that Schopenhauer combined Christian teachings of salvation with the Buddhist transmigration of souls and his metaphysical will into 'a new, a godless religion' (*BKS III* 620–1). Mauthner's interest in Buddhist thought is attested by his own godless mysticism of 'smiling resignation' and silence and the imaginative philosophical fiction on the Buddha's last days, *Der letzte Tod des Gautama*

---

[14] Like other philosophers Mauthner admired, Schopenhauer does not escape his critique for having stopped short of recognizing the limits of language, although Mauthner admits that he 'rattles often and hard on language critique'. Mauthner nevertheless accuses Schopenhauer of word fetishism in making of his will a mythological person (*BKS II* 478).

Buddha (1913) (The Last Death of Gautama Buddha), which he penned a few years after completing the *Beiträge*. Such an engagement with ancient Indian philosophy, as already noted, was not exceptional for thinkers, artists, and writers in the final decades of the nineteenth century and the first decades of the twentieth. Not only in Schopenhauer did Beckett encounter receptiveness to and a relay of Eastern thought.

When in his 1937 letter to Axel Kaun, Beckett amusingly likens language, or grammar and style, to the irrelevance of a 'Victorian bathing suit or the imperturbability of a true gentleman', after first commenting that his own language appears to him 'like a veil [*Schleier*] that must be torn apart in order to get at the things (or the Nothingness) behind it' (*Dis* 171), he could be echoing Mauthner's humorous put-downs in the *Beiträge* of concepts he rejects along with his Eastern-tinged nominalism, his 'Nebelhaftigkeit der Worte' (the nebulous/veiled quality of words;*BKS III* 626). The 'Nothingness' ('Nichts') Beckett posits as possibly to be found behind the veil is striking, of course, from both Schopenhauerian and Mahāyāna viewpoints. Whether adopted indirectly from Mauthner or directly from Schopenhauer, the veil metaphor was to stay with Beckett in his postwar writing. For Molloy, there is a mist that arises in him daily that 'veils the world from me and veils me from myself' (*Mo* 29), whereas the speaker of *Textes pour rien / Texts for Nothing* (French, 1955; English, 1967) speaks of 'words like smoke' (*CSP* 102). And in his 1948 essay 'Peintres de l'empêchement' (Painters of Impediment), Beckett describes the unrepresentable in the painting of Bram and Geer van Velde, in words reminiscent of the letter to Kaun: 'Un dévoilement sans fin ... vers l'indévoilable, le rien, la chose à nouveau' (An endless unveiling... toward what cannot be unveiled, nothingness, the thing anew; *Dis* 136).

The frequency with which Schopenhauer refers to the 'veil of *māyā*' no doubt accounts for Mauthner's comparison of the nebulous nature of words and metaphors to it. As previously noted, that in the view of several critics, Beckett's veil metaphor can be traced to the frequent allusions to the illusory 'Schleier der Maja' ('veil of *māyā*') in the *The World as Will and Representation* is further buttressed by an entry, in German, into Beckett's 'Clare Street' notebook of August 1936, a year before his letter to Kaun (Nixon 2011, 106, 166–70).[15] In his 'Clare Street' notes, Beckett

---

[15] Beckett's 'Clare Street' notebook (UoR MS 5003), which he began in July 1936 and wrote entirely in German, is the repository of his thoughts about 'all things German' (Nixon 2011, 106). The notebook's name refers to the Dublin street near Trinity College on which the quantity surveying office of Beckett's father, and later of his brother, was located. At times Beckett fled there to write.

summarizes and comments on a passage in which Schopenhauer maintains that we can only briefly free ourselves from the veil of *māyā* owing to our being enticed back into delusion by the 'temptations of hope' ('Lockungen der Hoffnung') and other worldly attractions (*WWR I* § 68, 406). In his summary in German of this passage, Beckett wittily condenses Schopenhauer's argument by creating the compound *Hoffnungschleier* ('veil of hope') and comparing it to the 'Geistes Star' ('cataract of the spirit') (qtd. and trans. in Nixon 2011, 170).

There remains, however, the matter of Deussen's Upanishadic *Nichtwort* (nonword), quoted by Mauthner in his early section on silence as a step toward a silence beyond silence. Basing his view on the marginal pencil markings in the three volumes of the *Beiträge* in Beckett's library and on Joyce's *Finnegans Wake* notebook, Dirk Van Hulle finds the *Nichtwort*, as already noted, to be 'reminiscent of Beckett's "Literatur des Unworts" (literature of the unword)' (Van Hulle and Nixon 2013, 159).[16] This view raises two unanswerable questions, and that's where the matter is best left: If Beckett read Mauthner before 1937, is his *Unwort* an echo of Deussen's *Nichtwort*? If he did not, did Beckett recognize the family resemblance when he read and reread Mauthner subsequently, eventually highlighting the section on silence in the 1960s?

Some critics detect irony in Mauthner and Beckett's use of words and metaphors to attack their lack of substance, but Beckett did not see it that way. In his letter to Kaun, he recognizes the usefulness of a method that mocks words through words, aware, it would seem, that reflexive or metalinguistic derision is language about language, not language about the world (*Dis* 172). It is a method he amply uses to write about writing and to unwrite the written. Similarly, comparing pure critique to articulated laughter, Mauthner finds laughter to be the best form of criticism (*BKS III* 632).[17] In his view, the mocking critique of language is the highest form of cognition in that it leads to a 'heavenly silent and heavenly serene resignation or renunciation' ('himmelsstillen, himmelsheiteren Resignation oder Entsagung'; *BKS III* 634). Mauthner thus claims that

---

[16] There is, however, some doubt about whether the marginal markings are Beckett's (Van Hulle and Nixon 2013 158–63). On the matter of the translation of Beckett's *Unwort*, in comparing Esslin's 'unword' translation with the 'non-word' rendition in the *Letters* (*LSB I* 520), Esslin's translation turns out to correspond to Beckett's preference for 'un-' as a negative prefix. Beckett translated the French *non-soi* (nonself) into the rarer 'unself' in his 1967 'For Avigdor Arikha' (*Dis* 152), also using the term in his short prose text 'neither' a few years later (*CSP* 258), with, in each case, the meaning of 'unself' corresponding to 'all that is not the self' or 'world'.

[17] 'Reine Kritik ist im Grunde nur ein artikuliertes Lachen. Jedes Lachen ist Kritik, die beste Kritik'.

his critique leads to the Indian path of sages, to which he refers elsewhere in the *Beiträge*, along with Eckhart's embrace of silence. The affinity with Nāgārjuna is equally striking, although the mocking stance that is Mauthner's and Beckett's goes beyond Nāgārjuna's and the other sages' language irreverence.

Beckett's Fiction and the Paradoxical Literature of Silence

Silence through words that are empty of meaning and reference or that unword themselves are maneuvers praised by Nāgārjuna, Mauthner, and the practitioners of the French literature of silence at the time Beckett composed his postwar fiction. Mauthner's agreement with Eckhart's critique of all saying as missaying, to put it in Beckettian terms, has major implications for understanding Beckett's 'being silent in writing' to which French critics drew attention as early as the publication of *Molloy* in 1951. The expression 'being silent in writing' ('se taire par écrit') is Jean-Paul Sartre's 1945 description of Jules Renard's economic style, seeing in its author – one of Beckett's Parisian literary ghosts – the forerunner of the modernist literature of silence and struggle with language (Sartre 1947, 271–2).[18]

In Sartre's view, the major proponent of the 1940s literature of silence was Maurice Blanchot, who, Sartre maintains, chooses words carefully to cancel each other out, a maneuver comparable to algebraic operations that add up to zero (Sartre 1947, 271). In the 1943 *Faux Pas*, Blanchot in fact describes the paradoxical situation of the writer 'doomed to write by the silence and lack of a language that assail him' Blanchot 2001, 3; translation modified). Blanchot, as is well known, ten years later, was to contend about the voice in Beckett's *L'Innommable* that, within it, 'le silence éternellement se parle' ('silence eternally speaks'; Blanchot 1953, 678; 1979, 116). This paradoxical silence evokes the silence 'murmurous with muted lamentation' of Beckett's novel (*Un* 393). The *Unnamable*'s narrator, though, would prefer the 'true silence' that cannot be broken, which has to be earned, liberating him from the murmurous voices within (393–4). This sought-after silence, on which the narrator embroiders for several pages, resonates with the theme of liberation from the world's woes.

---

[18] The twenty-eight entries in Beckett's 'Dream' notebook drawn from Renard's *Journal* (*DN* #s 212–39) and Beckett's frequent dipping into the *Journal* throughout his life underscore his fondness for this forerunner (1864–1910).

In another instance of relay, in his practice of silence in writing, Blanchot is aware of the silence beyond silence described in Shankara's story, which Mauthner found in Deussen's *Philosophy of the Upanishads*. In *Faux Pas*, at the end of his essay 'Autour de la pensée hindoue' ('On Hindu Thought'), Blanchot writes that Western audiences of mystical teachings should best renounce language and learn from Shankara's famous story declaring Ātman is silent (Blanchot 1943, 50; 2001, 36).[19] Nor was Blanchot unaware of the 'struggle with contradiction' and 'the passion of paradox' that prevent easy access to Indian thought, which, along with the mystical thought of Eckhart (the subject of another review in *Faux Pas*), he maintains, should remain unsettling (Blanchot 1943, 47; 2001, 34). This, too, he could have said both of himself and Beckett, the mutual respect for each other's writing no doubt in part owing to their embrace of paradox and maneuvers of silence in writing.

Sartre relates the self-implosion of language ('autodestruction du langage') (Sartre 1947, 272) to Blanchot and Georges Bataille's defense of skepticism, their unknowingness ('non-savoir') beyond knowing (274). The 'knowing unknowing' and the silence of self-cancelling words, which Sartre detected in Blanchot in 1945, were later asserted by the first critics – including Blanchot and Bataille – of Beckett's French trilogy of novels, Bataille entitling his essay 'Le Silence de Molloy'.[20]

The coming together of nominalist language critique of the East and West in the motif of empty words is encountered in Beckett with particular force from *Watt*, dating from the early 1940s, to *Worstward Ho* forty years later. When Watt, the eponymous protagonist of the novel, famously utters the words 'pot' or 'Watt', they no longer evoke a pot or himself, both self and unself (world) having become 'unspeakable' (*W* 82–3). The narrator of *The Unnamable* similarly proclaims that 'blank words' are the only ones he has to go on with, and famously, he continues with a litany of unwords or nonwords (and the near nonwords of onomatopoeia) – 'chuck chuck, ow, ha, pa, I'll practice, nyum, hoo, plop, psss, nothing but

---

[19] Blanchot's piece is a review of the 1941 special issue of *Les Cahiers du Sud* entitled *Message actuel de l'Inde* (Current Message from India), containing translations of essays by ancient and modern Indian thinkers and writers, including Shankara, Vivekananda, and Rabindranath Tagore, and contributions by Western authors.

[20] Rather than 'trilogy of novels' it would be more accurate to refer to Beckett's novels after *Murphy* as 'antinovels', that is, among the first exemplars of the French *nouveau roman* (new novel). Although Beckett contested the term 'trilogy' for the three novels penned from 1947 to 1950, it has been adopted by Beckett commentators for its convenience. Beckett, however, considered the novels from *Murphy* through *The Unnamable* as one series, as evident in the allusions in the later novels of the series to the characters in the earlier ones.

emotion, bing bang, that's blows, ugh, pooh, what else, oooh, aaah, that's love ... hee hee' – which are, for him, the final path to silence (*Un* 408).

In *Watt*, language critique takes still another form, this one poetic, in putting into effect the program announced in the letter to Kaun to launch an 'assault against words in the name of beauty' (*Dis* 173). Thus, in recounting to Sam the final period of his stay at Knott's domain, riddled as his story is with uncertainties and gaps, Watt proceeds to dissolve the 'materiality of the word surface' (*Dis* 172) by inverting the phonemes/graphemes in words, the words in sentences, and the sentences in paragraphs. His utterings, such as 'ot lems, lats lems, lats lems', consist on the surface of pseudowords without sense. This further linguistic decomposition is described in the text in terms of appealing to the ear and 'aesthetic judgement' (*W* 165), eclipsing the semantic sound–sense relation. It is another form of emptying out words, a practice announced in the letter to Kaun and increasingly adopted by Beckett's textual approximations to music and the speed of delivery he demanded in certain of his plays that precludes understanding the words uttered.

Beckett's debt to Schopenhauer's influential view of music is evident in the musical effects he envisaged for his writing. For Schopenhauer, music expresses the emotions in an abstract language thereby arousing a 'spiritual world' in the listener (*WWR I* § 52, 289). In his words, parodying Leibniz, music is 'an unconscious exercise in metaphysics, in which the mind does not know that it is philosophizing' (292); it reveals 'the deepest wisdom', incomprehensible to reason (288). The effect of music, for Schopenhauer, is paradisiacal and, more than any of the other arts, 'the panacea for all our sufferings' providing an 'imperturbable, blissful peace' (§ 51, 277; § 52, 289).

Empty words and the pleasure in sound repetition take on rhythmic force in *Worstward Ho*: 'Say a body. Where none. No mind. Where none ..... A place. Where none' (*Worst* 7). All saying consists of blank words: 'Enough [mind] still not to know. Not to know what they [words] say' (30). That this is an old motif is stated by *Worstward Ho*'s anonymous speaker: 'All of old. Nothing else ever' (9). Nevertheless, for Carla Locatelli, *Worstward Ho* differs from Beckett's previous works by the value it attaches to the saying of the always missaid, which, for her, corresponds to 'the positivity of linguistic failure' in its expression of the 'ignorance-imperative' (Locatelli 1990, 265).

This late work also sets itself apart by the importance attached to the value of a spoken (or written) silence. In recognizing that all saying is missaying and that, as already stated in the letter to Kaun, language is best used when most soundly misused, but nevertheless with an ear for musical effects (*Dis* 171), Beckett imagines an enthralling poetics of words by emptying words via oxymoronic couplings, such as the refrain 'better worse' (*Worst* 15ff.) that parallels the paradoxical 'it is and at the same time it isn't'. In this poetics of *śūnyatā*, silence is not the simple absence of saying but a paradoxical saying and unsaying and missaying, rhythmically aligned in gnomic stanzas interspersed with blankness.

In his close reading of *Worstward Ho* in his *Petit manuel d'inesthétique* (*Handbook of Inaesthetics*), Alain Badiou, perhaps picking up on the 'all of old', contends that Beckett consciously fashioned *Worstward Ho* as a 'testa-mental' text to recapitulate his entire 'intellectual enterprise' (Badiou 2003, 79–80). Badiou, surprisingly, argues that in remaining faithful to the old imperative of saying in this late text, Beckett resists an imperative of silence. For Badiou, one has to choose between what he conceives of as two opposing obligations: either a fidelity to saying, which accepts a poetic ill saying, or a fidelity to the silence evoked at the end of Wittgenstein's *Tractatus*. In Badiou's view, the latter imperative, based on the absolute failure of saying, corresponds to a mystic return to the pure being of the void (Badiou 2003, 90–2). Oddly, Badiou appears to be unaware of the unsaying maneuvers of the literature of silence or the 'being silent in writing'. He thus discounts the paradoxically simultaneous fidelity to (ill) saying and silence by Beckett who, moreover, contests the logical either/or of opposites by a both/and: it is saying and it is silence, a saying silenced by unsaying, or the speaking silence of nonwords. The narrator of the thirteenth and final *Texts for Nothing* thus cites the murmured, 'It's true and it's not true, there is silence and there is not silence' (*CSP* 154).

Challenging the Principle of Noncontradiction 2: It Is and at the Same Time It Is Not

Classical principles of logic famously censor such contradictory declara-tions as 'it's true and it's not true' and 'there is and there is not' by pronouncing that if one is true, the other must be false, and vice versa: contradictory statements cannot be simultaneously true nor simulta-neously false. Beckett, however, as we know, not only embraced such contradictory moves, but including Eckhart in the list of mystics he continued to read, he had strong praise for the mystics' 'illogicality' (Juliet 1986, 51). Indeed, Eckhart's use of paradox and repudiation of logical principles further substantiate Schopenhauer's view of the similar-ities between Gautama and Eckhart. In the sermon in which Eckhart imaginatively describes the dream of God's birth out of nothingness, he makes the paradoxical assertion, 'God is a nothing and God is a something (Got ist ein niht, und got ist ein iht). What is something is also nothing' (*DW* 71; *MEW II* 72; *CMW* 140).[21]

Beckett and Eckhart's contradictory claim of something that is and simultaneously is not concurs with the common challenge to logic adopted by the followers of negative theology in the West and, in the East, in Mādhyamika Buddhism. This further affinity between Eckhart and the Buddha is emphasized by the Kyoto School philosopher Shizuteru Ueda in his essay 'Nothingness in Meister Eckhart and Zen Buddhism'.[22] For Ueda, when it comes to ultimate reality, Eckhart's view of the nothingness of divinity (godhead) beyond God, in the sense that there is nothing that can be said about it, is akin to the Buddhist view of the ultimate as *śūnyatā* (emptiness). Yet, he claims that the Zen view is more radical than Eckhart's as it proceeds without reference to divinity (Ueda 2004 [1977], 158–9). Eckhart's paradoxical assertion about the nothing and something of God, too, resonates with the Buddhist view of reality as empty. Thus, Ueda explains to his mostly Western audience that 'everything that is, is in relationship to others, indeed in a reciprocally conditioned relationship. For anything "to be related", therefore, means that in itself it is a nothingness [is empty]' (161). This conjoining of relatedness and emptiness, Ueda continues, results in the Buddhist formula, 'It is and likewise it is not. It is not and likewise it is' and 'I am I *and likewise* I am not I' (161; emphasis in the original). The coincidence of affirmations and negations corresponds to *śūnyatā* in that neither of the contradictory statements (it is and it is not) can stand on its own to assert either being or non-being. Nihilism this is not.

When in *Dream* the narrator quotes Belacqua's aesthetic of the interval and hyphen in terms of relatedness, 'for me the one real thing is to be found in the relation: the dumbbell's bar, the silence between my eyes, between you and me, all the silences between you and me .... Me-You, One-minus One' (*Dream* 27–8), the family resemblance with Zen's empty space between related terms is remarkable. The narrator of *The Unnamable* confirms that 'between [words] would be the place to be ... bereft of speech, bereft of thought, and feel nothing, hear nothing, know nothing,

---

[21] In a striking example of paronomasia, Eckhart affirms a simultaneous nothing and something with only one sound difference *niht/iht*.

[22] Ueda's paper was originally presented at the 1976 international conference on the borderlines of philosophy and theology in Ludwigsburg, Germany. 'Emptiness' no doubt would be a more fitting translation than 'nothingness'.

say nothing, are nothing, that would be a blessed place to be, where you are'
(*Un* 374). For Ueda, addressing an audience that would be familiar with
Martin Buber's 1923 book *Ich und Du* (*I and Thou*), the definition of *śūnyatā*
in terms of relatedness and the consequent lack of inherent existence implies
that the 'selfless self . . . takes the hyphenated "between" of the I-Thou, as its
own existential inner realm of activity' (Ueda 2004 [1977], 163).

Beckett's contemporaries, too, who recognized their affinities with
him – Maurice Blanchot, Jacques Derrida, Gilles Deleuze, and the
Theodor Adorno of *Negative Dialectics* – embraced paradoxical logic no
less than Beckett and make of aporia a privileged method of undermining
conventional dualities. Derrida, in particular, noted the affinity of decon-
struction with the apophatic discourse of negative theology and its questioning of the propositional authority of the 'is', corresponding, for him, to
a critique of ontology, theology, and language (Derrida 1995, 49–50). Is it
surprising that Derrida would observe about Beckett, 'He is nihilist and he
is not nihilist' (Derrida 2009 [1992], 61)?

In the spirit of paradox, Beckett further asserts the identity of affirmation and negation when Murphy's question 'Yes or no?' is declared 'the
eternal tautology' in his second novel (*Mu* 41). And in the ninth of the
Texts for Nothing, the narrator declares, 'the yeses and noes mean nothing
in this mouth', the 'nothing', as usual taking on more than one possible
meaning (*CSP* 136). Little wonder, then, that Blanchot and Derrida
recognized that Beckett avoids nihilism by skirting the affirmation–
negation opposition (See Weller 2005, 15). The affinity with the
Mahāyāna Perfection of Wisdom literature is apparent in Conze's explanation that the 'secret of emptiness' in the Heart Sūtra is 'the identity of
Yes and No' (Conze 2001 [1958], 90).

But it is Beckett's novel *Watt* that, in particular, evokes parallels with
the Eckhartian and Buddhist 'it is not and likewise it is'. Incidents
described after Watt arrives in Mr. Knott's domain, such as the Galls
who came to tune the piano, take on the paradoxical nature of 'nothing'
and 'something'. Watt, the narrator informs us, could not accept that
'nothing had happened, with all the clarity and solidity of something', and
that this nothing with the attributes of something continues to befuddle
his mind (*W* 76). Emphasizing a 'positive nothing' within an Eckhartian
and Zen Buddhist perspective, Matoba pertinently draws attention to
Watt's conclusion about what he had learned: 'Nothing . . .. But was not
that something?' (*W* 148; Matoba 2003, 107). The first poem in *Watt*'s
addenda succinctly raises the question in asking, 'who may . . . the sum
assess / of the world's woes? / nothingness / in words enclose?' (*W* 247).

The mysterious Mr. Knott, with his multiple ties to something – his grotesque physicality, clothes, meals, and the arrangement of his furniture – which the narrator details in exhaustive lists of logical permutations leading to no certainty, comes to nothing in the end. Knott is but the source of 'naught' to which Watt brings his emptied self: 'this emptied heart. These emptied hands. This mind ignoring. This body homeless' (*W* 166). Avatars of Mr. Knott appear in Beckett's subsequent works of the 1940s and beyond, such as the Youdi of *Molloy*, the much puzzled-over Godot, the 'master' of *The Unnamable*, and 'the someone in another world' and 'the not one of us' of *How It Is*. They share the paradox of being something and at the same time nothing, resulting in visions of emptiness that have rattled readers and viewers ever since. The failure of logic and language to speak of the absolute accounts for the mystics' privileging the illogicality that Beckett not only prized but also practiced. If Beckett mercilessly mocks conceptions of an anthropomorphic deity, one that can be conceived of in terms of nameable somethings, whether in the guise of Knott or Godot, Beckett's famous 'perhaps' chimes more closely with apophatic mystical thought and even more so with nontheistic Buddhist conceptions of the absolute. So when Beckett quipped to Alan Schneider that if he had known who Godot was he would have said so in the play, he should for once be taken at his word (qtd. in Schneider 1967 [1958], 38). There is no knowing what is beyond knowing.

In a modernist foregrounding of fictionality, the paradoxical something and nothing further applies to Beckett's creatures. Already in his first novel, 'Mr Beckett' declares: 'There is no real Belacqua, it is to be hoped not indeed, there is no such person' (*Dream* 121). As we know, recantations of the narrator's previous proxies proliferate in *The Unnamable*, with his own existence no less in doubt. Having just resolved not to say 'I' again, he intones the paradoxical, 'Where I am there is no one but me, who am not' (*Un* 355). In disowning the protagonists from Murphy onward as so many failed representatives of his pains, the narrator declares that they are paradoxically both his invention and he theirs, that they tried to make him believe he was one of them, claiming him as their fiction as they are his (*Un* 303, 326, 377). Who then is narrating whom?[23] The boundaries of the different narrative levels of teller and told, inside and outside, are transgressed by such paradoxical, or 'aporetic', duplication, in which the told tell the stories that tell them, as no fixed identification is possible in the oscillation between narrator and narrated (Dällenbach 1989, 35). In Leslie

[23] Belacqua is unnamed here, but the narrator admits that Murphy 'wasn't even the first' (*Un* 390).

Hill's succinct conclusion about Beckett's metatextual paradoxes, 'There is, for Beckett's narrator, no respite from fiction, and no redemption from its paradoxes or from the aporia to which it leads' (Hill 1990, 77).

Beckett continued to refine aporetic doubling in the *mise en abyme* (self-reflexive, or recursive, embedding) of his late dramaticules *Not I*, *A Piece of Monologue*, *Ohio Impromptu*, and *Footfalls*, each involving storytelling. Beckett's pleasure in imagining the paradoxical slippage between narration and story is palpable as are its effects on the audience: anti-illusion, vertigo, and koan-like puzzlement, ultimately leading to emptiness.[24] (See Chapter 6.)

In *How It Is*, too, having first announced that he is moving toward his victim Pim, the narrator adds the paradoxical claim that 'he does not exist' (*How* 27), a claim repeated at the end by the work's torrent of yeses and nos: 'never any Pim no nor any Bom no never anyone no only me yes' (146), but this 'me' is tantalizingly derealized as a dream of 'someone in another world yes whose kind of dream I am yes' . . . his only story yes', before it too is denied as 'all balls' (145). At the end, 'yes' and 'no' collapse into each other.

The narrator's fleeting view of himself as someone's dream recalls the ancient Indian doctrine of emanation, which sees the world as the pha-tasmagoric dream and cosmic play world of a divine being. One mytho-logical story from the Brahmanic Purāṇas Beckett would have read in the already mentioned *Maya: Der indische Mythos*, by Heinrich Zimmer, depicts a god who out of the flowing dream narrative of his *māyā* – the creative force behind his dream – playfully spins out the world and its shadow beings. For this god, the world emanating from him is a phantas-magoria, whereas it appears real to those spun into it (Zimmer 1936, 47–8, 63). Buddhism's nonmythological concept of *māyā* as the illusory

---

[24] On Beckett's paradoxical *mise en abyme*, see Moorjani 1982, 15–67, for the fiction, and 1996, 89–95, for his late theatre. See also De Vos 2018, who discusses aporetic doubling in Beckett's theatre in terms of loops, the Möbius strip, and autopoiesis. Sharing Beckett's likely debt to André Gide's notion and practice of *mise en abyme*, Beckett's *nouveau roman* colleagues at the Éditions de Minuit during the 1950s and 1960s shared his fascination with textual mirrors. Aporetic doubling is a favored technique of other late modernist writers, Jorge Luis Borges, for instance, in his labyrinthine tales. In a stunning example of relay, Borges shared Beckett's appreciation (even if not always admitted) of Schopenhauer, Buddhism, Eckhart, and Mauthner. In fact, Borges's lifelong interest in Buddhism resulted in the book *Qué es el Budismo* in 1976 with the assistance of Alicia Jurado. The 1961 international literary Prix Formenter was split between Beckett and Borges, whose shared intertexts account partly for their flagrant assaults on logic. In a fascinating parallel, South Asian Buddhist psycho-cosmograms that model the world by techniques of recursive loops and homologies (Shulman 2020, 37) evoke effects on viewers similar to those elicited by Beckett's aporetic *mise en abyme*.

phenomenal world rather than the cosmic dream of a god would make it appear that Beckett was thinking of the Brahmanic rather than the Buddhist version of *māyā* in this instance. If in *How It Is* the Indian mythos of the world identified with the dream of a divine being is ultimately denied, so is the Christian belief in a transcendent 'pas des nôtres', which Beckett translated literally as 'not one of us', thereby losing the pun in French on *pater noster* (*Cc* 166; *How* 137). The two beliefs, of the East and the West, are both vehemently negated at the end of the novel.

Finally, having played his game of come and go, or of yes, it is/no, it isn't, with the fictional elements of *How It Is*, leaving only 'me' and its own voice, this final assertion is contradicted by the text's closing words, 'end of quotation'. In Leo Bersani and Ulysse Dutoit's remarkable reading of *How It Is*, the narrator's claim that he is quoting his story under dictation from an outside source implies that, this information, too, is part of the dictation, so that his claim corresponds to an infinite regress of sources (Bersani and Dutoit 1993, 59–60). Such a regress is apparent, moreover, since *Watt* (Moorjani 1982, 27–9) and applies as much to other fictions in which the narrators claim they are quoting, such as *The Unnamable* and *Company*. It is one of Beckett's ways of going on endlessly. And finally, doesn't *How It Is* echo Watt's 'nothing had happened, with all the clarity and solidity of something' (*W* 76)?

If we substitute the concept of 'fictional truth' for 'conventional truth', making it analogous to the Mādhyamika two truths, Beckett's protagonists exist in the 'as if' reality of fiction that corresponds to Mādhyamika conventional, but illusory, reality; but from the metatextual standpoint of the ultimately illusory nature of fiction, they do not exist.[25] But it is the contradictory 'I'/'not I' of the fictional voices of *The Unnamable* that in particular bears further exploration. That the narrator's 'I' is a 'not I' resounds throughout the last pages of *The Unnamable*: 'it's not I, not I, I can't say it, it came like that, it comes like that, it's not I' (*Un* 402).

This insistence on a 'not I' can be seen as an emptying out of the 'deictic center', in which the first person projects the central position that accrues to it in discourse into third-person (non-deictic) simulacra. As we know, in the egocentricity of discourse, deictic terms of person, place, and time, such as 'I' and 'you', 'here' and 'there', and 'now' and 'then', can only be understood by reconstructing the deictic center, that is, the position of the

---

[25] Scholars have similarly connected the is/is not, or the ghostly something that is also a nothing, to a metadiscourse about the paradoxes that inhere in broadcast media. See Bignell 2010, 125–42.

first-person speaker. In Beckett's fiction after *Murphy*, however, the deictic center is repeatedly emptied out and replaced by a proxy that speaks through a 'not I'.

Intriguingly, in a letter to Georges Duthuit that Beckett mailed in May 1949 from his country retreat in Ussy-sur-Marne, he replaces his *je*/I by the third person: 'Je fais du vélo avec frénésie, je veux dire celui que est censé ... me représenter' (I cycle frantically, I mean the one who is supposed to represent me) (*LSB II* 148).[26] The writer's 'I' is absent, replaced by someone else who is doing the cycling for him. This experience is familiar to seasoned automobile drivers who find themselves coming back to conscious control after moments of absence and wondering how it was possible to drive under such circumstances. Such dissociative, or automatic, states, well known to cognitive psychologists, occur commonly while absentmindedly carrying out well-learned actions or tasks, such as walking, cycling, or driving. What is striking about Beckett's letter is his imagining a *pauvre con* (bumbling fool) surrogate who represents him during these dissociative states so that he has the impression of his 'I' being doubled by a proxy who displaces him (148). It is the same 'existence by proxy' that Beckett later explained to Lawrence Harvey about his feelings of being 'absent' while walking and his impression that someone else is taking steps for him (Harvey 1970, 247). Beckett is, then, able to be aware of both psychic states – the dissociative (unconscious) and the conscious – and simultaneously and imaginatively personify them. Wilfred Bion asserted the same about his analysand 'A' who, some of us argue, is based in part on Beckett (Moorjani 2004, 26–8). As Bion reports, 'A' was capable of personifying his inner fractures in artful ways and thereby subjecting them to the scrutiny of his eyes and intellect (Bion 1967, 7–16).

In his letter to Duthuit, Beckett goes on jokingly to describe his proxy as cursing but happy at the (automatic) handywork (nailing, sawing, and so on) that he is best suited to do, but in wanting to transfer these skills to the page (measuring, anticipating, rectifying) acknowledges somewhat shame-facedly that this is not his place (*LSB II* 148).[27] The proxy's role, then, in the writing process is seen as limited to the dissociative dimension outside

---

[26] In citations of Beckett's *Letters* from here on, when the translation from the French is George Craig's, the translated text is enclosed in quotation marks. Otherwise, the translation is mine. At times, a note explains our differences.

[27] 'Le même pauvre con cloue, visse, scie et lime pestant et content. C'est de loin ce qu'il a de mieux à faire. Et devant la feuille, il voudrait s'affairer encore, se précipiter pour mesurer, prévoir et faire tenir debout. Mais un peu honteux quand même, sachant que ce n'est pas sa place'.

of conscious control, leaving space for the writer's control when he returns from his absence to the page. Having begun *L'Innommable* two months earlier, Beckett would seem to be playfully transferring the multiple vice-existers of his fictional narrator to his own blundering 'not I', or is it the other way around: his own sense of being represented by a 'not I' is being projected onto his fiction? And, intriguingly, in the fiction of the 1940s, the disorderly walking and cycling of Beckett's creatures, which call down on them the wrath of agents of order, can be read, on one level, as poetic analogues for the texts' limping and halting style, the work of the 'bumbling' proxy, or what Beckett referred to as a 'syntax of weakness' (Harvey 1970, 249). (More on dissociative creativity and the 'not I' in Chapter 6.)

The Paradoxical Ethics of Emptiness

If we return to Beckett's piece on Henri Hayden and the silence of his paintings that, in their near-effacement of subject and object, distantly echo the Buddha's paradoxical wisdom, the surmise that Beckett is writing as much about his own oeuvre as about Hayden's is borne out by his stating that he should have felt even more surprise and 'affection fraternelle' in front of the work of a painter who, enduring the 'mirages' of both self ('un soi tel quel') and nature ('une nature imprenable'), nevertheless paints (*Dis* 147).

In the following investigation of the ethical effects of Beckett's work, the compassionate side of his personality is rarely evoked, having been detailed by his biographers, the recipients of his generosity, and exegetes tracing his extensive political engagement throughout his life.[28]

In this connection, it is worth mentioning Beckett's 1946 letter to Simone de Beauvoir protesting her refusal to print the second part of the *nouvelle* 'Suite' (the later 'La Fin' / 'The End') in *Les Temps Modernes*. He ends this letter with the declaration of an ethical imperative to explain his insistence: 'Il existe simplement une misère qu'il s'agit de défendre jusqu'au bout, dans le travail et en dehors du travail' ('It is that there exists a wretchedness which must be defended to the very end, in one's work and outside it'; *LSB II* 40–42).[29] There are, as is well known, other aspects of Beckett's personality, such as the directorial compulsiveness that he projected onto such works as *Pochade radiophonique* / *Rough for Radio II*

---

[28] See Emilie Morin's *Beckett's Political Imagination* (2017).

[29] For the most persuasive reading to date of the 'Suite' controversy within the political climate of the times, see Morin 2017, 139–40, 168–70.

(written circa 1960) in which both the fictional torturer and victim are associated with autobiographical details recognizably the author's, so that he assumes the existence of the contrary identities for himself, echoing Schopenhauer's oneness of tormentor and tormented (*WWR I* § 62, 367; § 63, 381).

It is argued here that Beckett's texts, in their emptying out of self and unself (the 'rest' of the piece on Henri Hayden) and their intimations of an 'elsewhere', suggest, in a minor key, analogous effects to those offered by Mahāyāna's paradoxical path joining the wisdom of emptiness to the compassionate concern of introducing others to what Beckett terms a tentative 'way out'.[30] In his letter to Hans Neumann of 17 February 1954, Beckett admits that the reading experiences that marked him the most corresponded to his being 'à l'affût d'un ailleurs' ('on the lookout for an elsewhere'), that is, he was most affected by those readings, he writes, 'qui m'y ont le mieux renvoyé, à cet ailleurs' ('that were best at sending me to that elsewhere'; *LSB II* 462, 465). Because Beckett's statement flies in the face of the view held by many exegetes that he rejects an 'elsewhere', including some commentators aware of his affinity with Buddhism, it may take the close attention paid to his postwar and later texts in the remaining chapters of this study to convince readers. Also pertinent here is that prominent French philosopher Emmanuel Levinas holds metaphysics to consist in turning toward an *ailleurs* (elsewhere; Levinas 1974, 3).

Similar views to those Beckett expressed in his piece on Henri Hayden had surfaced in the frequently cited 'Three Dialogues' with Georges Duthuit. Beckett's discussions on art with the art critic and editor of the postwar *Transition* were originally published in *Transition Forty-Nine* (No. 5), in December of that year, with both Beckett and Duthuit listed as the authors. As a matter of fact, with the publication of the second volume of Beckett's *Letters*, it has become increasingly clear to what extent the 'Dialogues' are based on personal conversations and an exchange of letters in French between the two friends. Beckett, however, is the one who condensed and rescripted their discussions for the English-language *Transition*, writing into his role as B. some of the failings of the *pauvre con* in the letter to Duthuit of May 1949. Thus, he ends each of the three dialogues with a clownish protest of unsaying or silence on the part of B.

B. and D. devote the second dialogue to André Masson's recent concern with, in the words of D., 'painting the void' (*Dis* 139). At the time of the

---

[30] See the second and third parts of the next chapter, which discuss the theme of 'a way out' in the postwar fiction and *Le Dépeupleur / The Lost Ones*.

'Three Dialogues', Masson was engaged in his Asiatic period of 1947–57, leaving his violent surrealist paintings of the previous decade behind. His appreciation of Eastern thought and aesthetics parallels that of other Western artists drawn to Buddhist teachings in the aftermath of a brutal war. In the role of D., Duthuit, the author of the 1936 *Chinese Mysticism and Modern Painting*, quotes the beginning of Masson's recently published jottings about space: 'Inner emptiness, the prime condition, according to Chinese esthetics, of the act of painting' (139). Conversant with Zen Buddhism, Masson, in his 1949 article, briefly contrasts the depiction of space in Zen and Chinese Song art, on the one hand, and mostly modern European painting, on the other. That Beckett had carefully read Masson's 'Divagations sur l'espace' [Ramblings about Space] – Pages de journal (1936–1938)', is apparent when B. compares Masson's remarks on space with Leonardo's possessiveness in his notebooks (141).[31]

Surprisingly, however, B. does not respond to Masson's desire to paint the void with the 'fraternal affection' that Beckett expressed for Hayden three years later. And yet doesn't Masson's 'faire en soi le vide' (Masson 1949, 961) – literally, 'to create a void within oneself – which Beckett translates as 'inner emptiness', echo Belacqua's 'bel niente' and aesthetics of emptiness? Masson's void, B. argues, however, is not the void but 'perhaps simply the obliteration of an unbearable presence', a presence rendered unbearable to Masson, B. contends, by its resistance to expression (140). To this attitude, which, for B., is not to be confused with the void, he prefers the 'dream of an art unresentful of its insuperable indigence' (141), an impoverishment Beckett both practiced and praised in the pieces and tributes he composed on artists of his acquaintance, including Henri Hayden.

In the first of the three dialogues, B.'s famous argument about the 'obligation to express' in the face of the 'nothing to express', absent the means and the desire to express (*Dis* 139), echoes, as is well known, Maurice Blanchot's similar assertions in his 1943 *Faux Pas*. Could it be an instance of 'stolentelling'? In the introduction to his collection of his early essays and reviews, Blanchot gives this view of the writer's situation: 'L'écrivain se trouve dans cette condition de plus en plus comique de n'avoir rien à écrire, de n'avoir aucun moyen de l'écrire et d'être contraint par une nécessité extrême de toujours l'écrire' (Writers find themselves in the more and more comic situation of having nothing to write about, of

---

[31] A new translation of Leonardo's notebooks was the subject of a review by Blanchot in *Faux Pas* (2001 [1943], 71–5), not to imply that Beckett could not have read them in the original.

having no means with which to write about it, and of being compelled by utter necessity to write continuously about it; Blanchot 1943, 11; my translation).[32] Both Blanchot and Beckett's statements, as we can now see, resonate with Nāgārjuna's emptiness and negative dialectics. In words that parallel Beckett's paradoxical art of failure and decreation, Blanchot further maintains: 'The art of which [a writer] makes use is an art in which absolute success and utter failure, the abundance of means and their irremediable deterioration, the real and the nothingness of results must appear simultaneously' (Blanchot 2001, 5; translation amended).[33] But when Beckett rewrites Blanchot's 'nécessité extrême' as an 'obligation', this ethical turn at the time Beckett was writing L'Innommable suggests that the consonance with Mahāyāna's paradoxical bonding of emptiness to compassion is worthwhile pursuing.

The relation of emptiness to ethics has exercised many thinkers. In Mādhyamika, the cultivation of the mind through meditation on emptiness together with compassion and generosity comprise the path to liberation (Edelglass 2009, 389, 392). It is in particular the ethical path of the bodhisattvas, compassionate beings who dedicate themselves to liberating others from the ignorance that results in their suffering.[34] Two millennia later, in the contemporary view of the Vietnamese-American astrophysicist Trinh Xuan Thuan, the Taoist and Buddhist notion of emptiness concurs with the latest findings of modern cosmology. In his 2016 La Plénitude du vide (The Plenum Void), Trinh deduces infinite compassion from Buddhist interdependence or relatedness, which, in his view, resonates with the modern cosmological finding that we are derived from the vide plein (plenum void) that resulted in the big bang, the stars, and life (Trinh 2016, 277, 295). Theodor Adorno, too, in his notes on L'Innommable (in German translation) saw the ethical import of Beckett's works in 'the absolute emptiness of absolute egoity' that they propose, or, in other words, in the nonexistence of the 'absolute "I"' (qtd. in Weller 2010, 184). Interestingly, several other notes Adorno made on Beckett's novel in the 1960s overlap with Schopenhauer's philosophy and the Buddhist thinking with which he proclaimed his philosophy to be in agreement.

---

[32] For an alternate translation, see Blanchot 2001[1943], 3.

[33] 'L'art dont il [l'écrivain] use est un art où doivent apparaître à la fois la parfaite réussite et le complet échec, la plénitude des moyens et l'irrémédiable déchéance, la réalité et le néant des résultats' (Blanchot 1943, 14).

[34] See the analysis of Beckett's final fiction Stirrings Still in Chapter 8, in which the figure regrets that after his final liberation ('the one true end to time and grief and self and second self'), the sorrows of finitude will persist for others (CSP 261).

In one striking example, Adorno queries: 'something infinitely <u>liberating</u> comes from B[eckett] vis-à-vis death. What is it?' (Adorno 2010, 172; underlined in the original). It is a question that – from the Buddha to Schopenhauer and Beckett – is left unanswered. And in questioning whether 'nothingness' is the same as 'nothing' in *L'Innommable*, Adorno concludes: 'Absolute discardment, because there is hope only where nothing is retained. The fullness of nothingness. That is the reason for the insistence on the zero point' (Adorno 2010, 178).[35]

Beckett's 'obligation', which he compressed four decades later into 'Can't and must!' (qtd. in Shainberg 1987, 132), results in the paradoxical logic leaving his readers and viewers to contemplate the wisdom of emptiness.[36] Commentators have sought to understand Beckett's 'obligation' by drawing on Emmanuel Levinas's call for an ethical form of language fostering an openness to the other and privileging the saying over the said.[37] It is a matter of an ethical speaking to, not of, as we find in Mādhyamika, at once a commitment to others and a discourse emptied of deluded views.[38] Yet, the ethical effect does not end with the wisdom of emptiness, encompassing self, world, and words, but the 'new dimension' that Beckett attributed to his theatre after a passage through the void. It is envisioned, if not as liberation, in terms of the 'perhaps' of an unknowable 'elsewhere' or 'beyond' that has affinities with it.

Simon Critchley holds that Levinas's distinction between the saying and the said permits 'the performative enactment of ethical writing' (qtd. in Salisbury 2012, 174).[39] Among the first to draw attention to such an enactment of ethical and political processes in Beckett's texts are Peter Gidal, for the political, and Carla Locatelli for the performativity of saying

---

[35] In writing his notes on *L'Innommable*, Adorno (1903–69) had in mind composing an essay on the novel as he had on *Fin de partie / Endgame*.

[36] Shane Weller, however, hypothesizes that Beckett's repeated 'must' about going on, uttered by the narrator of *The Unnamable* and in his own voice, can be read not as an ethical imperative but as an act of compulsion (Weller 2009, 45). In fact, in reference to a time-consuming task he was about to undertake for *Transition*, Beckett explained in the already mentioned letter of May 1949 (without precise date) to Georges Duthuit, 'Mais je suis maniaque' (*LSB II* 149), which can be read as an admission of his compulsiveness but also his meticulousness about work. The translation given in the *Letters*, 'but I am by nature obsessive', is unwarranted in the given context (*LSB II* 150). In my view, compulsiveness about a task to accomplish does not preclude an ethical obligation.

[37] See, for example, Locatelli 1990, 130–1; Trezise 1990, 147–9, and for a summary of previous views on the topic, Salisbury 2012, 10–14 and 174–8.

[38] In his radical critique of language, Mauthner, too, has nevertheless much of usefulness to say about the pragmatic social function of everyday language. In recognizing that 'language is language use' ('Sprache ist Sprachgebrauch'), he compares it to a social game (*Gesellschaftsspiel*; *BKS I* 24–5).

[39] In 'The Death of the Author', Roland Barthes cogently argues that, in modern texts, the performative has replaced representation (1967, sec. 4).

and unsaying. The material/semiotic 'elements' of Beckett's theatre –
speech, gesture, body, temporal markers, mise en scène – Gidal argues,
effect 'a radical positioning' of the audience against accepted meanings and
meaning making, thereby occasioning resistance to patriarchal and other
historically and culturally/socially repressive scripts (Gidal 1986, 114).
Gidal's impressive and unsettling engagement with Beckett's texts situates
his own readers in a performative process similar to the one he uncovered
in Beckett – involving them in the thinking through and emptying out of
meanings that effect a change of conceptual horizons, a prerequisite to
envisioning political alternatives, an *ailleurs* of another order.

In more general (nonperformative) terms, Adorno contends that the
negation of a radically evil world in Beckett's works opens up a chance for
a different one (Adorno 2000a [1966], 380–1), an argument reprised by
Badiou, who sees in Beckett's subtractions from habitual ways of thinking
the possibility of an 'event' producing the revolutionary effects of a
previously unthought.[40]

Interesting in this connection is another trait shared by the three spoofers
of logic – Gautama, Eckhart, and Mauthner – with whose thought Beckett
was engaged: all three preferred the vernacular to the scholarly idiom of their
times, the former two in their preaching, the latter in his philosophical
writings: Gautama, it is said, privileged the spoken language over Sanskrit;
Eckhart formulated his German sermons in colloquial Middle High
German, while reserving Latin for his more formal philosophical writings,
and Mauthner adopted an informal and often humorous style. Beckett was
to do the same. Are we to understand that all four were intent on reaching
their audience by a way of saying that distances them from inherited
opinions and its power to reproduce the illusory worldview they are intent
on negating by their paradoxes? It is indeed a way of responding to the
paradoxical obligation to write in the face of nothingness by leaving intact
the commitment to the other while circumventing language's power to
mislead and missay. For Roland Barthes, by its social protest, the adoption
of a popular, as compared to a learned, idiom has an affinity with the 'zero
degree' of writing (Barthes 1953, chs. 5–7).

And the ethical import of humor? If one recalls Mauthner's praise of
laughter as the best form of critique, does Beckett's humor have a claim to

---

[40] For a general introduction to Badiou's thought on Beckett, see Badiou 1995; see Gibson 2002 for a
discussion of Beckett and Badiou's 'event', and Jean-Michel Rabaté's chapter 'Strength to Deny:
Beckett between Adorno and Badiou' for an incisive reading of the two philosophers' grappling with
Beckett's writing (Rabaté 2016, 134–57).

being an ethical practice? In Laura Salisbury's view, in her impressively thought-through study of the comic in Beckett's oeuvre, his postwar trilogy 'furiously spits out its given world' and thereby remains both humorous and a critique in the recognition that things should be otherwise (Salisbury 2012, 110–11).

In summary, Beckett's challenges to the principle of noncontradiction echo models of both the East and the West, from Gautama himself and the founder of the Middle Path Nāgārjuna to Eckhart and Mauthner. The effect of their paradoxical thought is not only to flout classical logic but to put their interlocutors into a perplexed frame of mind, which on freeing them from the grip of received knowledge, logic, and language, leaves them unmoored from conceptual anchors. Seen from a Mahāyāna standpoint, such actions are intended to extricate others from delusion and set them on the path to wisdom, compassion, and liberation. For Beckett, the uncoupling from certainties and the embrace of the Buddha's 'folle sagesse' involve the ethical obligation to engage with unknowing the known, with unsaying the said, while 'à l'affût d'un ailleurs' ('on the lookout for an elsewhere'). Despite his doubts, pragmatically, Beckett's paradoxical logic and unknowingness, rather than disconnecting readers, listeners, and viewers from his works, keep them engaged with the other dimension resulting from a passage through the void in which he situates his writing.

CHAPTER 5

The Coincidence of Contraries and Noh Drama

Contraries within Contraries

Beckett's taste for flouting classical logic and his critique of dichotomizing thought, which he knowingly shared with Buddhist and mystic philosophers, were apparent as early as *Dream* and its merging of the prenatal and posthumous into one mental retreat. In the later *More Pricks than Kicks,* the story 'Yellow' humorously engages with the paradoxical nature of affirming the union of contraries. In this story, an anxious Belacqua, who is facing an operation, contemplates John Donne's phrase that few of the wise would laugh at Heraclitus weeping, but that none would weep at Democritus laughing. Belacqua is then said to 'hazard a little paradox of his own account, to the effect that between contraries no alternation was possible'. In his view, laughter and tears come 'to the same thing in the end' (*MPTK* 175).[1] And yet, despite this declared sameness, differences persist between the two contraries, determining Belacqua to opt for laughter to avoid the social disgrace that would come with weeping (176–7).

Belacqua's ruminating about the weeping and laughing contraries corresponds to the Aristotelean distinction between contradictory and contrary pairs of terms. For Aristotle, contradictions involve affirmation and negation, whereas contraries refer to opposites in nature, such as living and dying, sleeping and waking, lower and higher, night and day, which, by definition, cannot both be true at the same time (Horn 1989, 6–7). Belacqua's weeping–laughing paradox flouts this logical principle in unifying opposites, for which Heraclitus is famous, but he disputes the Greek

---

[1] The two Presocratic thinkers were active about the time of the Buddha, Heraclitus, 'the weeping philosopher', around 500 BCE, and Democritus, 'the laughing philosopher', bridging the fifth and fourth centuries BCE. Beckett, in various works, engages with Heraclitus' doctrines of universal flux, the coincidence of contraries, and fire as the primary principle. Democritus, as evident from Beckett's *Murphy*, is renowned for his theory of atomism and the existence of the void.

philosopher's alternation principle, in which contraries change into each other. Described by Daniel Graham, the alternation of opposites is a 'transformational equivalence of opposites', or in Heraclitus' terms, 'As the same thing in us is living and dead, waking and sleeping, young and old. For these things having changed around are those, and conversely those having changed around are these' (Graham 2017, § 3). Beckett, on the other hand, has Belacqua first insist on the unchanging sameness of laughing and weeping, which is then ironically undercut by his awareness of their distinct effects, so that he adopts one rather than the other.

In this passage in 'Yellow', Beckett may be recalling Giordano Bruno's identified contraries that he noted in his 1929 essay on Joyce's future *Finnegans Wake* (*Dis* 20–1), although not mentioning Bruno's motto combining sadness (*tristitia*) with mirth (*hilaritas*), which famously made it into the *Wake* (Denham 2011, 7).[2] Bruno's claim that 'contraries are within contraries – which Aristotle and other Sophists could not comprehend' (qtd. in Denham 2011, 3), corresponds to the interpenetrating nature of oppositional terms in Beckett's works, with each retaining its difference. Whatever the case may be, the weeping and laughing paradox (among others) courses through Beckett's texts. In *The Unnamable*, the narrator compares the 'murmurous' silence, which is not as yet the true silence, to the 'exhaling of impossible sorrow, like distant laughter' (*Un* 393). And suffering joined to laughter is much in evidence in performances of *Endgame*. No matter how jarring the stage action and dialogue, audiences frequently respond with laughter to the comedy Beckett infused into the text. Nell's notorious line in the play, 'Nothing is funnier than unhappiness' (*End* 18), which Beckett repeated frequently in conversation, appears to be his preferred formulation of the paradox.

Beckett commentators have drawn attention to the dynamic quality of Beckett's paradoxical logic. Leslie Hill cautions against interpreting the union of contraries as a stable fusion, arguing instead that the intermingling of contraries in Beckett entails a continuing oscillation of differences within the sameness (Hill 1990, 4–8). Anthony Uhlmann (1999, 62–4) concurs, preferring however the Deleuzian 'inclusive disjunction', which in Deleuze's words is 'an art that no longer selects but affirms the disjointed terms through their distance, without limiting one by the other or excluding one from the other'. And Deleuze singles out Beckett for taking this art to 'its highest point' (Deleuze 1997b, 110–11). In terms reminiscent of

---

[2] Denham describes Bruno (1548–1600) as an influential philosopher and 'madcap free-thinker' who was burned at the stake for his heretical religious views (2011, 1).

Bruno's, Deleuze holds that opposites are inseparable and maintains that 'both are found in either' (Deleuze 1990 [1969], 79). The concept of the oxymoron offers still another approach to Beckett's unstable union of contraries. For Peter Gidal, oxymoron is a concept in which 'each portion is persistently weighted against another' resulting in an engagement with 'oppositionality *per se*' (Gidal 1986, 251).

The intermingling of contraries was to remain one of Beckett's preferred challenges to classical logic, challenges celebrated, as we have seen, by Buddhist, apophatic, and thinkers of his own time. Among ancient Buddhist examples of the unity of opposites is the already mentioned reconciliation of emptiness and fullness in Chapter 3, but more notorious is Nāgārjuna's assertion that there is no difference between *saṃsāra* and *nirvāṇa*, (*MMK* 25.19). In commenting on the Heart Sūtra's irreducible paradoxes, Conze wrestles with Nāgārjuna's conundrum, explaining that at one stage of self-discipline, it is useful to pay attention to the obviously distinct meanings of *nirvāṇa* and *saṃsāra*, the absolute and the empirical world. But for those seeking spiritual awareness, he continues, 'the identity of Beyond and not-Beyond' corresponds to the mystical identity of opposites (Conze 2001 [1958], 88–9). Other commentators hold that, when viewed conventionally, *nirvāṇa* and *saṃsāra* remain distinct states, but from the ultimate viewpoint, both are empty so that nothing can be claimed of them (Siderits and Katsura 2013, 303).

Beckett, as we have seen, consistently unifies the contraries of a before-birth and after-death state, birth and death, living and dying. These can be understood in their dynamic interdependency both linearly, one being transformed into the other or having been so transformed, and cyclically, in which case, birth turns into death, which turns into birth, and so on in the manner of the wheel of becoming,[3] and finally, their coincidence can be understood by resorting to the two viewpoints of the ideal real with its family likeness to the Buddha's two-truths doctrine. Conventionally or phenomenally, the distinctness of birth and death is maintained, but from an ultimate viewpoint, that of the *unborn* beyond birth and death, they coincide disjunctively.

Beckett's always renewed tropes for the collapse of birth and death point to an unstillable obsession, one shared by Schopenhauer when, as already noted, he writes that to think of ourselves as timeless, we must think of birth and death, in the same sense, as both beyond time, and therefore 'think of ourselves as *unborn*' (*WWR II* ch. 41, 503–4; italics in the text).

---

[3] The Buddhist wheel of becoming is a figure for cyclical existence.

'What birth is, death is as well', he writes, 'in essence and significance; it is the same line drawn in two directions' (504), having earlier asserted that death and life are included in each other (*WWR I* § 60, 357), and, more generally, that 'opposites always shed light on each other' (*WWR I* § 65, 394).

Brief discussions of the coincidence of contraries in two of Beckett's postwar works will highlight their inclusive disjunctions, final renunciations, and embracing of emptiness congruent with the Buddha's teachings. In *Eleutheria*, the play written in French in 1947 and published posthumously against Beckett's wishes, spatial contraries are visually portrayed on the dualistic stage of this disowned pre-*Godot* play: on one side of the stage, the cluttered bourgeois parlor of the Krap family, on the other, the bare room of their ironically named son Victor across Paris, the two joined onstage by a common backdrop and floor. The two merge 'imperceptibly', Beckett writes in the stage directions (*Eleu* 13), resulting in a blend of contraries without, however, annulling their divergent onstage portrayals. At the end of the play, whose title is Greek for 'freedom', Victor renounces, literally turning his back on the play's marked oppressive social hierarchies, the characters' indifference to the catastrophic suffering of the recent war, and the, at the time, popular terrorist Hegelian interpretation of history by Alexandre Kojève (Dr. Piouk in the play), all of which Beckett lampoons in the sense of laughter is the best critique. In allusions to Hegel and Schopenhauer, variations on the master-and-slave and tormentor-and-tormented opposites alternate and merge in this play and the next.[4]

In *Molloy*, written in French later in the same year as *Eleutheria*, Beckett transposes the play's dualistic stage to the two-part novel, narrated by two opposing and complementary figures of one writing persona. The first part's Molloy is declared to be 'just the opposite of myself' by the second part's Moran (*Mo* 113). Throughout the two parts, dichotomies multiply to ultimately coincide 'disjunctively'. In the mode of 'contraries are within contraries', in focusing on the novel's oscillating foreground and background, Moran's narrative is contained in Molloy's (part one), whose narrative is contained in Moran's (part two) without either losing its distinctness. Finally, both parts conclude in the characters' renunciations and end in the negation of what has been written. It is quite a *tour de force* that has puzzled readers ever since its publication in 1951 (French) and

---

[4] See Moorjani 2003, 69–88, and for different political readings of the play, see Morin 2017, 145–6, 162, 228.

1955 (English).⁵ Noteworthy, too, is the oscillating intermingling of other polarities throughout the novel, upending social hierarchies, gender among them, and demonstrating the 'both are found in either' of the conscious and unconscious, order and chaos, life and death, words and silence.

In the next two novels, contraries continue to collapse into sameness, or rather inclusive or oxymoronic disjunctions: in *Malone Dies*, birth and death meld throughout, but so do up and down and to and fro (*Ma* 219); in *The Unnamable*, Mahood and the 'anti-Mahood' Worm are declared to be the same and not the same (*Un* 346, 347); confounded too are the inability to die and be born (352), end and beginning (398), inside and outside (383), and the before and after in terms of the Heraclitean 'upstream, downstream, what matter' (352).

Three decades after *The Unnamable*, in *Mal vu mal dit / Ill Seen Ill Said*, the flouting of the principle of contradiction continues to gather force: 'Such the confusion now between real and – how say its contrary? No matter. That old tandem. Such now the confusion between them once so twain' (*Ill* 40). Because the narrator adds an 'ill' when he repeats the question, 'Real and – how ill say its contrary?' (40), whatever the contrary of the real could be 'ill' said to be – the ideal, the imaginary, the metaphysical, the absolute – Beckett is questioning their existence as simple contraries as compared to their dynamic confusion. Further, in startling ways, in *Worstward Ho*, failing 'better' is made to coincide with failing 'worse' and collapsed into the oxymoronic 'better worse' (*Worst* 7–8, 15ff.) Because of the obsessive collapse of the birth and death contraries into one throughout Beckett's oeuvre, this topos will be explored further in this chapter and taken up in detail in Chapter 7.

Beckett's Ghost Stories and Japanese Dream Noh

Among the several guises of the unbornness in his writing, Beckett introduced the theme of the embryonic and the undoing of birth as early as the Belacqua saga and, most dramatically, in 'Echo's Bones', with his reborn protagonist's avowal that, no sooner born, he sought to 'reintegrate' the womb, a pursuit to which only death put an end (*EB* 46). Expanding this theme in his four postwar *nouvelles*, Beckett imagined a posthumous

---

⁵ The complementary identity of Molloy–Moran was pointed out for the French version by Maurice Blanchot in his 1953 review of *L'Innommable* (Blanchot 1979 [1953], 118), and shortly after the publication of the English version of *Molloy* by David Hayman (1962, 100–1, 105). Many stabs at understanding the oscillating complementariness of the two figures were to follow. See, for instance, Moorjani 1982, 110; 1992, 183; Begam 1996, 101, 104; Uhlmann 1999, 58.

voice recounting variations of the relentless pursuit of such a 'reintegration'.

The four *nouvelles* were written in French in 1946 soon after Beckett's engagement in the French Resistance, his years of hiding in Roussillon, and his service with the Irish Red Cross in Saint-Lô after the war. They were conceived at a time when, in the aftermath of a brutal war and the testimonies of survivors of the camps, a traumatized French literary scene placed human values and the ethics of writing in question. 'La Fin' ('The End'), originally entitled 'Suite', was composed first in the series, but as the title suggests, it is the end piece in the novellas' eventual published presentation. The other three *nouvelles* – 'L'Expulsé' ('The Expelled'), 'Premier amour' ('First Love'), and 'Le Calmant' ('The Calmative') – were written in that order between October and December 1946, followed in quick succession by *Eleutheria* and *Molloy* the following year.[6]

In adopting, in his postwar fiction, the retrospective self-narration by a first-person narrator-protagonist, Beckett drastically unsettles this mode by the topos of the posthumous voice. The narrative split that comes with use of the deictic 'I', with the 'I' of the narrator divided from the 'I' of the narrated, is exacerbated by this posthumous voice telling of a former existence. In my reading of the four novellas, they share one anonymous first-person narrator-protagonist speaking from beyond the grave. 'I don't know when I died', the first words of 'The Calmative' (the story written last), would seem to leave no doubt about the matter (*CSP* 61). The other stories, too, intimate his ghostliness, when, for instance, in 'First Love', the speaker explains that the hat his father gave him, and which appears in all four novellas, 'followed me to the grave' (*CSP* 35). Does this posthumous narrator perhaps share Belacqua's fate in 'Echo's Bones' of being reborn into a spectral existence between life and death? The narrator's insistence on his present suffering and anxiety, admitting, for example, in 'First Love', 'What I understand best, which is not saying much, are my pains'

---

[6] The first part of 'La Fin', under the title 'Suite', was published in *Les Temps Modernes* in 1946, and an early version of 'L'Expulsé' in *Fontaine*'s 1946–47 issue. The 'Suite' notebook is witness to the turning point in Beckett's decision to write in French. Having begun the story in English, he switched to French on the twenty-eighth page (Cohn 2005, 129). Three of the French *nouvelles* appeared together only in 1955 in the order 'L'Expulsé', 'Le Calmant', 'La Fin'. The English versions followed the same pattern, but a decade later. 'Premier amour' / 'First Love', on the other hand, remained unpublished until 1970 and 1973 respectively. It was not until 1977 that the novellas appeared together in John Calder's *Four Novellas*, with 'First Love' preceding the other three. 'Premier amour', on the other hand, continues to be published separately. Beckett's first novel in French, *Mercier et Camier*, was written in between 'La Fin' and the other three *nouvelles*, but remained unpublished until 1970.

(32), suggests a speaker reborn into another *saṃsāric* cycle weighed down by his karmic fate. Toward the beginning of 'The Calmative', however, the narrator denies having come back to life after death, not that the reader necessarily has to believe him. Still, in view of the speaker's posthumous sufferings, could his be a purgatorial afterlife, one of many to follow in the Beckett canon? But what kind of purgatory, the Christian Purgatory of Dante – a stepping station to Paradise – or the Eastern hellish purgatorial afterlife – one of six realms of cyclical existence, from which purged ghosts will be reborn?

The narrator's anguish calls to mind the unquiet spectral characters of two forms of traditional Japanese theatre, the *shite* (protagonist), an ordinary mortal's ghost in the Buddhist influenced *mugen* noh, or dream noh, and the phantoms of Kabuki drama. Such spectral apparitions, in returning from the dead to the land of the living, seek to quiet the present torments they suffer in Buddhist purgatory by recounting the crimes they committed or the unresolved traumas and injustices they incurred during their lives, these, moreover, mirroring the misfortunes of the audience's world. In their tales, the boundaries are fluid between past, present, and a spirit world.[7]

Beckett's drama, if not his fiction, has long been thought to have affinities with noh.[8] But how familiar was Beckett with this form of Japanese drama or its adaptations in the West? When in 1980, Japanese scholar Yasunari Takahashi, who translated Beckett's plays and other works into Japanese, mentioned to him the resemblance he sees between his theatre and noh drama, Beckett replied, smilingly, that he was not consciously influenced by noh.[9] This denial, of course, leaves the question open as did his response concerning Buddhist influence on *Act without*

---

[7] This brief description of dream noh is taken from Takahashi 1983, 100–1; Keene 1990, 13–27; Okamuro 2009, 165–77; Charbonnier 2018, 16–17.

[8] See in this regard the fascinating article by translator Yoshiko Takebe on the effects on Japanese audiences of Beckett's late plays in Japanese translation and performed using traditional Japanese dramatic techniques. He details such a performance drawing on *mugen* noh's storytelling rituals in *Rockaby*, noting the importance of the off-stage ghostly voice. For Takebe, viewing Beckett's plays in the context of noh theatre brings out their affinity with Zen metaphysics involving the 'loss of egoism and aesthetics of silence' (Takebe 2011, 113). The East–West dialogue goes both ways. In regard to representations of ghosts on stage, a Japanese audience would be used to frequent depictions in the theatre and in the arts of ghosts situated in the gap between two rebirths. This audience would more easily identify May with her 'dishevelled grey hair' and 'worn grey wrap' in *Footfalls* with a ghost (*CSPL* 239) than a Western audience, owing to such spectral figures being depicted in popular Ukiyo-e prints.

[9] Beckett's response to Takahashi, published in the Japanese journal *Asahi* of 28 December 1989, is quoted in French translation in Kirishima 1990, 691.

Words I. In fact, Beckett used the same response in a letter to Takahashi of
13 December 1981, writing, 'If there are such elements [of noh] in my
plays I am not aware of them', and adding, 'Noh drama presupposes
audience complicity, mine audience resistance' (*LSB IV* 567–8). The latter
statement, of course, implies that Beckett was no stranger to noh. We may
well conclude that, as already proposed, such responses may imply the
amnesia of writers perturbed by their discoveries that they are uncon-
sciously repeating their forerunners or, it could rather be a way of prevent-
ing ready answers.

Could Beckett's early attraction to William Butler Yeats's noh-
influenced plays, *At the Hawk's Well* (1917) in particular, have served as
an introduction to elements of noh? Several scholars of Beckett's theatre
have concluded that this is the case, among them Takahashi, Japanese
professor of theatre Minako Okamuro, and British specialists of Irish
theatre Katharine Worth and Paul Lawley. In a perceptive article,
Okamuro (2009, 166–75) details the parallels between *mugen* noh and
Yeats and Beckett's purgatorial plays, maintaining that, in his television
play *...but the clouds...*, Beckett may have adopted Yeats's 'dreaming
back'. She quotes the definition of this concept in Yeats's book 3 of *The
Vision* (1925): 'In the *Dreaming back*, the *Spirit* is compelled to live over
and over again the events that had most moved it; there can be nothing
new, but the old events stand forth in a light which is dim or bright
according to the intensity of the passion that accompanied them' (qtd. in
Okamuro 2009, 169; emphasis in the original). Agreeing with Katharine
Worth, Okamuro maintains that in noh's 'dreaming back' the boundary
between the dead and the living is dissolved.[10] In addition to Yeats,
adaptations of noh drama were part of Western modernist practice
throughout the twentieth century: among others, Ezra Pound, who introduced Yeats to noh; Paul Claudel; Bertolt Brecht; and, more recently,

[10] Okamuro (2009, 169) is citing Worth's 'Enigmatic Influences: Yeats, Beckett and Noh', in *Yeats
and the Noh: A Comparative Study*, ed. by Masaru Sekine and Christopher Murray (Gerards Cross,
UK: Colin Smythe, 1990), 150. She also quotes from Takahashi's 'The Ghost Trio: Beckett, Yeats,
and Noh', *The Cambridge Review* 107.2295 (1986): 172–6. Paul Lawley describes several recorded
instances of Beckett's appreciation of *At the Hawk's Well* and, adding to the linkages made by critics
between Yeats's noh-influenced play and Beckett's theatre, analyzes the similarities between Yeats's
play and *Krapp's Last Tape* (Lawley 2015, 375–83). He further drew my attention to the letter
documenting Beckett's response to director George Devine's request for a play to accompany *Acte
sans paroles I* (first performed in Devine's production in 1957). In a letter of 5 December 1956
Beckett suggested *At the Hawk's Well* to Devine, 'where there is so much great poetry' (*LSB II* 683).
And Beckett's Irish biographer Anthony Cronin reports that in the 1920s Beckett was especially
moved by *At the Hawk's Well* at the Abbey Theatre (Cronin 1997, 58).

Robert Wilson are known to have drawn on aspects of noh theatre in their works.

Although he had tried his hand at *Human Wishes*, an abandoned drama on Samuel Johnson, at the time Beckett composed the four *nouvelles*, he thought of himself primarily as a writer of fiction and a poet. If in his stories he uses the noh-like dramatic technique of giving voice to a ghostly storyteller, he later, as we know, imagined such spectral narrators for the stage. In each case it is a matter of attempting to soothe a troubled mind: 'I'll try and tell myself another story', the narrator intones in 'The Calmative', 'to try and calm myself' (*CSP* 61). If the stories of the misdeeds that the inhabitants of Dante's *Inferno* or *Purgatorio* recount also come to mind, and even more so Murphy's 'Belacqua fantasy' – an equivalent of Yeatsian 'dreaming back' – in which the Belacqua of Antepurgatory dreams 'it all through again' (*Mu* 78), the soothing role given to the stories makes the noh analogy the more tempting one. In fact, in Takahashi's view, Dante's vision of purgatory best parallels the dream noh, even though in the manner of family resemblances, there are also differences (Takahashi 1982, 67).

Not only Beckett's later theatre, but his four posthumously narrated *nouvelles* of the 1940s share with dream noh a nightmarish 'dreaming back' and the intermingling of life and death. Beckett's later speakers, too, including those of his trilogy and *Texts for Nothing* are given 'the sensation of being beyond the grave', as Malone maintains about himself as he writes in his notebook (*Ma* 183). Before Malone, Molloy comments paradoxically about his life, 'at the same time it is over and it goes on' (*Mo* 36), whereas the narrator of *The Unnamable* speaks in Belacqua's limbic terms of 'the time of the ancient dead and the dead yet unborn' that 'buries you grain by grain neither dead nor alive' (*Un* 389). Theirs is the inclusive disjunction of death in life or life in death, so that the narrator of the novellas invents his stories from the posthumous space of writing in the paradoxical mode of Molloy's 'it is over and it goes on'.[11]

'We are needless to say in a skull', the storyteller assures us in 'The Calmative' (*CSP* 70), the novella that takes on the function of commenting on the series. The narrator's purgatorial existence corresponds to the mental suffering he is recording in his stories. Given the fear, anxiety, and pains he describes, the narrator cannot be in *Dream*'s haven of quietude, of which, nevertheless, he is aware. In 'First Love', he tells of anticipating,

---

[11] This limbic view is similarly evident in Blanchot's 1941 novel *Thomas l'obscur*, whose protagonist is as exiled from death as he is from life (Blanchot 1950, 40).

once no longer obsessed with Lulu/Anna in his former existence, 'the slow descents again, the long submersions, so long denied me through her fault' (*CSP* 41). What mattered to him was 'supineness in the mind, the dulling of the self and that residue of execrable frippery known as the non-self and even the world, for short' (31).[12] His preference was for the mental retreat familiar from *Dream*, with its eclipse of self and world, in consonance with Schopenhauer, the Buddha, and Eckhart, of which Beckett has here slipped a condensed and flippant version to hide its graveness. But the posthumous narrator of the novellas is rather telling his stories from a place of torment in the skull more suggestive of a purgatorial hell and, therefore, of Murphy's first rather than third zone of the mind, turning Belacqua's space of quietude and creativity in *Dream* into a regretted refuge.

In Beckett's work of the forties, writing is increasingly entrenched in historical, social, and personal trauma. The identification of life with suffering received such terrifying validation in the traumatic shock of the camps that scars, although occluded, bear witness to the disaster of the war, and oblique references to the camps and other war and postwar traumas in Beckett's postwar fiction are being continuously uncovered by commentators and related to questions raised by a literature of political testimony.[13] 'What is, [Beckett] says, is like a concentration camp', Adorno writes in his *Negative Dialectics*, and, as often pointed out, in his view, Beckett's practice of an anti-art is the only tolerable response to the camps (Adorno 2000a [1966], 380). In the view of French literary scholar Michèle Touret, Beckett's indirect postwar witnessing in his writings, shorn of a belief in the capacity of literature to do justice to such catastrophic events, is the testimony of a witness giving voice to a 'terrorized and atomized conscience' far from pretending to make sense of the events (2006, 28–9). In his *Writing History, Writing Trauma* (2014), placing Beckett alongside Kafka, Blanchot, and Paul Celan into the tradition of 'testimonial art', historian Dominick La Capra similarly maintains that each produced a 'writing of terrorized disempowerment as close as possible to the experience of traumatized victims without presuming to be identical to it' (qtd. in Morin 2017, 130). The spectral reciting of traumatic stories in dream noh provided Beckett with a form well suited to his indirect witnessing.

---

[12] In translating *Premier amour*'s *non-moi* as 'non-self', Beckett is using the term in the philosophical sense of 'all that is not the self', which also, 'for short' (or out of laziness, as the French version has it) is referred to as 'the world'.

[13] See, for instance, among others, Uhlmann 1999, 40–57, 91–97; Adelman 2004; Jones 2011; Morin 2017, 130–83.

Schopenhauer's view of the world 'as a place of penance, hence a prison, a penal colony as it were, a labour camp' was familiar to Beckett, having cited the essay in which it appears, 'On the Doctrine of the Suffering of the World', in his *Proust*. Schopenhauer associates this view with Ancient Greek and Roman philosophers, early Christian thinkers, and with Brahmanism and especially Buddhism, stating in a note at the bottom of the page, no doubt tongue in cheek, that one should repeat four times daily the Buddhist reminder '*This is Samsara*, the world of lust and craving, and therefore the world of birth, illness, ageing, and dying; it is the world that should not be' (*PP II* § 156, 272; emphasis in the original).[14] Around 1980, Beckett copied Schopenhauer's view of life as a 'pensum' and as a 'penal colony' into his 'Sottisier' notebook, views that obviously stayed with him all his writing life. If, in Beckett's 1946 stories, Belacqua's creative and blissful retreat in the mind is maintained, visions of hellish imprisonment with occluded allusions to a traumatic historical 'real' overshadow it to the point that it is often missed. Beckett at the time speaks of an 'art d'incarcération', as he termed the painting of the van Velde brothers in the 1948 'Peintres de l'empêchement' (Painters of Impediment) (*Dis* 137).

From the double vantage point of the ideal real (and of the Buddhist and Schopenhauerian two truths), writing then participates in the sufferings of *saṃsāra*, even as intimations of a way out persist. Reflecting on the paradoxical situation of the writer is given to Malone, who chronicles fierce brutalities in his stories, some reminiscent, in fact, of a penal colony or a concentration camp, and indicts the connivance of writing with terror and death throughout his entries into his notebook, wondering at one point how many characters he has killed and comparing the pencil of Lemuel (another variant on Samuel) to a murder weapon (*Ma* 236, 288). At the same time, he poetically reenvisions the mind familiar from *Murphy*: 'Words and images run riot in my head, pursuing, flying, clashing, merging, endlessly. But beyond this tumult there is a great calm, and a great indifference, never really to be troubled by anything again' (*Ma* 198). Beckett's knowing association of writing with terror and death, then, is

---

[14] Most likely, in referring to Ancient Greek philosophers, Schopenhauer had in mind the Platonic doctrine of the descent of the soul. In the view of Plato, the soul falls from a transcendent realm into imprisonment in the body, from which it reascends into the realm of Ideas. Paul Davies has suggested that the novellas dramatize this myth and the failed quest for a return home (Davies 2000, 83).

countered by an *ascesis* assimilated from Schopenhauer and Buddhist and mystic sources.[15]

In the 1946 *nouvelles*, an anonymous voice narrates what would appear to be four different accounts of events that happened to him in his lifetime, stretching from age twenty-five in 'First Love' and the prime of life in 'L'Expulsé' to the advanced years of 'The Calmative' and 'The End'. But such a traditional retrospective viewpoint is contested as is any realistic identity of the narrating voice. Corresponding to Beckett's modernist/ postmodernist ploys to draw attention to the illusory nature of his fictional worlds, this impression of a past recounted is undermined in 'The Calmative'. What he is telling in the mythic past tense is taking place in the present, the narrator insists, as he is telling it, situated in the 'distant refuge' or the dreamlike space of writing, as if, in a nod to Schopenhauer, temporarily freed from his present and past suffering by the act of telling his story as he dreams it (*CSP* 62). Similarly, in noh, the *shite* protagonist's story is dreamed by the *waki* (secondary character) on stage, usually conceived of as a Buddhist priest. The tales are but an illusion.

The novellas share similar locations, at times recognizably Dublin and its surroundings, at times Paris, in an oneiric mingling of localities, and the same corrosive humor and mordant hostility to Eros and birth mark the travails of the homeless and dispossessed protagonist, if at different ages. It is in these stories that the protagonist's characteristic hat and long coat, standing for indelible parental imprints, make their appearance along with his banishments from shelter and his increasingly failing body prone to falls. In their bleakness and episodic viciousness, despite their humor, these postwar stories indict human wretchedness far beyond Beckett's previous writings so that the destitute protagonist's dread of Eros and birth results in a quest for protective substitutes to reverse his repeated flights or expulsions from refuge.[16]

[15] Chris Ackerley has pointed out that Malone's 'beyond this tumult there is a great calm' echoes Thomas à Kempis's 'post tempestatum, magna serenitas' in *The Imitation of Christ* (Ackerley 2000, 90). Equally striking is its resonance with the Buddhist two-part mind: the nonenlightened of turmoil and the enlightened stillness of the *unborn*, which will be further explored in Chapter 7. Here the commonalities Schopenhauer sees between Eastern and Western quietism and asceticism are in evidence.

[16] Marjorie Perloff (2005) reads three of the 1946 novellas (excluding 'First Love') in terms of hallucinatory dream narratives chronicling the conditions in wartime Vichy, whereas Andrew Gibson (2015) sees the four novellas as an attack on the natalist and familialist politics of both the Irish Free State and the wartime Vichy regime, particularly the latter's nationalist promotion of the ideal body, glowing with health and vigor. For Emilie Morin (2017, 168–70) the novellas are 'narrative[s] of return' chronicling the postwar conditions in France for former internees of the camps, most clearly in the early versions of 'Suite' (later 'La Fin' / 'The End') and 'L'Expulsé'.

An impressive number of such psycho-spaces traverse the novellas, mostly rooms and sheds, but also more obvious tomb- and womblike psycho-objects: in 'The Expelled', a cab – 'a big black box, rocking and swaying on is springs' (*CSP* 53) – and, in 'The End', a boat with a lid found in a shed, in which the protagonist has an end-of-life vision of tossing on the waves as the water in his imagination rises to engulf him and, having swallowed his 'calmative' to tranquilize the will, envisions sea, sky, mountains, and islands crushing him and dissipating into 'the utter-most confines of space' (*CSP* 99), a vision recalling Schopenhauer's of the disappearance of the phenomenal world with the negation of the will.

The boat metaphor, on which Beckett draws repeatedly after 'The End' (as he does on the rocking chair after *Murphy*), bears some discussion in relation to the theme of undoing birth. For Gaston Bachelard, it is the poetic trope that even more than the rocking chair evokes the sensation of being cradled in the womb: 'Water cradles us', he writes, 'water gives us back our mother' (Bachelard 1973 [1942], 178; my translation). In Beckett's early poem 'Calvary by Night', inserted into *Dream*, where it is not attributed, however, to Belacqua but to the 'homespun poet' of his acquaintance, water and womb are likewise condensed into one poetic image, the poet envisaging a pansy from its leaping in 'a womb of water' to its 'sprouting forth' and 're-enwombing' (*Dream* 213–14). In Bachelard's view, not only does boat imagery conjure up the cradling in the womb, but the fusion of water and sky invokes free-flowing poetic reveries (Bachelard 1973, 179). (Discussion of more boat scenes is to follow.)

The physical womb- and tomblike refuges in the novellas, however, are only simulacra, or poor reflections, of the metaphysical inner space of timelessness and generativity. Hence, the protagonist in 'First Love' finds that the disposition of his 'carcass' stretched out on a bench was only 'the merest and most futile of accidents' in regard to the 'supineness in the mind' that matters most to him. This observation, which in *Premier amour* is expressed in terms of 'le plus lointain et futile des reflets' (the most distant and futile of reflections) provides two variations on the Platonic theory of Ideas, according to which sensible phenomena are reflections or copies of the Essential or the Idea (*PA* 21; *CSP* 31). Disparaged in 'First Love' in Platonic terms most likely borrowed from Schopenhauer and his view of art (*WWR I* § 35, 204; § 38, 219), Beckett's psycho-objects, then, waver between the status of 'futile' icons of the metaphysical space of writing in the mind and simulacra that only simulate what they appear futilely to resemble. As such, they are the targets as much of the pro-tagonist's wishfulness as of his aggressiveness. In 'The Expelled' he is tempted to set fire to the stable in which he has found refuge, and in 'The End', stretched out in the boat inside a shed, he comically exclaims, 'To contrive a little kingdom, in the midst of the universal muck, then shit on it, ah that was me all over' (*CSP* 98).[17]

In the novellas, the protagonist's always failed attempts to reach a lasting material sanctuary are countered by the motif of the calming effects of storytelling. In 'The Calmative', the narrator not only speaks of the soothing effect the story he is about to tell will have on him but also movingly recalls the bedtime story of Joe Breem or Breen told to him night after night by his father to calm his fears (*CSP* 63–4). Such tranquilizing effects of storytelling resonate with Beckett's childhood memory of his own night terrors and the bedtime story of Joe Breem or Breen his father used to read to him, the story itself being about dangers overcome at sea permitting the safe return to harbor (Knowlson 1996, 336). In *Proust,* on the other hand, Beckett describes the voice of the protagonist's mother, at the beginning of 'Combray' in *Du côté de chez Swann* (*Swann's Way*), reading to her young son to soothe his terror of night associated with separation and death. Beckett may have remembered his description of the mother's voice, 'muted and sweetened almost to a lullaby' (*P* 53), on asking actor David Warrilow to read the sad tale in his late play *Ohio Impromptu*, as if it were 'a bedtime story', in a voice, 'calm, steady, designed to soothe', it too intended to still the character's renewed terrors of night following a death he is mourning (Letter of 19 February 1981, *LSB IV* 545). It is then the calming musical effect of the voice telling the tale, an effect Beckett aimed for in his late texts, that contributes to inducing quietude in the listener. The father's nighttime reading of the Breem/Breen story makes another appearance in the first of the *Texts for Nothing.* Frequently portraying the roles of speaker and listener joined into one ghostly figure, notably in 'The Calmative' whose narrator is both storyteller and listener to the tale he is imagining, Beckett has the narrator of *Texts for Nothing* mutter, 'Yes, I was my father and I was my son' as he holds himself in his own arms drifting into sleep (*CSP* 103–4).

In giving the performative role to calm the mind to imaginative art, Beckett is in consonance with Schopenhauer, who, as Dorothea Dauer recognizes in her study *Schopenhauer as Transmitter of Buddhist Ideas,*

---

[17] For an insightful reading of the novellas, partly drawing on Rankian birth trauma and Bachelard's concept of shelter, see Baker 1997, 64–105. Additionally, Baker cogently analyzes the fantasized boat scene of 'The End' in terms of Freudian oceanic dissolution (1997, 88–90). Amanda Dennis perceptively investigates the merging of physical and textual spaces in the novellas and the transformations the character effects of the spaces he occupies (2015b, 43–55).

assigned to music and art, more than to Buddhist meditation, the liberation from the suffering associated with self and time and world (Dauer
1969, 23). For Beckett, however, calmness of mind by way of silence and
music is paradoxically effected by means of words themselves, by emptying
them by unsaying but leaving their musicality in an aesthetic and ascetic
release from human torments. Not that meditation is excluded or the
performative telling of a tale leading to an 'elsewhere'.

Around the time Beckett wrote to Matti Megged about the difference
between the 'real' of experience and the Proustian 'ideal real' of writing,
Beckett explained to Lawrence Harvey that the many autobiographical
reminiscences pervading his writing do not mean that his work depends on
experience: 'Work . . . is not a record of experience. But of course you must
use it', furthermore, as already noted, candidly admitting to Harvey, 'Of
course, I say my life has nothing to do with my work, but of course it does'
(qtd. in Harvey 2006, 136–7). H. Porter Abbott's 'autography', which he
contrasts with the always dubious recovery of the past, aptly evokes the
'mode of action taken in the moment of writing' of such modernist
interweaving of life and fiction as Beckett's (Abbott 1996, x). It is a mode
we are familiar with from the narrator's claim in 'The Calmative' that his
story is taking place as he is composing it.[18] As such, it is something to
keep in mind in reading Beckett's postwar work in light of his wartime and
postwar experiences. The real, as he holds, is to be viewed from his distinct
perspective at the moment of writing, a fusion of the imaginative and 'the
ideal' with the empirical. To exclude one or the other does not do justice
to his writing.

Emptying Out and the Postwar Poetics of Elsewhere

As the title *Malone meurt* / *Malone Dies* intimates, Malone narrates his
'being given . . . birth to into death' (*Ma* 283), or nearly so, as he makes his
ongoing near-demise coincide with the suspension of the story he is
writing. If *Molloy* famously ends with a retraction of what has been
written, *Malone Dies*, anticipating *The Unnamable*'s repudiations, proceeds
with an emptying out of his present and past incarnations, beginning with
Murphy, as they disappear in a tossing boat heading out to sea at night
under the stars and the distant lights of land. Beckett situates this colossal

---

[18] Beckett's emphasis on the performative effect of storytelling anticipates the postmodern emphasis
on performativity, such as Roland Barthes's in the already mentioned 'Death of the Author'
(Barthes 1967, sec. 4).

Figure 5.1   The beacon on the East Pier of Dún Laoghaire.
Photo © David H. Davison

emptying out of his past fictions on Easter weekend as if announcing that this is and is not the end of Malone and cohort, who will be resurrected as specters in the next novel. At the same time could he be alluding to Eastern cyclical rebirth? This question will be explored in Chapter 7.

In both 'The End' and *Malone Dies*, in the personages' hallucinatory farewell to the lights on land and to the stars overhead, the poetically evoked beacons, buoys, and fires of the burning gorse in the hills identify the imagined site as Dublin Bay near Beckett's place of birth. In consonance with Bachelard's poetics of space, in which our first shelter – *la maison* (home) in a corner of the world – subsequently haunts our inner space after undergoing poetic and oneiric transformations (Bachelard 2009 [1957], 24, 26), Beckett's indirect invocations of Dublin Bay appear to be an instance of such a poetic psycho-geography. The earlier psycho-objects are increasingly reenvisioned in the postwar fictions in cosmic terms. Figure 5.1 shows an artful portrayal of the East Pier of Dún Laoghaire (pronounced 'Dunleary'), one of Beckett's psycho-spaces on Dublin Bay and the location of Krapp's vision in *Krapp's Last Tape* (Knowlson 1996, 319).

In the first part of *Molloy*, Dublin Bay, referred to indirectly by the eponymous narrator-character as a part of his region, recognizably the surroundings of Dublin, is the site of his paddling a skiff out into the sea, from which, dreamlike, he cannot recall returning (*Mo* 68–9). Since this voyage follows Molloy's stay in a cave by the seaside, in the later radio play *Cascando*, Maunu/Woburn's leaving his shed and heading out to sea echoes Molloy's imagined departure without return and the similar scenes in 'The End' and *Malone Dies,* all four evoking the same psycho-geography. Their leave-taking brings to mind Schopenhauer's famous words about the disappearance of the world 'with all its suns and galaxies' when the will has turned and abolished itself, leaving nothing of the phenomenal world. Akin to Bachelard's phenomenological poetics of space, 'home' in Beckett's writing is evoked as a place in which to wander in memory in a finite world (the everyday 'real' imaginatively transformed). Simultaneously, however, from the standpoint of a metaphysical poetics of elsewhere, 'home' is envisioned as an 'unspeakable home' (*CSP* 258) consonant with the Buddha's unknowable metaphysical realm beyond birth and death and Schopenhauer's adoption of it.[19]

That Beckett's echoes of Schopenhauerian nothingness of the empirical world are no more nihilistic than the philosopher's is apparent in *Cascando*, in which Voice's story is suspended, the character heading perhaps into 'nowhere', 'anywhere', or 'elsewhere'. The traditional allegorical journey to salvation has become a postmodern allegory of uncertainty.[20] With this radio play for music and voice, Beckett provided another brief 'codicil' of sorts, or an addendum, this one to his postwar fiction, although he called it a 'residuum', that is, a distillation.[21] In the radio play, originally written in French in December 1961 (English, 1963), an Opener alternatively turns on and off the performances of Voice and Music, which begin in midstream and taper off into silence at the end. Throughout Beckett's theatre, emptiness is similarly foregrounded by fade-ins and fade-outs, voice and image coming out of and returning into the stage silence and darkness. In *Cascando*, Voice, attempting to tell the 'right story' in a quest for inner peace, labors (in vain) to conclude one about a

---

[19] The distress Beckett expressed in his 1946 letter to Simone de Beauvoir about her refusal to publish the concluding part of what was to become 'La Fin' / 'The End' can be understood in terms of the ubiquitous theme of reaching 'home'. When he writes that without the second part, his character is 'frustré de son repos' (*LSB II* 40), the 'rest' in 'deprived of his rest' would appear to refer to the character's peace of mind in tranquilizing his will and imagining his death.

[20] On postmodern allegory in Beckett, see Campbell 2012, 89–103. Beckett's use of allegory can be explained by his critique of an exclusively realistic standpoint.

[21] Beckett first suggested the title 'Cascando and other residua' for the volume eventually published by Grove Press in 1969 under the title *Cascando and Other Short Dramatic Pieces* (Zilliacus 1976, 125, n. 20). Because of the briefness of this play, page references are omitted. The text of *Cascando* is found in *CSPL* 137–44.

character named Maunu, in French, and Woburn, in English (the names suggesting pain and woe), a story in which it is easy to recognize elements of Beckett's postwar fiction.

In his letter of 21 September 1962 accompanying his gift of the original French manuscript and typescripts to the Theatre Collection of Harvard College Library, Beckett comments: 'It is an unimportant work, but the best I have to offer. It does I suppose show in a way what passes for my mind and what passes for its work' (qtd. in Zilliacus 1976, 118; letter not collected in *LSB IV*). Clas Zilliacus, the author of an impressive genetic analysis of *Cascando's* many variants in both French and English, contests the author's claim about the unimportance of the play, but did Beckett not imply the contrary himself? Finding it to be paradigmatic of Beckett's art and its longing for the peace of silence, Zilliacus dubs *Cascando* 'a key text in the Beckett canon' (119).

In line with Beckett's comment about the play passing for his mind's work, *Cascando* stages figures representing elements of the author's mind 'working' at producing a play. Morphing from what was 'Voix 1' in an early French draft, Opener plays the role of soliciting Voice and then Music, at first separately, then together, resulting in a quasi-musical composition. (Zilliacus 1976, 122).[22] Voice's words, modulated by tonal and rhythmic prosody and marked caesuras and counterpointed by Music, accentuate once more the role of music in fashioning a story to calm the mind.[23]

In *Cascando*, the Opener throughout is the controlling element, opening and closing, as he says, 'at will', a will, however, weakening toward the end, along with the volume of Voice and Music, as foreshadowed by the title's meaning of diminishing volume and tempo. The wearing down of the will and vitality suggests Schopenhauer's turning of the will that opens the way to resignation and an elsewhere, a theme familiar since *Dream*. Beckett introduced a similar weakening into the last part of *Comment c'est / How It Is*, written shortly after the radio play, in which 'imagination [is] on the decline', and the voice, too, is becoming 'fainter weaker but still audible less clear' (*How* 104, 126).[24]

---

[22] For a discussion of the metatheatrical convergence in *Cascando* between the performance of the script, on the one hand, and allusions to the medium of performance, on the other, see Zilliacus 1976, 140–3.

[23] Konrad Körte, the sound engineer for the 1977 Beckett-directed production of *Geistertrio* (*Ghost Trio*) in Stuttgart, aptly describes the coming together of the television play's 'two levels of music', that is, excerpts from the Largo of Beethoven's Piano Trio No. 5 and the melodic and rhythmic prosody of the spoken text. In his view, Beckett heard the two levels as a musical whole (Körte 2017, 111). *Cascando* would appear to be an earlier experiment in combining the two levels.

[24] In his essay 'L'Épuisé' ('The Exhausted') Deleuze famously reads Beckett's texts in terms of an exhaustion of possibilities, which is another reading of the loss of will and vitality in Beckett's texts (Deleuze 1997a [1992], 152–74).

Voice alternates between telling the story of Woburn and commenting anxiously on whether it is the 'right story' required to be at peace. Voice's present story – claimed to follow 'thousands and one' ending in a failure that comically outnumbers Scheherezade's feat by thousands – begins with Woburn leaving his shed at night to walk through the dunes down to the sea in search of an 'elsewhere' ('*ailleurs*'). The shed is familiar from the postwar fiction as are the coat and hat Woburn is wearing and the stick he carries. Evoked by Woburn's three falls in cruciform pose is the obsessive theme of guilt and redemption that runs through Beckett's oeuvre. Woburn's posture, recalling Macman's in the pouring rain in *Malone Dies*, as he ponders the relation between punishment and guilt (*Ma* 239–40), is repeated in the speaker's final posture in *How It Is*, prone in the mud, arms outstretched. In fact, in one of the French drafts of *Cascando*, Beckett had sought to include the theme of guilt, innocence, and absolution in Voix's ruminations about the need to tell the right story (Zilliacus 1976, 130–1). The three falls, evocative of the Way of the Cross, described in Voice's spoken text, appear to be a substitute for Voix's words on the theme of guilt and absolution haunting Beckett's oeuvre, as they did Schopenhauer's, in both its Christian and Buddhist forms.

The obsessive topos of the cross in Beckett's work has been much remarked on.[25] From the standpoint of the dialogue between Buddhism and Christianity since the mid-twentieth century, the theological doctrine of Christ's *kenōsis* – from the Greek *kenōs* (empty) – which holds that, by his incarnation and death, Christ emptied himself of his divine attributes, is a possible basis for discussion between the two religions. Such, for instance, is the view of Buddhist philosopher Masao Abe in his essay 'Kenosis and Emptiness' (Abe 1990, 5–25). A *kenōtic* analysis of *Watt* from both a Christian theological and a Buddhist nontheistic standpoint would thus result in an overlapping of the two views in the dissolution of the Watt–Knott tie, the repeated allusions to Watt as a *kenōtic* Christ figure, and the final emptying out of Knott and Watt and world, all slipping into namelessness and emptiness comparable to the *via negativa*'s '*kenōsis* of discourse' (Derrida 1995, 50) and Buddhist *śūnyatā*.[26]

In returning to *Cascando*, Voice asks three times what is in Woburn's head and provides the answers: the first speaks of memories of refuge

---

[25] David Hesla sees in Watt's journey to Knott's house a close parallel to the Stations of the Cross (Hesla 1971, 62). See also Bryden 1998, 138–48.

[26] In *Watt*, the narrator Sam, for instance, sees himself mirrored in Watt, whose bloodied face and hands and thorns in his scalp make of him the icon of the Man of Sorrows (*W* 159).

encountered in previous fictions; the second, refers to 'peace again...in his head', which the shelters only simulate; the third tells of Woburn drifting in a boat, without known destination, face down, arms extended, his back turned to the lights onshore and the stars overhead. This suspended ending of *Cascando*, as the will to life weakens and the phenomenal world fades into nothing, opens up the perhaps, but only that, of the release from the guilty cycles of birth, suffering, and death. But the story peters out with a 'nearly there', leaving both Voice's and Woburn's salvation as uncertain as it is in the thousands and one stories already attempted. The always suspended stories are, then, so many literary simulacra of the path to an untellable, unknowable, and perhaps unreachable 'nowhere' or 'elsewhere'.

Coming together in the poetic visions of drifting out to sea of 'The End', *Molloy*, *Malone Dies*, and *Cascando* is the coming home to a habitat never left in the imagination, the figural 're-enwombing' in water of the early 'Calvary by Night', the simultaneous advancing toward death and regressing toward birth, and intimations of the timeless beyond, of which nothing can be known or said, analogous, for Schopenhauer, to Buddhist liberation. In less tentative terms about the play's relation to Buddhist *nirvāṇa*, for Paul Davies, Voice's attempt to narrate Woburn into an elsewhere records the failure 'to drift into selflessness' in the direction of enlightenment (Davies 2000, 201–2).

'Those calm wastes' of *The Lost Ones*

The question of a way out of our distressing condition haunts Beckett's writing from his earliest fiction onward. Thus, in the ninth of the *Texts for Nothing*, the narrator utters the wish, 'let there be no more talk of any creature, nor of a world to leave, nor of a world to reach, in order to have done, with worlds, with creatures, with words, with misery, misery', which is then at once contradicted by the possibility of saying that 'there's a way out somewhere', and further, if he could say so, he would find a way to get there and, alluding to Dante, 'see the stars again' (*CSP* 137, 140). But since this vision ultimately depends on the performative act of saying it, it is as uncertain as the capacity of Voice in *Cascando* to narrate Woburn into an elsewhere. When at the end of the play, the Voice fades out, the audience is left with an image of Woburn in his boat, his back turned to the stars, a pose suggesting that since the novellas and *Texts for Nothing*, a view of the stars – Dante's sublime vision in *The Divine Comedy* – has lost its aura as a trope for the way out.

Nevertheless, a view of the stars and a refuge in nature are the ends that determine the search for a way out in *Le Dépeupleur* / *The Lost Ones*

(French, 1970; English, 1972), Beckett's fiction of an imaginary cylinder-world, one among the several miniaturized worlds he composed a few years after *Cascando*.[27] The search of the cylinder's inhabitants, however, is condemned to collapse, as are the searchers themselves, the text indicting their misguided attempts to conceive of the ideal of an 'inviolable zenith' in terms of 'a way out to earth and sky'. Qualifying them as 'amateurs of myth', the narrator intimates that, owing to their fixation on these ends, their search is bound to founder (*CSP* 207); the way out is to be conceived otherwise than immanence in the earth or transcendence in the sky.[28] Nevertheless, for the strangely detached observer describing the world inside the cylinder, should they forego their joint outbursts of violence, cooperation among the inhabitants might lead to a way out (207), bringing to mind the ethics based on the connectedness of all in the philosophy of the Buddha and of Schopenhauer. A hint of a way out comes in the final paragraph, added four years after the composition of the rest of the fiction, in which a man, 'if a man', described as 'the last of all', approaches the first vanquished woman to contemplate in her eyes 'those calm wastes' ('ces calmes déserts') before all ends in silence (*CSP* 223; *D* 54–5).

The literary motif of a woman's eyes as windows, if not to the soul, then to a mystical elsewhere, is one Beckett turned to as early as the Belacqua saga, where it no doubt comes with a dose of irony. In the 'Walking Out' story of *More Kicks than Pricks*, Belacqua finds in the paralyzed Lucy's eyes 'better worlds than this' (*MPTK* 121). Several decades later, both *Krapp's Last Tape* and the radio play *Words and Music* tell of visions in a woman's eyes, in the latter play, a 'glimpse / of that wellhead', or source of all, beyond the 'trash' or 'scum' of earthly existence (*CSPL* 133–4). In *Le Dépeupleur / The Lost Ones*, however, 'ces calmes déserts' / 'those calm wastes' the last man sees in the woman's eyes recall Eckhart's trope of 'still waste' and 'simple stillness' for the ultimate unknowable ground, which Beckett found cited in Inge (1899, 158). (See Chapter 2.) Or possibly, Beckett may have found the trope in his subsequent reading of Eckhart, as the mystic philosopher's 'stille wüeste' can be translated as either 'calm desert' or 'calm waste'/'wasteland' (Eckhart *DW* 48; *MEW I* 508).

---

[27] Beckett told Michael Haerdter, his production assistant for the 1967 *Endspiel* (*Endgame*) in Berlin, that he had turned to writing works of the imagination, as compared to novels, because they permit creating 'un univers à part' (a separate universe), a simpler world in which to satisfy one's need for order and understanding (qtd. in McMillan and Fehsenfeld 1988, 230–1). Beckett shared a preference for this postmodern fictional mode with other writers of the time.

[28] In *Watt*, too, the narrator explains, 'And if there were two things that Watt loathed, one was the earth, and the other was the sky' (*W* 36).

In his reflections on the mystics' *via negativa*, Derrida discerns in the frequent mystical trope of the desert a figure of 'pure place', akin to the *khōra* as interval or spacing, that is, a figure of emptiness or *kenōsis* (Derrida 1995, 56–7). Such, too, is the conception of Eckhart who likened the *khōra* to something 'pure' that is neither in nor out of the world, neither in nor out of time, an analogue of the 'stille wüeste' of the ultimate ground (*DM* 23; *MEW I* 323; *CMW* 131–2), an emptiness and stillness that Buddhist philosophers recognize as confluent with *śūnyatā* without the theology. In *The Lost Ones*, intimations of the silence and emptiness of 'ces calmes déserts' are by way of a vision that transports the last man, unlike the cylinder's 'amateurs of myth', to an experience of the contemplative emptiness of Christian mystics and Buddhist philosophers.[29]

A mystical ending to this dystopian tale, which is hard to resist given the allusion to Eckhart, an ending, moreover, Beckett long hesitated to append, is not intended to ignore this alternate world's allusions to the real of the human predicament, as once again this fiction evokes Schopenhauer's view of the world as a penal colony.[30] Further, in an impressive study of *Le Dépeupleur*, Antoinette Weber-Caflisch sees in the phrase 'si c'est un homme' ('if a man') repeated thrice in the final pages of Beckett's text, an allusion to Primo Levi's testimonial memoir of the Buna concentration camp – *Se questo è un uomo* – translated into French as *Si c'est un homme* (Weber-Caflisch 1994, 41–2).[31] Still, the evocation of the abominable machinations of a hellish world and its 'misery, misery' is not Beckett's final word – as it was not the Buddha's or Schopenhauer's – on the possibility of way out. Termed an 'inviolable zenith' in *The Lost Ones*, the way out is intimated by the vision of 'those calm wastes', consonant with the emptiness and stillness of the mystics and Buddhist *śūnyatā* and liberation from misery.

This chapter's probing of the disjunctive collapse of contraries in Beckett's texts extends the previous chapter's investigation of his paradoxical logic and its Buddhist, apophatic, and poststructural parallels. From

---

[29] Lack of space precludes exploring the possibility that the 'last of all' alludes to Nietzsche's 'last man' introduced in the prologue of *Thus Spoke Zarathustra* (1883–5) as a foil to his superhuman *Übermensch*. The 'last man' was under much scrutiny at the time by French thinkers, among others in the writings of Bataille and Blanchot. A further question to be investigated is whether *The Lost Ones* could be contesting the ridicule heaped on the Buddha's ethics of compassion and renunciation in *Zarathustra* 1.9.

[30] For Gary Adelman, *The Lost Ones* echoes Kafka's story 'In der Strafkolonie' ('In the Penal Colony') (Adelman 2003, 164–9).

[31] See also David Houston Jones (2011, 38–43) on the testimonial dimension of *The Lost Ones*.

this perspective, Beckett's life-in-death and death-in-life postwar fictions are viewed in their analogy with *mugen* noh's dreamlike narratives of the traumas endured in their life by ghosts returned from Buddhist purgatory. The *nouvelles'* motif of a story to tell that would approximate peace in the mind will go through numerous versions in subsequent works, as seen in this and the next chapter, together with the topos of an uncertain way out.

CHAPTER 6

The No-Self Staged and Voices from Elsewhere

The Voices of *Not I*

Among the spectral storytellers that Beckett imagined for the stage, the one that has intrigued theatre practitioners, audiences, and critics most intensely is the disembodied Mouth of the 1972 play *Not I*, accompanied by the shadowy figure of the Auditor that listens to her torrent of words. 'Nice posthumous feel', Beckett wrote to Ruby Cohn about the play on 24 April 1972 (qtd. in *LSB IV* 299, n. 2). The ghostly vision of a spotlit mouth is heightened by the jolting rush of words streaming into the stage darkness during the fifteen minutes or so a performance lasts.[1] See Figure 6.1. The harrowing life story, seemingly from birth to death, and the feelings of guilt and need for absolution that pour out of Mouth parallel the dramatic situation of dream noh. Japanese professor Futoshi Sakauchi has identified *Not I* 's distressing story with concerns in the Ireland of the times about the social stigma imposed on disadvantaged women owing to 'childbirth out of wedlock, adoption and misery in a church-run institution, powerlessness in society, and the lack of mercy' (Sakauchi 2008, 372). Similar to dream noh, the story uttered by the spoken-through ghostly Mouth mirrors the social conflicts of the times. In an instance of the metatheatrical overlapping of stage situation and story told, much experimented with by Beckett, the onstage spotlit Mouth stands synecdochically for the woman whose story is gushing out of it; the stage image doubles the woman's 'mouth on fire' in the story and its logorrheic speech resulting from a loss of all other bodily sensations: 'whole body like gone...just the mouth' (*CSPL* 220, 221).[2]

---

[1] The stage image of a mouth is less startling when one recalls paintings of disembodied heads, eyes, and mouths, among other body parts, as well as film close-ups, with all of which Beckett would have been acquainted.

[2] The metatheatrical 'counterpoint' between stage and text in *Not I* was impressively detailed by Paul Lawley (1983). See Cohn 2005, 316–17, for her reading of the audience's experience of the play

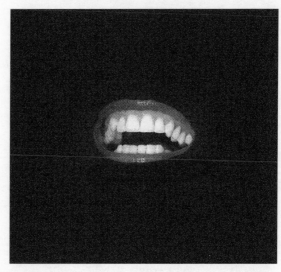

Figure 6.1   Lisa Shawn in *Not I* in the Royal Court Theatre production of *Not I*, *Footfalls*, *Rockaby*, directed by Walter Asmus, Brooklyn Academy of Music, Brooklyn, NY, 2014. Photo © Richard Termine

For Yasunari Takahashi, the mysterious spectral apparition of the play's Auditor – *'tall standing figure, sex undeterminable, enveloped ... in loose black djellaba'* (*CSPL* 216)[3] – suggests the noh-like configuration of a priestly *waki* listening to a 'voice (Shite) arriving out of an alien time-space dimension' whose torment he tries to calm (Takahashi 1983, 103–4). Torment in *Not I*, recalling the spotlight of the earlier purgatorial *Play*, is suggested by a beam of light focused on the mouth of the woman in the dictated story and on the onstage Mouth uttering it and, further, occasioned by the voice itself: 'Suffering begins with voice', Beckett points out in his holograph analysis of *Not I*.[4] Beckett's note at the beginning of the play's published text, describing the Auditor's gestures of 'helpless compassion' at the moments of Mouth's rejection of the first person, would point in the direction of an empathetic *waki*.

converging with Mouth's utterance. The convergence of 'fictional and theater situation' is Cohn's definition of the 'theatereality' of Beckett's post-*Play* plays (Cohn 1980, 28).

[3] James Knowlson (1996, 521–2) reports the origin of the Auditor in a seemingly intensely listening woman wearing a djellaba Beckett saw in Morocco, and in the figure of a woman in Caravaggio's *The Beheading of St. John the Baptist* in Malta.

[4] UoR MS 1227/7/12/1, reproduced in Pountney 1998 [1988], 245. There are two holograph and six typescript drafts of *Not I* housed at the Beckett International Foundation, University of Reading.

In the play, the Auditor's arm movements progressively weaken, and tellingly, in *Pas moi*, his French translation of the play, Beckett adds blame to the 'pitié impuissante' (helpless compassion) of the Auditor's gesture (*Pm* 95). He thereby renders the interpretation of the figure more uncertain, undecidability, in any case, being something Beckett prefers to maintain or augment. In making his Auditor hard to tie down, the author has left his audiences and exegetes unconstrained in their understanding of the figure so that in addition to the compassionate *waki*, some see in the Auditor the origin of the unheard admonitions and corrections that repeatedly interrupt Mouth's monologue, thereby turning the listening figure into a confessor, psychoanalyst, accuser, judge, or even an inquisitor. In still another reading, he is compared to Mouth's other half or Jungian shadow.[5]

In my view, though, there are three voices intimated in *Not I*, none of which belong to the Auditor, whether viewed as a projection of the interrupting voice or not. Emphasizing the crucial importance of listeners in Beckett's late plays, his role of a more or less compassionate listener assimilates him to the listeners of *Ohio Impromptu* and *That Time*. In the three plays, listeners react nonverbally to the reminiscences they hear in order to introduce pauses, emphasis, and emotional responses.[6]

In Not I, of the three voices, Auditor and audience hear only the voice streaming out of Mouth, who is trying to catch the dictation of an unheard (by the audience) inner voice (1). That Mouth can only half follow this voice is apparent from the panting speed of her delivery and its disjointedness, reiterations, and gaps. Beckett in his note before the published text, calls the ventriloquized voice 'MOUTH' (2), although it is not as such her voice but the inner voice she partially 'mouths'. So let's follow the author and call the echoing voice 'Mouth' in the sense of uttered by Mouth, the situation, after all, of all speakers voicing their inner speech, which they only echo in their utterances, after undergoing editing. Another unheard voice is the source of the '22 inner promptings' that Beckett noted in his fifth typescript draft of the play (UoR MS 1227/2/12/6, qtd. in Pountney

---

[5] On early interpretations of the Auditor, see Lawley 1983, 407. For a discussion of the many readings of the Auditor, see Wynands 2007, 87–9, 102–3, 106.

[6] In reply to the question by two American directors of whether the Auditor could be omitted, as he sometimes was in performance, Beckett explained: 'He is very difficult to stage (light, position) and may well be of more harm than good. For me the play needs him but can do without him' (Letter of 16 November 1986, *LSB IV* 680). Despite the figure's 'undeterminable sex', Beckett stated in a 1972 letter to director Alan Schneider that the Auditor is 'a man' (*LSB IV* 311).

1998 [1988], 96). In a letter to director Alan Schneider of 16 October
1972, in attributing this contentious prompting to the mind (*LSB IV* 311),
Beckett is drawing attention to the interiority of this interrupting and
controlling voice (3), which is often attributed instead to the silent
Auditor. When the prompting voice is dissatisfied with the storytelling
inner voice, it contradicts, corrects, adds, and censors by interrupting the
rapid flow of disjointed sentence fragments that stream out of Mouth.[7] In
summary then, the inner voice (1) is being mouthed piecemeal by the
ventriloquized Mouth (2) and interrupted and corrected by the directing
voice (3), a censor in the mind.

In light of the spoken-through drama of *Not I*, the Auditor's compassionate gesture, weakening with each repetition, remains ambiguous. Are
we to understand, as often surmised, that he is sympathizing with the inner
narrating voice's difficulty to accept the story she tells is about herself, or
could he not rather be showing compassion for the continued efforts she
has to make to refute the prompter's imposition of the first person? In
other words, is the blame (in the French version) directed against the inner
voice, or is it rather aimed at the mind's prompting interrupter? In
focusing on the play's staging of an inner drama, the Auditor could
possibly be identified with what has been persuasively hypothesized as an
inner hearing or an 'inner ear' (Riley 2004, 59).[8]

In his above-noted letter to Alan Schneider, who was preparing the
1972 premiere of *Not I* in New York City, Beckett clarifies that the inner
prompting voice he associates with 'mind' is to be distinguished from the
inner narrating voice, not from Mouth, as Schneider supposed. Mouth's
speech, Beckett tells Schneider, is 'a purely buccal phenomenon without
mental control or understanding, only half heard', adding, 'The only stage
apprehension of the text is the Auditor's' (*LSB IV* 311, 313). Beckett, then,
conceives of Mouth as the theatre of two antagonistic inner voices, one
coming vaguely from within and the other from a prompting and controlling mind. And the Auditor is described as an apprehending listener.
Judging from commentaries on the play, some critics find it difficult, as

---

[7] My use of the feminine pronoun for Mouth as well as for the narrating voice 'she' is echoing
erratically follows the author.

[8] British poet and philosopher Denise Riley has written brilliantly on the ventriloquy and
'autoventriloquy' of inner speech, which are marked by 'echo, repetition, and dictation', social-
ideological and otherwise (2004, 73). Her poetic assertion, 'The dead chatter away as the inner
speech of the living' is particularly apropos for Beckett's postwar and late writings.

did Schneider, to assign the tension between the two voices to interior voices and to view Auditor as an apprehending listener.[9]

Not I's two adversarial voices dictating Mouth's utterings shed light on the puzzling question of voices in Beckett's oeuvre and the role they play in the spoken-through subjectlessness of its speakers. That an interior monologue, or inner speech, actually consists of a dialogue between two antagonistic voices was already the young Beckett's view in his 1931 lectures on Racine's plays at Trinity College Dublin. For him, the dialogues between Racinian protagonists and their confidants are interior monologues, or rather interior 'poliloquies', that give utterance to the protagonists' inner conflicts (Le Juez 2009, 59; *Dream* 45). Such poliloquies keep the mind in flux, without congealing into monologues of self.

How are we to conceive of the conflicting voices of *Not I*? In my view, the inner voice whispering its story to Mouth suggests the voice from an alien inner space that murmurs to us outside of our control and whispers stories to storytellers, imagining their fictions for them or engaging them in 'dreaming back' their lives, as frequently occurs in Beckett. And the inner censoring voice, challenging the murmuring voice, corresponds to the mental archive made up of acquired social scripts – linguistic, discursive, conceptual, ideological – whose controlling function was emphasized by Mādhyamika thinkers, Eckhart, and Mauthner, and continued to be probed by pragmatic, poststructural, and contemporary philosophers of mind. The two antagonistic voices in tandem would then constitute the dictated character of discourse, which, for Roland Barthes and Michel Foucault, calls into question the subject and authorial functions as central and foundational (Barthes 1967, n.p.; Foucault 1969, 73–104). In this sense Mouth is only a stage for the warring interior voices, which from the 'outside' turn storytellers into ventriloquist dummies, Beckett having adopted this trope in the eighth of the *Texts for Nothing*, whose narrator asserts, 'all I say will be false and to begin with not said by me, here I'm a mere ventriloquist's dummy' (*CSP* 133).[10] The narrators' spoken-through

---

[9] There are other exegetes who have postulated an inner voice for Mouth. See Cohn 1980, 70–1; Ben-Zvi 1986, 166; Pountney 1998 [1988], 96; and Campbell 2005, 163. Cohn sees a conflict between Mouth's monologue and a probing brain; for Julie Campbell, the voice from within is 'an emancipated voice from the unconscious' in the Jungian sense.

[10] Foucault famously begins and ends his 1969 lecture 'Que'est-ce qu'un auteur?' ('What is an Author?') with an echoic 'spoken-through' quotation from the beginning of the third text of Beckett's *Textes pour rien* / *Texts for Nothing*: 'Qu'importe qui parle, quelqu'un a dit qu'importe qui parle' ('What matter who's speaking, someone said what matter who's speaking'; *Textes* 129; *CSP* 109). In fact, the thirteenth and last of the *Texts for Nothing* concludes with quotations from the murmuring voice. *Text* 8 was featured in the same 1967 issue of the avant-garde journal *Aspen* in

condition, which is further compared to a haunting by phantoms both in *The Unnamable* and the *Texts for Nothing*, is reiterated by the narrator of the latter's fifth text: 'It's they [the phantoms] murmur my name, speak to me of me . . . . Theirs all these voices, like a rattling of chains in my head' (*CSP* 120). The insistence on the 'not I', then, is to be understood by the spoken-through character of discourse that makes of the speaker, instead of an agent, an empty subject, with a family resemblance to the Buddhist sense of the no-self's conditioned and relational nature.

Not only poststructuralist philosophers but contemporary philosophers of mind who have integrated the investigations of cognitive science into their thought come to a similar conclusion about the no-self. Thus, philosopher of consciousness Daniel C. Dennett, who, moreover, is aware of the overlap of his cognitive-scientific view with poststructuralist philosophy (Dennett 1991, 410–11), maintains that 'selves are not independently existing soul-pearls, but artifacts of the social processes that create us' and therefore in constant flux (423). And about the narratives we invent to represent our selves to the world, he holds that: 'Our tales are spun, but for the most part we don't spin them; they spin us. Our human consciousness, and our narrative selfhood, is their product, not their source' (418). The psychological or narrative self, for Dennett, is along with the biological self only an 'abstraction' (418). His cognitive-biological view, then, is congruent with the Buddhist no-self, and with both Beckett's top-down domineering and bottom-up whispering voices that speak through an empty subject.

In a parallel development, scholars of Buddhism have begun to query the overlap between Buddhist thought and the insights gleaned from cognitive science. In his study *Brains, Buddhas, and Believing: The Problem of Intentionality in Classical Buddhist and Cognitive-Scientist Philosophy of Mind* (2014), Dan Arnold explores to what extent the Buddhist denial of the self is comparable to such contemporary philosophical projects in cognitive science as Dennett's. In a separate article, he draws attention to the overlap between the Buddhist two-truths doctrine and the two levels of description used in cognitive science: on the one hand, the intentional that corresponds to a phenomenological and common-sense view that includes a first-person perspective, and on the

---

which Barthes's 'The Death of the Author' first appeared in English translation (a year before the French original). In his fictions of the 1940s, even before *Text* 8, Beckett conceived of the eclipse of the author two decades before Barthes's notorious essay.

other hand, a scientific level of description that denies the existence of a self (Arnold n.d., § 2a).

About the voice that whispers their texts to writers, H. Porter Abbott reminds us that it is 'one of the commonest tropes in the discourse of writers about their art' (Abbott 2008, 83). He cites modern writers who speak of being taken over by their characters and quotes the experience of the poet Ka, in Orhan Pamuk's novel *Snow*, who, after hearing a poem about to appear, wrote it out 'as it came to him, word by word. It was like copying down a poem someone was whispering in his ear' (qtd. in Abbott 2008, 84). In fact, Beckett told Deirdre Bair that the narrative voice in *Not I* is a composite of the 'old crones' he knew in Ireland, adding: 'And I heard "her" saying what I wrote in *Not I*. I actually heard it' (qtd. in Bair 1978, 622). Some of the modern writers Abbott quotes are elated by such experiences, as were writers throughout history by their Muse, whereas others, and he cites J. M. Coetzee among them, find it more of a curse, as do Beckett's narrators who prefer emptiness and silence. Abbott similarly compares the writing of fiction and poetry to a bottom-up behavior, emphasizing, nevertheless, authorial editing and shaping, comparing this process to the scientific concept of 'emergent behavior' and moments of emergence of the Beckettian voice (2008, 84–7).

Beckett's anonymous voice is frequently compared to Blanchot's 'neuter' narrating voice, which in his 1953 review of *L'Innommable*, which mattered most to Beckett, is an impersonal utterance arriving from the void, a voice haunting writers who seek in vain to escape from it (Blanchot 1953, 681–2; 1979, 119–20). For Blanchot, in his later *L'Entretien infini* (1969) / *The Infinite Conversation* (1993), the 'neuter', masked by the third-person pronoun, tells the work from an abstract space that calls into question divinity, the 'I', words that could affirm being, and writing itself, having been disengaged from discourse. Something speaks outside of the subject, he repeats, outside of discourse (Blanchot 1993 [1969], xi–xii, 379–87). Blanchot specialist Joseph Kuzma thus aptly defines the 'neuter' as 'a lexical placeholder for the trace of what remains outside of being and non-being' (Kuzma n.d., sec. 1d), which, as you recall, is the Buddhist and Eckhartian definition of emptiness or nothingness. Compare the utterance of the ventriloquized narrator of the thirteenth text of *Texts for Nothing*: 'there is nothing but a voice murmuring a trace' (*CSP* 152).

Adopting Blanchotian terms, Roland Barthes, in his 'The Death of the Author' essay, finds in the 'special voice' of literature, a 'neuter' composite of voices without assignable origin and 'the trap where all identity is lost' (Barthes 1967, sec. 1). Beckett reiterated the desubjectification staged in his works when, a few years after completing *Not I*, in conversation with Charles Juliet, he comments that in his writing, at the end, 'on ne sait plus qui parle. Il y a une totale disparition du sujet' (one doesn't know who is speaking. The subject totally disappears), further observing that withdrawing from the work as an individual is demanded of the artist (qtd. in Juliet 1986, 39).[11] For Beckett, the anonymous and domineering voices interpenetrate to disperse a unified subject, but it is the anonymity and exteriority of the inner voice that account for Beckett's refusal to hold his creatures to a uniquely human identity that excludes the *unborn* outside of lived categories. More on this topic in the next chapter.[12]

The two contesting voices that dispossess the subject and turn writers into mediums or ventriloquist dummies take on new masks in work after work. The dictated nature of Mouth's voice in *Not I* thus recalls the complex narrative situation of *Watt*, one of whose narrators, no longer 'Mr Beckett' but the more familiar 'Sam', writes in his notebook the fragments he can catch of the stream of words gushing out of the mouth of Watt at a speed anticipating Mouth's breakneck delivery. Watt, in turn the narrator of his time at Knott's house, is described as 'speaking to dictation' by an inner voice that is ill heard, ill transmitted, and then ill transcribed by Sam, a powerful expression of the experience of writers with unfathomable inner voices dictating to them from an unconscious exteriority (*W* 156).[13]

The writing process, then, as Beckett and other writers repeat, involves a 'non-pathological' split into writer and dissociative voices, which are and are not the writer's own. Subject to authorial control and shaped into a text for an audience, these voices are not to be confused with symptoms of

---

[11] Although some critics detect a hegemony of the Blanchotian 'neuter' in Beckett criticism in France, this view is countered by the investigations by French and other scholars of testimonial postwar writing, among whom Beckett and Blanchot have privileged places. (By way of example, see Michèle Touret (2006) on this topic and the discussion of *Le Dépeupleur / The Lost Ones* in Chapter 5.) The metaphysical does not preclude the political nor the political the metaphysical (or the psychoanalytic), especially not in Beckett. Au contraire!

[12] In contrast to the anonymous murmuring voice, the domineering voice issuing from an inner archive of social scripts has been read in terms of the symbolic 'Other', Jacques Lacan's term for the internalized discourse of social constraints that Freud theorized as the 'superego'. In fact, in his postwar work of the 1940s, Beckett alludes obliquely to the Freudian superego on which he had taken notes in the 1930s. On the notes, see Frost and Maxwell 2006, 160. Llewellyn Brown gives a perceptive Lacanian reading of the two Beckettian voices, one the voice of the 'Other' speaking the subject, the second an inscrutable voice, outside the subject, related to the Lacanian unrepresentable 'Real' (Brown 2011, 172–94).

[13] For an analysis of *Watt's* abysmal, or nested, narrative structure, entailing multiple embedded narrators, from the omniscient third person to the first person to the whispered voice, see Moorjani 1982, 26–39.

clinical hysteria or schizophrenia, as such splittings often are. Unlike many writers, Beckett, however, is intent on transmitting the flavor of the dictated words by means of a syntax of dispersion (he famously called it a 'syntax of weakness'; Harvey 2006, 135), resulting in a repetitive, fragmented text, punctuated with gaps, in which there is no deictic center, no identifiable first-person speaker, and which, more often than not, unravels at the end in an approximation of silence, until the next round.

Not I's spoken-through Mouth evokes Sam's faulty recording of Watt's increasingly incomprehensible utterances. Because Watt's murmuring voice is dictated by yet another voice, one can imagine an unending chain of partial inscriptions comparable to the Derridean archival traces that 'are *always already* transcriptions' (Derrida 1972 [1967], 92; emphasis in the original). Intriguingly, both Derrida and William S. Waldron, a scholar of Buddhism and philosophies of mind, refer to Freud's mystic writing pad trope for the psychic apparatus in their descriptions of archival traces (Freud 1961 [1925], 227–32; Derrida 1972 [1967], 92; Waldron 2003, 231, n. 18). Inscriptions on the mystic writing pad, which are erased when the pad's cover is lifted, remain recorded on the underlying base. From Waldron's Buddhist perspective, such psychic inscriptions correspond to the traces in the *ālayavijñāna* – the Buddhist equivalent of the unconscious – which linger from previous transmigrations, adding thereby the dimension of guilt and penance. Intriguingly, in a repetition of *Watt*'s unending narrative structure, in *Not I*'s story, which Mouth echoes in fits and starts, the figure of the old woman reduced to a mouth, is spoken through in turn by memory voices that introduce feelings of guilt that are out of her control.

In *Watt*, Beckett further experiments with a form, 'disordered' and 'broken', both to evoke human weakness and suffering, as he explained to Lawrence Harvey, and to grapple with the artist's task 'to find a form that accommodates the mess', as Beckett told Tom Driver.[14] He experimented with such a chaotic form in *Watt* and the postwar French fiction, spectacularly reprising it in *Not I*.

In summary, the narrative situation, which has migrated from *Watt* to the play thirty years later, consists in a spoken-through voice (Sam's, Mouth's) telling in turn of a spoken-through voice (Watt's, the woman's in voice's story of *Not I*), with suggestions of endless repetition. The

---

[14] The need for a more chaotic form of which Beckett spoke in his conversations with Harvey in the early 1960s is summarized in Harvey 2006, 133–6. The quotation from the interview with Tom Driver dating from the same period is found in Driver 1979 [1961], 218–19.

situation of the author's homopseudonymous Sam in *Watt* is echoed in the subsequent fictional narratives of *The Unnamable, Texts for Nothing, How It Is,* and *Company*, all dictated narratives, or a saying as it is heard, dispossessing the subject. Critics have further investigated Beckett's late romance with recording media, in which the reverberating voices are increasingly encoded and distanced.

In addition to *Watt*, it is in particular *The Unnamable* that is echoed in *Not I*. Insisting that he is obliged to speak with voices that are not his, the novel's narrator wonders, 'Where do these words come from that pour out of my mouth, and what do they mean?' (*Un* 370). His insistent denial of the first person, 'it's not I, not I, I can't say it, it came like that, it comes like that, it's not I' (*Un* 402), reverberates with the refusal of *Not I*'s narrating voice to accept the first person, which, after being repeatedly prompted to her, is rejected by her impatient 'what?..who?..no!..she!'. And intriguingly, the startling stage image of Mouth is foreshadowed by the resolutions of *The Unnamable*'s narrator:

> Assume notably henceforward that the thing said and the thing heard have a common source . . .. Situate the source in me, without specifying where exactly . . .. Evoke at painful junctures . . . the image of a vast cretinous mouth, red, blubber and slobbering . . . extruding indefatigably . . . the words that obstruct it. (*Un* 390)

Beckett was to adopt the trope of the ventriloquized mouth for his own experience of writing. Patrick Bowles, reporting on his conversations with Beckett during the early 1950s, recalls: '[Beckett] talks of his books as if they were written by someone else. He said that it was the voice to which he listened, the voice one should listen to.' Admitting that 'there are many things I don't understand in my books', Beckett, as reported by Bowles, concluded that 'his books become no more than the mouth speaking, then the voices, coming from one cannot tell where' (Bowles 2006 [1994], 109). Beckett is here speaking of his own writing in terms of the spoken-through mouth of *The Unnamable*'s fictional speaker, an image he projected onto the stage some twenty years later, but in the transgendered image of a ventriloquized female mouth.[15]

---

[15] The transgendered Mouth in *Not I*, especially in televised close-up, has been frequently interpreted as a vaginal trope, which, in my view, instead of alluding to lack and castration (Wilson 1990, 195), is an image of birthing a text. See also Van Hulle 2009, 48, who cites the view that 'Beckett may have used Mouth as a way of describing his position as an author', attributed to Wilma Siccama, who made this suggestion in her book *Het waarnemend lichaam: Zintuiglijkheid en representatie bij Beckett en Artaud* (Nijmegen: Vantilt, 2000), 121.

Beckett's Voices and the Brain

Beckett's two voices – the top-down controlling and the bottom-up murmuring – correlate in fascinating ways with cognitive-scientist investigations of brain network dynamics and creativity. At the beginning of the twenty-first century, following the renewed interest by cognitive scientists (after decades of behaviorism) in the interrelation between unconscious and conscious thought, neuroscientists identified two dynamically interacting brain circuits dubbed a 'default network' and an 'executive network'.[16] In their probing of the brain, they found the default network to be active during daydreaming and other dissociative activities, such as the walking and cycling and to some extent writing, that Beckett, as noted in Chapter 4, describes as the acts of a proxy. The 'executive network', on the other hand, which is largely quiet during creative and imaginative activity, becomes active, in their description, during the subsequent evaluation process by its oversight. It suggests Beckett's prompting voice in *Not I* and its many tyrannical superego avatars imposing their commands. The writer's oversight is inevitably enmeshed with the controlling voice.

In this connection, Beckett's answer to my question about how he goes about writing is apropos: 'One decides what elements to use and puts them together.' He appears to be describing the directing role that his *pauvre con* proxy was unable to furnish in his 1949 letter to Georges Duthuit (see Chapter 4). The bottom-up 'elements', involving imagination and the creative faculty that give voice to unconscious traces, Beckett implies, are not his doing, a view that sheds light on his refusal to talk about the 'meaning' of his works, claiming that he is as much outside his written texts as any reader. On the controlling role, there is a telling entry into Beckett's German Diaries (notebook 4, 2 February 1937), in which, discouraged by his depression, he expresses the hope of being equal 'to the relatively trifling act of organisation that is all that is needed to turn this dereliction, profoundly felt, into literature' (qtd. in Knowlson 1996, 235).

Where does this leave the question of transtextual and autobiographical 'elements' that Beckett weaves into his texts? Depending on whether these are involuntary hauntings or are voluntarily imported, they would appear to be the province of one or the other voice. Interestingly, involuntary autobiographical retrieval of the Proustian type is considered part of the function of the 'default network' (Beaty et al. 2016, 88), so that the many

---

[16] See Beaty et al. 2016, 87–95; and Dewey 2018, ch. 3.

autobiographical echoes in Beckett's oeuvre are attributable in part to the bottom-up voice as appears from the late texts *This Time* and *Company*. The same can be said of the remembered life scenes of the woman in the story of *Not I* 's narrating voice, which intrude outside of conscious control. And perhaps the hauntings by previous authors arrive in the same way as the involuntary memories.

Anticipating the two networks, the portrayal of the unconscious displacing consciousness, or doubling it in the guise of a doppelgänger, became a familiar tale beginning with Romantic writers. A late instance is found in Jules Renard's *Journal* into which Beckett would regularly dip from the 1930s onward, recording some of his witty remarks in his 'Dream' Notebook. In his journal entry of 23 December 1896, Renard tells of the impression that during waking dreams the images that suddenly appear are by another self or a double, that his consciousness is being taken over by his unconscious. Such dissociative feelings are similar to Beckett's impressions of 'existence by proxy' and the theme of an unborn twin/ double that speaks through a 'no-self'.[17]

Beckett's ironic use of a fantasized unborn twin is evident in the previously mentioned *Pochade radiophonique* / *Rough for Radio II*, written in French circa 1960 and first performed in both languages in the mid-1970s. Outrageously spoofing both the artistic process and a psychoanalytic session, the play assimilates both to torture.[18] In the appropriately named *Rough*, a male figure's refusal to utter as directed, even under duress, is doubled by his failure to give birth to an imaginary twin (*CSPL* 113–24).[19] Further, in Beckett's 'Foirade 2' / 'Fizzle 4', 'J'ai renoncé avant de naître' / 'I gave up before birth' (French, early 1960s; English, 1976), a male figure is ventriloquized by an unborn double inside him who will continue to speak in his stead through several existences (*CSP* 234–5). In fact, psychoanalysts from Freud (1959 [1908], 150) and Otto Rank (1971 [1914], 75–6) to Wilfred R. Bion (1967, 8–9) see in the imaginary twin fantasy of writers a personified split in the psyche in the form of a double, or a doppelgänger, a common-enough literary device permitting writers to adopt a distance from their own viewpoints. The

---

[17] There is no dearth of articles linking the Beckettian 'voice' to a rift in the subject, or in the author. See, for example, Clément 2008, 89–101, and Brown 2011, 172–96.

[18] In Emilie Morin's view, the *Rough* stages a detective's investigation, and the terms that are often taken as applicable to the author and the creative process are rather euphemistic expressions pertaining to political torture (2017, 220–4). As is the case in Beckett's other 'torture' plays, the one reading does not preclude the other.

[19] On this failure in the *Rough*, see Lawley 1989, 1–10.

imaginary twin's role in Beckett's texts and his comments at about the same time to Lawrence Harvey about his intuition of an embryonic being that 'might have been but never got born' and his attempts to get down into the dark, to hear the unborn's 'infinitesimal murmur' (qtd. in Harvey 1970, 247) suggest that the unborn twin fantasy is related to the author's grappling with the voice in the writing process, which, irrupting from the outside inside, dispossesses writers from any semblance of a unified subject. (For further discussion of the role of dissociative states in the Buddhist concept of the *unborn*, see Chapter 7.)

Some exegetes see in Mouth's discontinuously and repetitively quoted inner dialogue evidence of a 'schizoid voice'. However, even though the traits associated with the 'default network' in creative writing – interiority, dissociation, splitting, and voices and visions outside conscious awareness – are, when in excess and out of control, symptoms of the incapacitating conditions and suffering of schizophrenic illness (Sass 2017, x, 325–6), the writer's organizational abilities, as Beckett contends, make the difference between a debilitating disease and an act of the imagination turned into literature.[20] From this perspective, what is viewed as a 'schizoid voice' (or hysteria) in Beckett is rather the voice that murmurs and dictates to writers, whose translation into disordered speech is carefully crafted by the author.[21]

Beckett himself was aware of the partial convergence between dissociative writing and schizophrenia as, in his conversations with Lawrence Harvey, he followed his description of 'being absent' with recounting his experience with the extreme vacuity of a schizophrenic patient in a London mental institution (Harvey 1970, 247).[22] Such associations are, as we

---

[20] Even if Gilles Deleuze (with or without psychotherapist and anti-psychiatry activist Félix Guattari) attempts to bypass the 'havoc' that schizophrenia 'wreaks in the person' by conceptualizing it as an imaginative process (qtd. in Keatinge 2015, 84), there is a fundamental distinction to be made between an imaginative process and the severe psychosis and suffering caused by schizophrenia. If you abstract the 'havoc', you are no longer talking about a schizophrenic illness but about an imaginative or creative process involving dissociation for which the clinical term 'schizophrenia' is misleading. The latter involves other factors, such as disturbances in neural communication, traumas, and genetics resulting in an incapacitating psychosis. Keatinge is citing Deleuze,'s *Two Regimes of Madness: Texts and Interviews 1975–1995*, ed. by David Lapoujade, trans. by Ames Hodges and Mike Taormina (New York: Semiotext(e), 2007), 27.

[21] On the schizoid voice, see Ackerley 2004, 39–49. Shane Weller, detailing Beckett's knowledge of schizophrenia from a number of sources – psychoanalytic and poetic – and reviewing the critical literature on the schizoid voice in Beckett, similarly comes to the conclusion that Beckett made conscious use of languages of 'derangement', while keeping a distance from them and exercising control over them (Weller 2009, 32–44). See also Denise Riley's overview (2004, 62–5) of the neurological basis for distinguishing between delusion and sanity in hearing inner voices.

[22] See other instances of Beckett's awareness of this convergence in Weller 2009, 41.

know, put to imaginative use in his writings, such as Murphy's attraction to the schizophrenic Endon and the narrator's description of his 'schizoid voice' (*Mu* 185). But does the partial overlap between inner voice and schizoid voice justify indulging in hypothetical diagnoses of individual writers or of their creatures?[23] Often enough, the characters' illnesses of mind and body evoke the sufferings of the 'human predicament' and the perhaps of a way out with which Beckett's writing is engaged. Such are the 'woes' imagined for the woman in the story pouring out of Mouth and her search for deliverance.

Not I 's Tale of Woes

Beckett counted on the jarring stage image of a spotlit mouth and, as he wrote to director Alan Schneider, its nearly unintelligible 'panting' to work on the nerves of the audience, which, he adds, 'should in a sense <u>share her bewilderment</u>' (Letter of 16 October 1972, *LSB IV* 311; underscored in the original). The bafflement no doubt is augmented by the 'spoken-through' Mouth's subjectlessness, which the audience of Beckett's late plays is made to share, such a non-subject, or no-self, in Peter Gidal's view, contesting fixed subject positions within established power hierarchies (Gidal 1986, 129–30).

Beckett composed a story for the narrating voice evoking the misery of a woman in an identifiably contemporary place and time, even though Mouth's syntactically disjointed and breathless delivery prevents it from being consumed as straightforward Ibsen. Beckett decried the likelihood of such a response from actors and audience in his previously cited answer to Alan Schneider's questions about *Not I*: 'All I know is in the text . . .. The rest is Ibsen' (*LSB IV* 311). In responding to questions about his plays, Beckett tended, more often than not, to limit discussion to their theatricality, or to the directing function, this, of course, being only one dimension of the contrapuntal four-part composition of his texts. Mouth's quoted story corresponds to the everyday empirical dimension of *Not I* and, despite Beckett's dismissive words, it can be taken as a nod in the direction of Ibsen's plots about women's social situation at the time he wrote his plays. Paradoxically, the author's 'the rest is Ibsen' leads us there. 'An enumeration of woes' is what Beckett calls Mouth's story in his analysis of *Not I* (UoR MS 1227/7/12/1, reproduced in Pountney 1998

---

[23] In his book *Madness and Modernity*, psychologist Louis Sass lists as 'markedly schizoid', Baudelaire, Kafka, Pessoa, Wittgenstein, and Beckett, among others (2017, 304–5).

[1988], 245). Unmistakably, *Not I*'s compassion-evoking tale is a far cry from the scornful and cruel depiction of women in the Belacqua saga. The distancing techniques introduced into the tale as dictated to and quoted by Mouth function to moderate its pathos.

In counterpoint to the play's down-to-earth story are its inner stage of voices, its other-world purgatorial setting, and its metatheatrical convergences. All four dimensions are intricately combined into one contrapuntal composition despite Beckett's adhering to the uniquely theatrical dimension in his letter to Alan Schneider. All four are 'in the text'.

Reiterating the Beckettian theme of birth into death, *Not I*'s posthumous narrating voice starts on her story several times, beginning with the premature birth and abandonment of the 'tiny little girl' and after a quick dismissal of the rest – 'no love of any kind' and 'nothing of note' – focusing closely on what appears to be the character's death or near-death seventy years later in a field on an April morning. In paying attention to what follows when 'all went out' (*CSPL* 216), the woman's symptoms suggest a stroke: lack of suffering, her inability to tell what position she is in, her slow recovery of speech after feeling is restored to her mouth but not to the rest of her body ('whole body like gone. . .just the mouth'; 221). Her logorrheic speech – a common consequence of stroke – is something she at first cannot accept as coming from her own mouth, taking it to be another's, and failing to understand what she is saying. The woman reduced to a mouth spewing out logorrheic speech hears an inner voice begging her to stop, while at the same time 'dragging up the past' (220).[24] Among the memories surfacing outside of her control are tears shed at dusk in Croker's Acres (near Beckett's birthplace), disconsolate supermarket and court scenes ('guilty or not guilty'; 221), reclusiveness and search for listeners (222), and, repeatedly, the field where 'all went out'. Finally, the five 'life scenes' in this enumeration of woes' as Beckett refers to them in his synopsis and analysis of *Not I* (qtd. in Pountney 1998 [1988], 245, 247) are an instance of Beckett's declared ethical concern with defending the powerless and the miseries inflicted on them (*LSB II* 41, 42).

What is one to make of the 'buzzing' in the skull, a noise, which, on being prompted, the narrating voice repeatedly affirms about the protagonist in the story she is telling? For Simon Critchley, it is 'the tinnitus of existence', an apt phrase, when one recalls, as he does,

---

[24] The neurological investigations Denise Riley cites on inner voices elucidate many of the symptoms described in *Not I*'s story (Riley 2004, 62–5).

Malone's description of the 'noises of the world' merged into one continuous 'buzzing' in his head: 'The noises of nature, of mankind and even my
own', Malone explains, 'were all jumbled together in one and the same
unbridled gibberish' (Critchley 2004, 203, 206–7; *Ma* 207).[25]

Reduced to the sensation of a phantom mouth and to buzzing noises
and memories racing through her brain, the woman in the narrated story is
spoken-through as is the onstage Mouth. She appears to be going through
a 'life review', as it is practiced late in life or when death is near, the
situation of many of Beckett's characters beginning with the postwar
fiction and later theatre. In *Just Play*, Cohn comments that *Not I* 'continues the death's threshold re-view of a lifetime, which started in
1958 with *Krapp's Last Tape*' (Cohn 1980, 129). Even earlier, as we have
seen, the four *nouvelles* stage life reviews in the form of 'dreaming back'.

More drastically, though, the woman's remembering resembles a near-
death or a *bardo* experience in the interspace between death and the
afterlife. The out-of-body sensation, the flickering light beam, the
thoughts, memories, and past sins flashing through the woman's brain
are elements of what are described as near-death experiences.[26] Beckett
most likely knew of the *Bardo Thödol* of Tibetan Buddhism – popular in
the West since its 1927 translation/adaptation as the *Tibetan Book of the
Dead* – for intimations of the *bardo* and the dreamlike visions and
sensations that are chronicled in it.[27]

Toward the end of *Not I*, the narrating voice picks up the earlier theme
of the fear of punishment and the belief in a merciful God, vestiges of the
protagonist's upbringing in a church-run orphanage. A '*Good laugh*', as per
the stage directions, greets this evocation of God's mercy (*CSPL* 217),
which is amply acted on in performance and reminiscent of Mauthner's
'laughter is the best critique'. Later in the play, the forgiveness the
protagonist seeks from a loving and merciful God is but 'grabbing at straw'

[25] In an interview with Tom Driver, Beckett spoke of 'this buzzing confusion' as the 'mess' that is the
artist's task to let into form (qtd. in Driver 1979 [1961], 218).
[26] In an article in the journal *Frontiers in Human Neuroscience*, in which the authors investigate the
findings about possible brain functions in relation to near-death phenomena, they define near-death
experiences as 'an altered state of consciousness that occurs during an episode of unconsciousness as
a result of a life-threatening condition'. 'Under these circumstances', the authors continue, 'patients
often report perceiving a tunnel, a bright light, deceased relatives, mental clarity, a review of their
lives, and out-of-body experiences (OBEs) in which they describe a feeling of separation from their
bodies and the ability to watch themselves from a different perspective' (Facco and Agrillo 2012, 1).
[27] For a brief introduction to the *bardo*, see 'Life after Death, and *The Book of the Dead*' in Conze
1959b, 227–32. Conze bases his brief excerpts on a Tibetan manuscript and several translations of
the *bardo* material (222).

(221),[28] yet neither can anything she might think or tell bring her forgiveness. Rather, salvation could possibly come from 'something she didn't know herself...wouldn't know if she heard...then forgiven' (221). Increasingly, the narrating voice's repeated imperatives, 'imagine', 'keep on', apply as much to her composing her story as to her protagonist (222–3). Similar to the ending of *Cascando*, in which Voice's failure to tell the right story to find peace overlaps with Woburn's drifting into an uncertain elsewhere, the narrating voice's monologue, or rather 'poliloquy', in *Not I* is suspended with the imperative, 'pick it up'. The begging in the brain to stop the woman's stream of words having been denied, storyteller and protagonist are left with the sole possibility to keep on trying 'not knowing what' to perhaps 'hit on it in the end' (222–3). The obligation to pursue the 'not knowing what' leaves us unconstrained to imagine what it may be. A merciful God and thoughts and words having been devalued as means of redemption, it suggests the view Schopenhauer shared with the Buddha: 'It is the point forever inaccessible to all human cognition' (*WWR II* ch. 44, 576). In his article on Zen in *Not I*, Kyle Gillette states his Buddhist interpretation more emphatically, suggesting that the attempt by Mouth (actually the mouth in voice's story) to stop her stream of words aligns it with the Zen practice of reaching the emptiness beyond the jabbering delusions of *saṃsāra* (Gillette 2012, 289).[29]

The woman in the voice's story, reduced to a mouth, comes to admit that the voice she is hearing 'straining to hear...make something of it', along with her thoughts, must be her own (219–20). The onstage spotlit Mouth and the 'mouth on fire' in the story she is doubling (220), each spew out words dictated from inside by a voice that is their own, but which, coming from an alien space, neither understands, but only echoes. For Beckett, such is the situation of the composition process. Storytellers are not the sources of their tales but the conduits of other voices that whisper their stories to them, signaling the absence of the first person by

---

[28] In Beckett's synopsis of *Not I*, he reiterates the point: 'Brain grabbing at straws (e.g. God's mercy)' (UoR MS 1227/7/12/10, rpt. in Pountney 1998 [1988], 247).

[29] Some commentators have read *Not I* in terms of Christian mysticism. Hélène L. Baldwin sees in Beckett's texts a 'continuing process of stripping away, of detachment, as preliminary to the mystic encounter', and reads *Not I* as 'an almost conventionally religious play about judgment, in a purgatorial existence' (Baldwin 1981, 7, 137). Reading Beckett's artistic vision in terms of 'a metaphoric depiction of emptiness', Sandra Wynands, while impressively bringing to bear Buddhist *śūnyatā* on Beckett's late theatre, opts to interpret *Not I* mainly in terms of Christian *kenōsis*: 'The subject empties itself in a torrential outpouring of that which constitutes its ego-centered subjectivity and in this process the divine likeness can emerge' (Wynands 2007, 82, 106–7).

their insistence on the second or the third. This distancing maneuver is
repeated in Beckett's late plays and fictions, whose affinity with the
Buddhist doctrine of the no-self will continue to be explored in the
next chapters.

The convergence, then, of the spoken-through onstage Mouth and the
mouth in the story suggests that Mouth is being dictated her own story,
distanced as that of an other's or a doppelgänger's, to the snippets of which
the Auditor-*waki* or inner hearer listens with increasing helplessness,
unable to soothe the ghostly storyteller's pain. But even without his
hard-to-stage presence in the play, the story clearly fails to bring relief, as
Voice's story did not in the earlier *Cascando*, while leaving open whether
another one might, possibly the thousands and third. Is there then in the
reiterated perhaps of finding the right story in the face of failure after
failure an encore of the day-after-day promise that Godot will certainly
come tomorrow? Finally, though, could it all be a nightmarish dream, as in
delusory *saṃsāra* or in noh drama, a nightmare from which one awakens?:
'*Voice ... ceases as house lights up*' (223) is the playwright's final
stage instruction. The infliction of tales of woe on the empty conduit of
a no-self can be taken as so much illusion, doubling that of the
theatrical performance.

'Nothing is left to tell': The Voice of Memory in *That Time* and *Ohio Impromptu*

The out-of-body experience of *Not I* appears in other Beckett texts: *Malone
Dies*, *Film*, *That Time*, and his last piece of fiction, *Stirrings Still*, each
involving figures close to dying. In fact, the 1976 play *That Time*, with its
disembodied 'old white face ... as if seen from above' and streams of
memories consisting in a life review, so closely resembles *Not I* that Beckett
barred it from being performed together with the latter play (*CSPL* 228;
Cohn 1980, 30).[30] A few years after completing *That Time*, Beckett was to
bundle the play's three separately recorded 'moments' of the Listener's
own voice (227), corresponding to the traditional three stages of life, into
one voice in *Company*. Continuing *Not I*'s avoidance of the first person,
the voices in both works recount the Listener/Hearer's past using the
'you'/*tu* form. In *Company*, the narrator's description of the voice also

---

[30] The subsequent parenthetical page numbers in my discussion of *That Time* refer to the text of the
play in *CSPL* 227–35.

pertains to the voices of *That Time*: 'Another trait its repetitiousness. Repeatedly with only variants the same bygone' (*Co* 16).

That Time's voice A tells of the adult Listener searching for the ruin in which he hid as a child; voice B recounts a love scene of young adulthood, and voice C's stories are of old age. The reminiscences, linked to three specific psycho-habitats that haunt the Listener – a ruined folly, a stone in the sun, public spaces of refuge – interweave in achronological order, one taking over from the other by association, as memories tend to do. Thus, echoes chime from the voice of one segment to the next: A's attempt to remember whether his mother was alive the last time he looked for the ruin, 'was your mother ah for God's sake all gone long ago', is repeated word for word by C at the beginning of the next segment (229). And C's telling of the marble slab on which he would dry off at the Portrait Gallery is picked up by B's description 'on the stone together in the sun . . . at the edge of the little wood' (228). B's later elaboration about the meeting of the lovers on the stone leads to A's description of hiding in the abandoned ruin on a stone all day long (229).[31] More than in *Not I*'s life review, *That Time*'s three narratives interweave the writer's autobiographical memory with invention. The mixture is apparent, for example, in the richly alliterative name of Foley's Folly for the ruined tower in A's narrative. The actual ruin was named Barrington's Tower, but as Eoin O'Brien reports, for Beckett, 'there was no music in that name, so he changed it to Foley's Folly' (O'Brien 1987, 71).[32]

In another instance of stage and text counterpoint, the voices tell of the Listener, at various ages, inventing other voices or characters to people his aloneness and 'to keep the void from pouring in on top of you the shroud' (230). Toward the play's end, forgetfulness, will-lessness, and the increasing uncertainty of the who, where, and when bring the voices to a contemplative end-of-life renunciation, whose pathos is carefully avoided by means of a number of devices Beckett uses to this effect, swearing and obscenities among them. Thus, voice A tells of abandoning his search for the ruin where he hid as a child, preferring to get 'the hell out of it all and never come back' (235). In his last speech, voice B, at a loss for words to

---

[31] For a different and more elaborate analysis of this repetitive pattern in the play and of the three stones recalled by the three voices, see Connor 2007 [1988], 151–2. For me, the same motif picked up and developed by different voices evokes a musical composition.

[32] In *The Beckett Country*, a photograph of the imposing Barrington Tower depicts Beckett's childhood hideout approximately one mile from his childhood home (O'Brien 1986, 28). As O'Brien (29) points out, the ruined folly also appears in 'The Calmative' (*CSP* 61). 'Folly' is an architectural term for fantasy constructions, often with no set purpose, following no particular style.

keep out the void, tells of letting it in 'and nothing the worse ... little or nothing the worse' (234). And C has a final hallucinatory vision that concludes the play, in which the Public Library's reading room fills with dust from top to bottom, as he hears something like, 'no one come and gone in no time gone in no time' (235), evoking a preferably toothless smile from the Listener. It is a near-death vision of the void of existence, in which the words enclosed in books are so much dust, and the 'you' is a no-self, or 'no one', come from and going into timelessness.[33]

Emptiness of mind is dramatically staged in the 1981 *Ohio Impromptu* when the reading from the final pages of the book of memory, recounting the loss of a loved one, comes to an end. The importance of storytelling as a means of reaching the wished-for calm and peace in the mind is staged once more in this short play for a Reader and a Listener, both of identical appearance.[34] See Figure 6.2. In fact, as mentioned earlier, in his letter of 19 February 1981, Beckett advised David Warrilow, who played the part of Reader at the world premiere, to read the story in a voice, 'calm, steady, designed to soothe' (*LSB IV* 545). Contrapuntally, the stage image and actions parallel (with variations) the actions in the story read, resulting in a 'ghostly off-stage doubling' in Steven Connor's words (Connor 2007 [1988], 170). Or, in my view, the play is an example of aporetic doubling, the tale the Reader reads is about his reading it.

Reading the mournful tale he finds in the final pages of the volume placed in front of him, the Reader cites a distraught mourner dreaming of a departed loved one's 'unspoken' promise: 'My shade will comfort you.' The ghostly reader in the story, dressed like the Reader on stage, arrives on several evenings to read the sad tale, disappearing in the morning, until one night he announces he will not come again. At the end, the comforting shade and mourner in the story, doubled by the onstage Reader and Listener, remain sitting as if absent to the world – 'as though turned to stone'– 'buried in who knows what profounds of mind. Of mindlessness'.

---

[33] Steven Connor glosses C's 'in no time' at the end of the play as 'abruptly', referring to lived time, and to the 'non-time' of dramatic representation (Connor 2007 [1988], 154). To these, my reading adds the third sense of the timelessness that precedes and follows life, the metaphysical dimension missed by commentators convinced, as Connor was to be subsequently, of Beckett's 'radical finitude' (Connor 2008, 35–50). See also Lawley 2002, 173–86, for an incisive analysis of *That Time*'s repeated allusions to attempts to escape perceivedness, which Beckett (following Berkeley) associates with being.

[34] Written for the 1981 symposium at Ohio State University in honor of Beckett's seventy-fifth birthday, the play's tableau of Reader and Listener seated at a table, bowed heads propped on their hands before an open book, was met by laughter. It must have reminded the Beckett scholars in the audience, as it did this one, of the many hours spent poring over Beckett's works. The play covers less than four pages in *CSPL* (285–8).

Figure 6.2   Sam McCready as Reader and Walter Bilderback as Listener in *Ohio Impromptu*, directed by Xerxes Mehta, Maryland Stage Company, Baltimore, 1990. Photo courtesy of Theatre Department records, University Archives, UMBC

Here the story read by the onstage Reader ends as after a pause he reads the words 'Nothing is left to tell'. With the commanding knock of the Listener, which takes on the nonverbal interrupting role throughout the play, the Reader reiterates 'Nothing is left to tell' and closes the book. A further knock is met with silence as the two figures seemingly merge into one, doubling what in the story read is said of the mourner and the shade reading to him: 'With never a word exchanged they grew to be as one.'[35]

That Beckett staged the reading of the book of memory as a dream sequence suggests itself by the ghostliness of the character(s), who as in dreams, can be considered two versions of the dreamer. Reminiscent of the narrator of 'The Calmative', the phantom dreamer repeatedly tells himself a story to be comforted for the loss of a loved one, after which, the two-in-one dreamer – voice of memory and inner hearer – imagines descending into the peace and nothingness in the mind that has been the preferred space of Beckett's personages from Belacqua onward. For this play, the affinity with Zen's 'no-mind/no-language' state (*mushin*) was pointed out by Yasunari Takahashi who tentatively added: 'We might imagine that [the characters] could at last surrender themselves to that great void, which

---

[35] The statuelike ghostliness at the end brings to mind not only the return to the mineral evoked in Freud's *Beyond the Pleasure Principle* and Echo's voice turned to stone but the Romantic and Surrealist dreamlike motif of statues that hover between lifelessness and life. The motif recurs in *Mal vu mal dit* / *Ill Seen Ill Said*, which Beckett was writing at the same time as the play.

Zen teaches us is the ultimate reality of human existence' (Takahashi 2001, 39–40). Takahashi remarks that although 'probably no other writer in the twentieth century has delved deeper than Beckett into the void that exists before, within, and beyond the rational mind', it is important, he observes, to emphasize that Beckett refused the temptation of *nirvāṇa* (40–1). Nevertheless, even if, for himself, Beckett at times denied the Eastern solution of liberation, the 'perhaps' of an elsewhere or a beyond sounds in his late writings.

The movement beyond thought in *Ohio Impromptu* echoes the suspicion or limits of conceptual thought that Beckett shared with Christian mysticism, philosophical self-critique, and Buddhist thought. A passage from an early discussion of emptiness in the Buddhist canon in the Mahāsuññata Sutta makes explicit the connection between an inner void and quietude of mind: 'Then that bhikkhu [Buddhist devotee] should steady his mind internally, quiet it, bring it to singleness, and concentrate on that same sign of concentration as before. Then he gives attention to voidness ... internally and externally .... He gives attention to imperturbability' (qtd. in Garfield 2011, § 1). The 'sign of concentration' of Beckett's characters, however, involves less the usual meditative absorption (although that too occurs) than, as noted, the act of telling the right story in order to reach, by means of renunciation, the different dimension of Malone's 'great calm' and 'great indifference'. And the act of storytelling aims to provide the gift of quietude for the child terrified of night, or the writer feeling 'beyond the grave', or the distressed mourner, or the audience of Beckett's fiction and theatre.

In affinity with dream noh, the ghostly voices in the three short memory plays scrutinized in this chapter search for an end to their telling and pain. They each abdicate the first person in the life- or end-of-life stories they tell in a purgatorial-, *bardo*-, or dreamlike space-time. Each of the three plays involves listeners who react to the voices that address them in an inner colloquium involving memory. We are, in these plays, once again in the inner playground of the skull with its cast of shades that do not add up to a self but that mirror the creative and controlling functions of the brain. Whereas in *Not I*, the search for the right story to tell is suspended as the voice ceases as the house lights come up, the later plays *That Time* and *Ohio Impromptu* conclude in the peace of resignation and descent into an inner void and timelessness confluent with *śūnyatā*.

CHAPTER 7

Rebirth and the Buddhist Unborn *in the Fiction and Drama*

'Born the dead of night'

Echoing Malone's birth into death, Pozzo's pronouncement in *Waiting for Godot* is among the most memorable and stark of Beckett's visions of the simultaneity of birth and death: 'One day we were born, one day we shall die, the same day, the same second . . . . They give birth astride of a grave, the light gleams an instant, then it's night once more' (*WfG* 57b). Beckett was to rewrite Pozzo's poetic night-to-night trope, with its brief glimmer of light, in visual terms in subsequent dramas. Such is the case of *A Piece of Monologue* whose opening line, 'birth was the death of him', and punning 'born dead of night' (*CSPL* 265) continue to startle in their oxymoronic blurring of contraries that bond birth to death.

Prior to this dramatized monologue, the intermingling of birth (or of a birthday) and death, takes on numerous forms in Beckett's oeuvre, often quite unobtrusively. Hence, toward the end of *Krapp's Last Tape* (1958), on his sixty-ninth birthday, the protagonist listens for a second time to the end of what was to become his 'last tape', recording his 'farewell to . . . love' thirty years earlier (*CSPL* 57). In his recall of the 'farewell' scene, we hear the younger Krapp, in a rhythmically cadenced voice, tell of drifting in a punt, as he asks the woman he loves and is about to lose to let him look into her eyes. Unlike the earlier and later variations on this motif in Beckett's texts, what Krapp sees is at first left to the imagination of the audience. It is omitted on the tape. For Beckettians, familiar with the obsession with women's eyes in Beckett's writing, amply rehearsed throughout this play, it is not difficult to imagine an encore of Belacqua's 'better worlds than this' glimpsed in Lucy's eyes, minus the irony, or 'the wellhead' of *Words and Music*. We eventually learn what the sixty-nine-year-old Krapp recalls seeing in the eyes of the woman in the punt thirty years earlier. Recording his reaction to the tape made on his thirty-ninth birthday, Krapp begins with a disabused, 'Just been listening to that stupid bastard I took myself for thirty years ago', but he soon pauses to recall, 'The eyes she had!', and after a brooding silence, to muse, 'Everything there, everything on this old muckball, all the light and dark and famine and feasting of. . .[*hesitates*]. . .the ages' (62). This vision evokes moments of immersion in Beckett's works: Arsene's in the cosmos (*W* 42) and Molloy, losing his sense of self and 'the thread of the dream' in merging with Lousse's garden, the planet's cycles of seasons, and night breaking into dawn, abolishing the difference between self and nonself in their mingling (*Mo* 49). Such episodes recall the Schopenhauerian peaceful contemplation of natural sights that results in similar metaphysical selfless and will-less and timeless raptures as art and the asceticism of mystics (*WWR I* § 34, 200–1).

In Krapp's recall of the boat scene, Beckett fuses the erotic with the mystical while undercutting it by Krapp's swearing and scatological 'old muckball'. At the end, as Krapp listens to the boat scene again, the renunciation of Eros, the vision in the eyes, and the gentle womblike rocking on the water come together with Krapp's drifting, on his birthday, into the final silence, his last tape running on wordlessly. With this play, Beckett has furthermore fashioned an early instance of a character listening to ghostly recorded voices recounting the past, each later play intriguingly adapting the voices' stories to the medium involved in the performance.

In *Happy Days* (1961), one of his most frequently performed plays, Beckett projects onto the stage the startling image of fiftyish Winnie progressively sinking into a mound of scorched grass under a 'hellish sun' (*HD* 25). The play's staged mound has a topographical similarity to the circular sepulchral mounds, dating from pagan times, that are scattered throughout the Irish landscape. In a powerful projection of the Beckettian obsession with an enwombing tomb, only Winnie's head protrudes from the mound in the second act, a stage image suggesting a progressive descent into the tomb envisioned simultaneously as a return to the womb. See Figure 7.1. This ancient motif is interwoven in the play with intimations of a hellish existence that Winnie does her utmost to disguise by the ways she finds to pass the time. In her puzzling double consciousness, linear time is 'the old style' that has beginnings and endings and wears down mind, body, intimacy, and the environment, whereas she is simultaneously aware of existing in timelessness. It is one of many instances in Beckett's works staging the Buddha and the mystics' awareness of the simultaneous passage of time and an ultimate timelessness. Beckett further expressed such simultaneity of being in time and out of time in terms of spatial distance, telling Charles Juliet of the necessity of being here (and

Figure 7.1   Fiona Shaw in the National Theatre of Great Britain production of *Happy Days*, directed by Deborah Warner, Brooklyn Academy of Music, Brooklyn, NY, 2008.
Photo © Richard Termine

now) and, at the same time, at a remove of millions of light years (Juliet 1986, 48),[1] calling to mind Winnie's imprisonment in earthly finitude and simultaneous sensations of infinity, of 'float[ing] up into the blue' (*HD* 33).

A Piece of Monologue

In the late play *A Piece of Monologue*, composed in English in 1977–8, Beckett joins the aversion to the first person to the theme of the simultaneity of birth and death and intimations of an end to cycles of existence. In his allusions to rebirth, beginning with the early 'Echo's Bones', he was, as we know, in the company of other modernists who allude to this doctrine popularized in the West by Schopenhauer: W. B. Yeats, Proust, T. S. Eliot, and Borges, among others. Beckett's involvement with the rebirth

---

[1]   'Il faut être là – index pointé sur la table – et aussi – index levé vers le haut – à des millions d'années-lumière. En même temps...'

topos extends from the early 1930s to his last fiction of 1987, that is, over six decades. (More on rebirth below and in the next chapter.)

A Piece of Monologue features a diffusely lit room, in which a ghostly Speaker, white from head to toe, is doubled by a ghostly lamp of equal height, with the white foot of a pallet bed visible on the side. In the familiar counterpoint between stage and text, the Speaker's appearance converges with that of the protagonist in the story he is narrating, whereas the latter's imagined movements about a room are in contrast to the stillness of the Speaker on stage facing the invisible fourth wall. Recalling Beckett's other late theatrical texts, *A Piece of Monologue*'s two-part counterpoint – stage and story – introduces variations from one to the other as suggested by its musical parallel.

The ghostly double in the Speaker's account comes only at night to a dimly lit room to peer out of the window into the darkness and emptiness, to light and relight a lamp, and to stand facing a bare wall. Written at the request of the remarkable bilingual actor David Warrilow (1934–95), who had asked the author for a play in which a man is 'talking about death', the monologue repeatedly portrays a birth scenario reminiscent of Beckett's own birth at the family home Cooldrinagh and funerals recalling the Protestant graveyard at Graystones where his parents were buried (Knowlson 1996, 572–3). 'My birth was my death. Or put it another way. My birth was the death of me' are Speaker's opening lines in the first holograph draft of the play (qtd. in Krance 1993, xvii), which evolved in later drafts into 'Birth was the death of him'.

Given the resemblance of the ghostly Speaker to his protagonist, Speaker is recounting the doings of a ghostly doppelgänger while gazing at the absent fourth wall and beyond as he tells his tale. Intriguingly, the protagonist in the second half of the Speaker's story, 'Stands staring beyond half hearing what he's saying. He? The words falling from his mouth. Making do with his mouth', and this double of the Speaker is said to wait for always the same first word, 'birth', and, at the end, to wait for the 'rip word' – *requiescat in pace* – announcing his death (*CSPL* 268–9). The protagonist, and the Speaker by implication, then, are not the agents of their tales but once again spoken-through. No pronoun corresponds to this ventriloquized emptiness, and throughout the monologue pronouns are mostly avoided or questioned.

The ghostly room in which the protagonist is said to appear nightly is the room of his birth, in which an oil lamp with low-turned wick provided a faint light as night was falling. In his present nightly visits, when the lamp goes out, he relights it and turns the wick down low in a nightly ritual of reliving his birth. He repeatedly is said to be 'staring beyond', facing a wall in the east, and 'staring out' of a window facing west (266ff.), the opposite directions of birth and death. The bare wall he faces has been stripped of the family photographs reminiscent of similarly torn-up photographs in Beckett's *Film*. The bits, swept under the bed like so much dust, are a memento mori and a form of detachment and emptying out as death nears.

In the Speaker's story, birth is evoked by the relighting of the lamp and the protagonist repeatedly articulating the word 'birth'. As David Warrilow explained, the Speaker twice describes the physical actions involved in pronouncing the word 'birth'– 'Parts lips and thrusts tongue forward' – suggestive of the act of birth. Because the French word *naissance* does not lend itself to the same analogy between the articulated word and birth, Warrilow recounts, Beckett told him at the time that there may never be a French version of the monologue (Warrilow 1986, 253). In fact, the eventual French *Solo* leaves parts of the English monologue untranslated. Beckett's pleasure in the phonetic aspect of words, their feel in the mouth and effects on speakers and listeners, as evident in this play and Krapp's 'Spooool!' (*CSPL* 56), is a modernist celebration of the materiality and sensuality of language, eclipsing to some extent its ready meanings.

In the play, birth is insistently associated with night and the dying light of the lamp. In the narrated room, light and dark intermingle and give way to the faint light of the lamp, which is alternatively extinguished – 'Gone. Again and again. Again and again gone' (*CSPL* 268) – and relit, until it is 'gone' once and for all as the narrative ends and the onstage lamp goes out followed by silence. In this brief monologue of barely five print pages, the dying from birth on, pictured as a 'ghastly grinning ... up at the lid to come' (265), is doubled by the dying of the light of the lamp, which, in its repeated renewals suggests cycles of birth, death, and rebirth until the final 'gone'. The alternating scenes of birth and funerals along with the extinguished and relit lamp, either by the protagonist or by the hands he sees in his mind's eye on the first night of his birth, are variations on the merging of the contraries of life and death, with which the narrative opens and closes. At the end, the protagonist 'half hears' that there was, 'Never but the one matter. The dead and gone' (269), 'Gone' being the title of the play originally envisioned by Beckett (Cohn 2005, 355).

The signs of impending death, suggested by 'As if looking his last. At that first night' (268), make of the monologue's ghostly room the site of the first night and the last night. The evocation of 'ghosts beyond. Beyond that black beyond' (269) and the trope of *nirvāṇa*, the lamp extinguished and 'gone' once and for all, intimate that he may be heading beyond the repetitions of births and deaths. The pervasive light and dark imagery in this play brings to mind once again Beckett's words to Tom Driver, 'Where we have both dark and light we have also the inexplicable. The key word in my plays is "perhaps"' (qtd. in Driver 1979 [1961], 220).

The 'staring out' and 'staring beyond' sounded throughout the play demand further scrutiny. The 'staring out' scenes, repeated three times, occur at the western window looking out at 'that black vast'. 'Nothing stirring' is what the Speaker reports, after which the figure returns to the relighting of the lamp (*CSPL* 265ff.). During the second scene at the window, the Speaker explains that there is 'nothing stirring' that he can see or hear (267), suggesting, in the manner of Schopenhauer, that the 'nothing there' refers to the phenomenal world, but not denying a possible beyond. In both the second and third iterations at the window, the figure has difficulty tearing himself away from the black vastness, surmising that his will has stopped willing: 'staring out as if unable to move again. Or gone the will to move again' (268), thereby hinting at the Schopenhauerian negation of the will to life and the metaphysical beyond that follows it, which the author of *The World as Will and Representation*, as we know, likened to Buddhist *nirvāṇa*, about which, he repeats, nothing can be known.

In the five repetitions of 'staring beyond', facing the eastern wall, the Speaker reports first, 'Nothing stirring there either', and then, 'Nothing. Empty dark' (266, 267). The scenes of wall gazing are interrupted by the word 'birth' and the memories it evokes of first and last nights, of birth and funerals. In a variation on these scenes, in the fourth repetition, the figure at the eastern wall is said to shift focus from one dark to the further dark outside the western window and then back to the darkened room (268), merging the various darks into a 'beyond that black beyond' (269), suggesting the beyond birth and death timelessness of the Buddha and Schopenhauer.

Could the 'staring beyond' while facing the wall perhaps evoke Zen wall gazing? Even though a contested practice, it fits, in the view of Buddhist scholar Sam van Schaik, into the tradition of peaceful meditation involving an object to focus on (Schaik 2018, 118).[2] There can be no doubt that Beckett was aware of this type of meditation in portraying Murphy staring

---

[2] Schaik bases his discussion of Buddhist meditation practices on his translation from the Chinese of the early Ch'an/Zen manuscript *Masters of the Lanka*.

up at an 'iridescence splashed over the cornice moulding, shrinking and fading' while rocking himself into a trance (*Mu* 2), and in picturing Arsene sitting on a step gazing at the light on a wall during his mystic experience (*W* 42). And in *Endgame*, in answer to Hamm's question about what he sees on retreating to his kitchen to look at the wall, Clov responds, 'I see my light dying' (*End* 12), a line echoed by the wall gazing in *A Piece of Monologue*. But when Shainberg, who reported Beckett's 'I know nothing about Buddhism', told the author about his own practice of Zen wall gazing, Beckett retorted, 'you don't have to know about Zen to do that, I've been doing it for fifty years' (qtd. in Shainberg 1987, 112). Most likely, Beckett was aware of Leonardo da Vinci's famous wall gazing, if not for the purpose of peaceful meditation, in the interest of stimulating the imagination, and had discovered, by the time he composed *Murphy*, the calmness it can bring. However, in a note to Shainberg of 28 March 1981, Beckett tells of a different effect on him of this practice: 'When I start looking at walls I begin to see the writing. From which even my own is a relief' (*LSB IV* 546). This allusion to the writing on the wall appeared earlier in Hamm's question to Clov about what he sees on the wall, 'Mene, mene? Naked bodies?' (*End* 12), the 'mene, mene' ('numbered, numbered' in Aramaic), referring to the biblical story, in Daniel, chapter 5, that tells of a hand writing a cryptic warning of impending doom on a wall. If Beckett wanted to prove to Shainberg that his wall gazing leads to visions of world catastrophe instead of to peaceful meditation, the point was made. Yet, in the monologue he wrote for Warrilow a few years before the note to Shainberg, had he not rather implied both types of vision, the trauma of birth into death, on the one hand, and on the other, the 'nothing stirring', reminiscent of Malone's 'great calm' or the Buddhist 'stillness without name' that comes with sitting firmly without moving, gazing at a wall to attain peace of mind (Schaik 2018, 124–5)?

In the penultimate 'staring beyond' in *A Piece of Monologue*, Beckett once more draws on the veil trope, as the staring at the wall gives way to staring at a 'black veil', while the figure is said to listen to half-heard words, inviting visions of what may be beyond the veil (269). What remains in the room after the lamp is extinguished and the room falls silent is an 'unaccountable' and 'unutterably faint' dimness said to be from 'nowhere' (269). The preternatural light remaining, without a known source, which was to appear in subsequent works, suggests Inge's mystical 'dim consciousness of the *beyond*' (Inge 1899, 5; emphasis in the original) and Beckett's 'perhaps' about what both the Buddha and Schopenhauer, too, found to be an inexplicable beyond.

The repetitions of 'gone' and 'beyond' in the play chime uncannily with the final mantra of the Perfection of Wisdom Heart Sūtra, which, in the words of one of its translators, is 'Buddhism in a nutshell' (Red Pine 2004, 5). This mantra, in the Conze translation, reads, 'Gone, gone, gone beyond, gone altogether beyond. O what an awakening, all hail!' (Conze 2001 [1958], 113). The coincidence is such that one could almost imagine that Beckett was familiar with the mantra, although the haunting asso-nance of 'gone' and 'beyond' could in itself serve to explain the repetitions of the two words to suggest an unknowable existence beyond death. Conze glosses 'beyond' (*pāra* in Sanskrit), as 'a technical term [that] is opposed to a Not-Beyond', explaining the latter in terms of, '(1) suffering, (2) its basis, i.e., the rounds of births, (3) the place where suffering takes place, i.e., the skandhas [the five temporary and conditioned constituents of our (no-self) psychophysical personality], and (4) its cause, i.e., craving and other bad habits' (Conze 2001 [1958], 119). He explains 'awakening' (Sanskrit *bodhi*) as corresponding to 'enlightenment, wisdom, emptiness, and Nirvana' (119). That Beckett was aware of this sense of 'awakening' can be gleaned from his final message to Linda Ben-Zvi a year before his death: 'Hope we may meet again before the rude awakening' (4 November 1988, qtd. in Ben-Zvi 2017, 68). Death conceived of as an 'awakening', albeit a rude one, suggests both the Schopenhauerian and Buddhist awakening from the dream of existence into an unknowable beyond whose emptiness in the play is suggested by the 'nothing stirring'.[3]

In comparing the wall gazing in *Monologue* to Zen meditation, one has to take into account that in Beckett's play the figure, instead of sitting, 'stands staring beyond', a detail repeated more than once. Beckett's use of wall gazing in his earlier works makes it likely that he had its calming effects in mind, but whether he was alluding necessarily to Zen meditation on writing the play remains open to question. Yet, the crisscrossing of family resemblances is so striking between the figure's staring beyond while facing an empty wall and Zen wall gazing that it adds another strand of kinship with the Buddhist concepts that are wound into Beckett's texts, without denying the differences and the tentativeness that accompany it. And as such it helps elucidate another of Beckett's intricate texts.

If wall gazing is double-edged for Beckett, evoking calamitous as well as calming visions, the same doubleness is attributed to the void in *That Time*

---

[3] The 'nothing stirring' further resonates with the end of Eckhart's sermon, *DW* 48, poetically abridged in Inge, portraying the nothing and stillness of divinity in the ultimate ground, a vision close to the Buddha's *śūnyatā* minus the divine.

until merged into one. As we have seen, the play's memory voice B first attempts to ward off the void, imagined as a shroud pouring on top of him, until at the end, renouncing his efforts, he lets it in, with 'little or nothing the worse' (*CSPL* 234). If from the viewpoint of finitude, the void evokes death, from the metaphysical standpoint, it is more often than not, and increasingly so in the late work, a vision of 'home at last' (*Ill* 31). In testifying to the both terrifying and calming aspects of wall gazing and the void, Beckett is reprising his description of Malone's two states of mind and the promise of a 'great calm' beyond its turmoil.

Given the overall ghostliness of Speaker, stage set, and their equivalents in the Speaker's incantatory narrative, 'Ghost light. Ghost nights. Ghost rooms. Ghost graves' (269), the audience listens to an account of the birth and dying of a phantom delivered by a phantom, a variation on the Schopenhauerian 'dream of a shadow' (*PP II* § 139, 245), an amalgam of imagination and memory, as is the old woman of *Ill Seen Ill Said* written shortly thereafter. As suggested in Chapter 3, the ghostly figures are a poetic reprisal of the liminal state of the spectral Belacqua in the 'Echo's Bones' story of forty-five years earlier (minus the grotesquerie), as he too is said to be 'at last on the threshold of total extinction', the Buddhist *nirvāṇa* further evoked by the flame of a lantern's candle extinguished (*EB* 36, 51). Yet, what a remarkable distance between the style of the early 'Echo's Bones', concealing the Buddhist echoes behind a dense screen of parody, and this late play's abstract poetry, which although just as concealing, intimates a beyond where there is 'nothing stirring'.

Company

Banning the first-person pronoun as resolutely as *Not I*, *That Time*, and *A Piece of Monologue*, Beckett's late prose fiction *Company*, composed in English in 1978–9, a year after *Monologue*, stages another mental colloquy of three facets of the writer's mind – hearer, voice, and deviser – that are called together for company. Point of view is projected onto an unnamed narrator who recounts the scene, which he asks the readers to imagine. Beckett commentators have drawn attention to the piece as a piece of mental theatre parodying Cartesian doubt and contesting the *cogito*'s association of being with the first person whose authenticity is guaranteed by the existence of a perfect God. In addition to the Cartesian intertext, Beckett's fable has been compared to David Hume's description of the mind as 'a kind of theatre, where several perceptions successively make their appearance; pass, repass, glide away, and mingle in an infinite variety of postures and situations'. Just as apropos is Hume's conclusion that the undecidable questions of personal identity are grammatical rather than philosophical in nature, a view anticipated, as we have seen, by Nāgārjuna and anticipating Mauthner, pragmatics, and post-structuralism.[4] From a Buddhist perspective, as we know, the eclipse of the first person does not represent a loss but corresponds to the very nature of the ultimate reality of *śūnyatā* according to which the interdependent components of the mind do not add up to a self. *Company*, in its voiding of a self-creating author-creator from the space of writing, echoing the earlier parodic undermining of divine inspiration, and in foregoing linguistic reference to an 'I', dramatizes once again the empty theatre of the self.[5]

A critique of Cartesianism is only one of several obsessive themes in Beckett's writing that are recapitulated in *Company*, as if at this late stage of his career, the author was intent on a life review of his own, comprising both his writings and his life. *Company* is the first piece of what is considered Beckett's late prose trilogy, composed between 1978 and 1982, followed by *Ill Seen Ill Said*, and *Worstward Ho*. In condensed form, the three can be characterized as recapitulating the previous works' *kenōsis*: the first, of the 'I'; the second, of the 'eye'; and the third, as we have seen, of words themselves.[6]

Although at the end of *Company*, the voice bids farewell to Dante's Belacqua who has haunted the author for half a century, the namesake in *Dream* of the slothful inhabitant of Antepurgatory is evoked by *Company*'s figure in a tomblike and womblike space. Recalling the ideal refuge of Beckett's first novel, this space in *Company*, however, abounds in allusions to suffering and decreation. In lieu of a haven of quietude, it is a mournful place, in which, rather than 'achieving creation', the hearer is shown once more to 'labour in vain at [his] fable' (*Co* 62).

The hearer, 'one on his back in the dark' (7), is the first 'figment' on *Company*'s inner stage, recalling the before-birth as much as the posthumous specters of *Dream*'s space of writing in the mind.[7] At the same time, the first figure's position is reminiscent of the coveted 'supineness in the

---

[4] On the Cartesian intertext of *Company*, see Beplate 2005 and Roesler 2012. Hume's *A Treatise of Human Nature* (1739–40) is cited in Beplate 2005, 153–4.

[5] Paul Shields has perceptively plumbed the allusions to Genesis in *Company* countered by Beckett's textual decreation (Shields 2001, 478–85).

[6] On the Beckett exegetes who have written about the auto-allusions to Beckett's own works and about other literary allusions in *Company*, see Cohn 2005, 350–1.

[7] For H. Porter Abbott, the text's figments are similarly 'bound within the original womb in which the text in effect delivers itself' (Abbott 1996, 11). Andy Wimbush, on the other hand, argues for an afterlife without denying Abbott's womb interpretation (Wimbush 2020, 238).

mind' of 'First Love', but of a more troubling cast, as the supine hearer, both silent and unnamed, is imagined ghostly in his 'bonewhite' nakedness, with 'hands invisibly manacled' as if a victim of punishment or martyrdom (*Co* 57). The figment recalls the ghostly white bare body of *Bing / Ping* (French, 1966; English, 1967) enclosed in a white box which, to Ruby Cohn, suggests an upright coffin (2005, 300), whose wounded state is evoked in such phrases as, 'White scars invisible same white as flesh torn of old given rose only just' (*CSP* 195). For David Lodge, this figure may be 'Beckett's version of "The Man Who Died"' or 'Christ in the tomb' (Lodge 1979 [1968], 298). This, then, is a more fearful ghostliness than the shades in Belacqua's psychic retreat and wellspring of creativity in *Dream*.

The wounded state of *Company*'s supine figure and his before-birth and after-death postures further recall *Watt*'s simultaneous unborn state, as intimated by the addenda's 'never been properly born' (*W* 248) and his iconic likeness to the 'Man of Sorrows', here in an entombed state. In this late piece, the entombed Christ is repeatedly called on to depict the abandonment and dispossession in which Beckett's creatures find themselves with only a distant 'perhaps' of salvation. Envisioned in terms of an unknowable beyond, it is left unsaid in *Company* but not in the contemporaneous *A Piece of Monologue* and *Ill Seen Ill Said* nor in Beckett's final prose piece *Stirrings Still*.

Positions of body receive repeated attention in *Company*, the hearer's shifting between supineness and the Dantean Belacqua's 'embryonal repose', as it is called in *Murphy* (*Mu* 78), of legs clasped in his arms and head bent, until the hearer permanently adopts the supine position (*Co* 62). *Company*'s hearer, progressively abandoning the embryonal for the postmortem pose, inhabits *Dream*'s generative-turned-degenerative space in the mind in which the before-birth and after-death states shade into each other. But, unlike Dante's Belacqua, amusingly imagined perhaps singing among the blessed as he is bid farewell at the end of *Company*, the hearer, joining Beckett's other failed fabulists, is doomed to labor in vain in a purgatorial space that belies the pleasure and generativity of the retreat of the Dantean Belacqua's namesake in *Dream*.

Company features startling instances of what H. Porter Abbott terms 'autography', which, you will recall, he defines as 'a mode of action taken in the moment of writing', as contrasted with an autobiographical life review (Abbott 1996, x). In *Company*, the supine hearer listens to a voice that, using the second person, narrates a number of scenes from the past, while constructing them in the present, as memories are known to be, and all seemingly situated in or around the author's birthplace. These vignettes evoke Beckett's birth, childhood, and early adulthood, interspersed with a meditation on the 'woes of [his] kind' (*Co* 57) and alternating with imagined treks of the hearer as an old man walking the back roads and nearby pastures with or without his father's shade for company. Echoing *That Time*'s life reviews, the memories, recounted in the second person, suggest that the supine hearer lacks control over them; they are assembled by the proxy voice that dictates to the spoken-through figures of Beckett's fictions and dramas. Like them, the hearer would prefer silence (*Co* 10).

The hearer and voice are joined by the 'deviser' or 'creator' who supposedly invents the hearer, voice, and himself, using the narrative third person for all. Reminiscent of *Not I* and *A Piece of Monologue*, he 'speaks of himself as of another' (*Co* 26). This figure, however, is lampooned as a crawling and falling figment unable to create. He is chased off the stage as if to be done with the trope of pseudo-creator, from Knott to the 'not one of us' of *How It Is*, all so many projections of the controlling parts of the mind and ultimately illusory. Finally, the figments of *Company*'s ghostly trinity seemingly add up to one, as so frequently in Beckett. Shortly before beginning *Company*, Beckett outlined a similar situation in his 'Sottisier' notebook: imagining a speech by A that B overhears and recounts to C, he concludes that all three are one and the same.

In *Company*, the aporetic embedding found in the trilogy once again complicates this sameness, as the deviser, one in an infinite regress of devisers, who invents himself and the hearer and his voice, is finally said to be devised by the hearer 'alone', the last word of the piece. This claim, however, is contradicted in that the hearer gets word of this state from the voice. As in *How It Is*, the voice has the last word, and the reader is left with the usual paradoxical situation, which with its aporia and coincidence of affirmation and negation, corresponds to a theatre emptied of self.

The Rebirth Topos in Beckett's Postwar and Later Fiction and Theatre

Having staged Belacqua Shuah's rebirth and escape from *saṃsāric* existence in the parodic mode of 'Echo's Bones', Beckett returns to the rebirth topos beginning with the postwar fiction of the 1940s and ending with the shorter prose fictions and plays of his last decade. In the trilogy, he not only projects his own authorship of earlier novels onto his successive narrator-protagonists, but he ascribes to them partial inklings of previous existences as one of his earlier creatures. Unlike the Belacqua of 'Echo's

Bones' or the narrator of the novellas, their reminiscences, however, are not of former lives of their own, as in Dante's afterworld or in dream noh; rather, they recall their previous incarnations as Beckett characters. Consequently, in the beginning pages of *Malone Dies*, to take this novel as an example of the rebirth motif, the eponymous narrator, tells of one night, while studying the stars, suddenly and vaguely remembering himself in London (*Ma* 184). It is left to the reader to understand Malone's former incarnations as Murphy and then as Molloy, the latter suggested by a number of clues that exegetes have easily caught (*Ma* 182–3, 258). There are other intimations of transmigration in the novel. Malone at one point speaks of the impression of having died without knowing it and gone to hell or rather of having 'been born again into an even worse place than before' (*Ma* 227). Or he wonders whether the line of M and W characters of previous novels will end with his demise or whether it will stretch on beyond the grave (*Ma* 236), a question, as we know, left in suspense at the end of the novel. In *Malone Dies*, then, Beckett is drawing on the rebirth topos to figuratively suggest that his post-Belacqua creatures are reincarnations of previous fictional characters issued from the limbic space of writing. The author's creatures are born again one after the other into a hellish existence resembling the purgatorial hells of the Eastern wheel of becoming.

Although exegetes have taken note of the birth into death theme in Beckett's theatre and fiction, they have less frequently remarked on its prolongation into cycles of rebirth or the tentative suggestions, in some instances, of an end to cycles of existence. Some notable exceptions include the readings of *How It Is*, discussed later in this section, by Richard Coe early on, followed by Andy Wimbush's attention to rebirth in this and other postwar and late fictions; Paul Davies's discussion of *Stirrings Still*, to be examined in Chapter 8; and brief comments by two of Beckett's close associates, Martin Esslin, the producer and director of Beckett's radio plays commissioned for BBC Radio Drama in the 1960s and 1970s, and Beckett's British publisher John Calder. In a meditation on timelessness in Beckett, Esslin draws attention to Nietzsche's eternal return and the wheel of becoming from which, he maintains, Beckett sought release in the tradition of Indian philosophy, Buddhism, and Christian mysticism (Esslin 1986, 114, 121–3). John Calder, on the other hand, surmised that the three heads protruding from urns in the 1963 one-act *Play* are possibly waiting for reincarnation (Calder 2001, 35).[8]

---

[8] Similarly, in my reading of *Play*, the three atoning shades in their womblike funereal urns, reminiscent of Egyptian canopic jars, are entrapped in cycles of transmigration. The allusions in

Figure 7.2　*Act without Words II*, directed by Peter Brook, The Young Vic, London, 2007.
Photo © Donald Cooper/Photostage

There are other short plays, however, whose portrayal of the rebirth cycle, has to my knowledge not been noticed. Preceding *Play*, Beckett's mime *Acte sans paroles II / Act without Words II* (*CSPL* 49–51), dating from 1959, stages the brief span of time between birth and death and their repetition in seemingly endless rounds of rebirths and redeaths. In this mime to be performed on an intensely lit platform surrounded by stage darkness, two sacks containing the characters A and B are placed close to the right wing. A goad, reminiscent of the Schopenhauerian will, 'strictly horizontal' (*CSPL* 49) prods the two characters enveloped in their sacks to crawl out of their womblike containers, one after the other, and after a few minutes of activity to reenter the same sacks. See Figure 7.2. Character A has to be prodded twice before he reluctantly relinquishes his sack to perform his activities broodingly and without zest, except for the pills

this drama, however, appear to be to the Egyptian *Book of the Dead* – a book of particular interest to modernist writers – rather than to Schopenhauerian or Indian accounts of rebirth (Moorjani 2008, 127–30). In *Dream*, Beckett alerts us to the interest in the Egyptian underworld in literary circles in the first part of the twentieth century by having the Alba, one of Belacqua's three loves, ask the character modeled on Beckett's Trinity College Professor Thomas Rudmose-Brown to tell her about the *Egyptian Book of the Dead* (*Dream* 164).

(tranquilizers?) he swallows, before crawling back into his sack. He, it is implied, would rather not have emerged. B, on the other hand, needs only one thrust of the goad to begin a vigorous program of exercise and grooming. Obsessed with self, time, and space, he inspects himself in a mirror and repeatedly consults his watch, a map, and a compass before reentering his sack. Two ways of living – on the one hand the contemplative and will-tranquilizing (in the Schopenhauerian sense) and, on the other, the active and will-consenting – result in the same brief interlude between womb and tomb. But the mime does not conclude at this point. The goad proceeds once more to prod A's sack, twice over, situated by then on the opposite side of the stage, to which the sacks have been carried. The re-emergence of A suggests another round in the turn of the wheel of birth and death and rebirth.

In the playlet *Breath* of 1969 (*CSPL* 211), Beckett shortened the brief span of time from birth to death to rebirth to a few seconds: a cry is heard in faint light on a rubbish-strewn stage, followed by an intake of breath as the light comes up, then an expiration of breath as the light dies down, followed by another birth cry as before, the drama of birth, life, death, followed by rebirth, captured in less than a minute, although Beckett termed it a 'farce in five acts' (qtd. in Cohn 2005, 298).

These short plays, in addition to *A Piece of Monologue* and the rebirth trope in the postwar trilogy and later fictions (to be examined subsequently), underscore Beckett's allusions to the rebirth topos and the wheel of karma first introduced in 'Echo's Bones'.

How It Is

In Beckett's *How It Is*, the narrator's imposed recall of a former existence 'above in the light before I fell' (*How* 109) led to comparisons with the damned in Dante's *Inferno* and Milton's fallen Satan in *Paradise Lost*. Several exegetes have associated the work's chain of tormentors and tormented in the mud with the damned in the swamp of canto 7 of the *Inferno*, whose punishment for their sullenness and wrath consists in endless mutual aggression.[9] For Richard Coe, however, the crawling chain of tormentors and victims suggests karma and, 'the "wheel" of birth, death and reincarnation from which there is no escape save through Nirvana'

---

[9] See Abbott 1996, 98–9, for a summary of the Dantean and Miltonean echoes adduced by early critics of *How It Is*. Later critics have followed their lead.

(Coe 1970 [1964], 26), a view seconded half a century later by Andy Wimbush who identifies passages throughout the novel that suggest a process of life, death, and rebirth (Wimbush 2013, 129).

The rebirth theme in *How It Is* suggests a further infernal afterlife to blend with Dante and Milton's Christian hells. One of the six realms of karmic rebirth, or six realms of existence that Buddhism shares with Hinduism, is, as noted, a purgatorial hell, an abode of the damned, leading to a return to the cycles of transmigration. In an astonishingly close parallel to Dante's canto 7, the most gruesome of the six realms of existence punishes the damned for their anger in their former lives with unceasing torture. But would Beckett have been aware of the six karmic realms as he was of Dante and Milton's afterworlds? He would most certainly have read about them in the already mentioned *Maya: Der indische Mythos* by Heinrich Zimmer. The three sheets of notes Beckett took at Joyce's request, listing seventy-seven keywords from throughout the thick volume, give evidence of the thorough reading Beckett gave Zimmer's book. Zimmer's presentation of the transmigration into multiple existences, one among several overlaps between Hindu and Buddhist concepts Zimmer discusses, is likely to have brought Dante to Beckett's mind, Zimmer, moreover, referring several times to the author of the *Divine Comedy*. On the topic of rebirth, Zimmer recounts a conversation in his first chapter, in which Kamadamana, the son of a mythic king, tells his father of the thousands of births he has lived through, detailing his incarnations into plants, worms, wild animals, women and men, demons, benevolent and evil ghosts, and gods (Zimmer 1936, 38). 'Vyasa's story of Kamadamana' is duly noted in Beckett's list for Joyce.[10] These births correspond roughly to the six realms of karmic existence, the punishing ones of hells, hungry ghosts, and animals, and the rewarding realms of humans, demigods, and gods. None are permanent, and, for Buddhists, only enlightenment permits escaping these karmic paths of *saṃsāra*.

The parallels between the Buddhist purgatorial hell as described in *sūtras* and figured on pagodas and temples in Southeast Asia, on the one hand, and Christian hell as envisioned in Christian apocryphal texts and medieval figurations, on the other, prompted French archeologist Paul Gendronneau to postulate a Buddhist influence on the representations of Christian hell (Gendronneau 1922, 6–8, 32–6). There is in particular an astonishing family resemblance between the circles of Dante's Inferno and the subdivisions of Buddhist hell that are assigned to the punishments for

---

[10] In Beckett's list, reprinted in Connolly 1955, 45–7, Kamadamana appears on page 46.

particular categories of evil deeds, with penalties corresponding to the crimes committed.

To find Western and Eastern visions of diabolical torments informing Beckett's imaginative fiction is encouraged by Beckett's text and the references to Eastern thought and rebirth. Beckett's Schopenhauerian trope of human existence as hell merges Dante's *Inferno* and *Purgatorio* with Eastern views of the karma of a purgatorial hell. The unending chain of tormentors and tormented in *How It Is*, however, could alternatively be a fable of the narrator's self-inflicted sufferings, claiming as the narrator does at one point that it was not before, with, and after Pim, but before, with, and after himself that his story is about (*How* 105).

There is, in fact, a possible explanation for the alternating views of mutually and self-inflicted torments. Just as some Western writers, Dostoevsky and Beckett, for instance, assimilate the three parts of their characters' minds to heaven, purgatory, and hell, Buddhologist Ken Holmes, among others, maintains that the karmic wheel of becoming can be taken to be an allegory of states of mind and of the interactions with the outside world that follow from them (Holmes n.d.). This psychological interpretation, connecting the six karmic realms with states of mind, is found in traditional Buddhist texts, but to designate the realms as primarily or exclusively psychological is uniquely modern, an effect of the modern demythologization of religion (McMahan 2008, 46). It is also a matter of philosophical versus popular Buddhism. Accordingly, Professor of Religious Studies David L. McMahan draws attention to popular rituals pertaining to the wheel of becoming that are still being practiced, as if its six domains were a factual description of the cycles of rebirth (49). In addition, popular imagery of deities and demons connected to the karmic realms – especially in Southeast and East Asia – and practices of *bhakti* – the veneration and devotion accorded relics and iconic images of the Buddha and *bodhisattvas* – are part of popular Buddhist practice. These have their parallels in Christian imagery of heaven and hell, in icons of divine figures and saints, as well as in the popular reverence for relics in some Christian denominations. In fact, popular religious practices in many cultures vouch for the need for emotional contact with the sacred in iconic form and the commemoration of the dead by venerating relics and seeking their protection (Moorjani 2000, 45).

The hellish visions of *How It Is*, then, are an imaginative rendition of the punishing Christian afterworlds of Dante and Milton and of Eastern purgatorial hells in a visionary indictment of the human existence that Beckett found in Schopenhauer's 'Suffering of the World' chapter in 1930.

He copied it into his 'Sottisier' notebook four decades later: 'The world is simply *hell* and human beings are on the one hand its tortured souls and on the other its devils' (*PP II* § 156, 270; emphasis in the original).[11] In having the narrator of *How It Is* declare his story an illusion, as he has quoted it, leaving only himself in the mud, with his murmuring voice, in the same posture as the character at the end of *Cascando* awaiting death, Beckett has left the question of atonement in another cycle of rebirth or the attainment of peace suspended, as he will again in the play for radio composed at the same time.

Into the hellishness of *How It Is*, Beckett has slipped a lyrical tribute to the narrator's sack, turning it into another of his inventive psycho-objects, this one reminiscent of the earlier *Act without Words II*. Throughout the novel, the sack that accompanies the narrator as he crawls through the mud is the focus of his unflinching attention. It nourishes and comforts him, in imagination it enshrouds him, as well as containing the can opener that serves both life-preserving and deadly functions. Calling the sack 'this life first sign very first of life' and his 'sole good', he clutches the sack while in a fetal position, tying it around his neck with a cord so that it is bound to evoke the amniotic sac and umbilical cord, which together with the shroud image unites the two into the paradoxical oneness of the before-life and after-life (*How* 8, 10, 11).

The sack of *How It Is* corresponds to what French psychoanalyst Didier Anzieu has theorized as a fantasized skin that alternatively repeats and heals the tearing away from uterine shelter (Anzieu 1985). The gruesome training imagined in *How It Is*, inflicting a name, a language, a cultural script, and religious belief on the victim, consists of attacks on the skin – the tormentor, among other ferocities, incising the victim's skin with his finger nails, pounding him on the head, and, in repeated acts of anal sadism, stabbing his buttocks with his can opener until bloody. Congruent with Schopenhauer's 'the world is simply *hell*' and Eastern and Western diabolical apparitions – how not to think of Hieronymus Bosch's infernal nightmares paralleled by Buddhist depictions of purgatorial punishments? – the hellish tortures of *How It Is* dramatize the punishment of being born 'back into the muck' (*EB* 3), depriving the narrator of 'hearing nothing saying nothing capable of nothing nothing', of the unborn state (*How* 61). The sack, too, just another simulacrum, is finally said not to exist.

---

[11] Adding to the occluded allusions to the political use of torture in Beckett's texts, Emilie Morin discusses covert allusions in *Comment c'est*, and particularly in its earlier drafts, to the Algerian War and the French use of colonial warfare and torture (2017, 232–5).

Ill Seen Ill Said

In *Ill Seen Ill Said* (first written in French as *Mal vu mal dit* between late 1979 and 1981), more than hearing and saying nothing, it is a matter of seeing nothing. In this late prose fiction we are, as in Beckett's earlier *Film*, anchored to the eye of an observer observing an observer observing. Beckett's filmic imagination in this late prose piece adds to the impression that he is recapitulating his career-long fascination with filmic techniques and the impulse to escape the scopic drive: unseeing as much as unsaying annuls illusion in the interest of emptiness.[12]

The gluttonous eye of the observer-narrator of *Ill Seen Ill Said* recalls the 'voracious' camera eye of *Film* pursuing his other self, intent on escaping visibility, the seeing as much as the being seen, tied as they are both to being by Berkeley.[13] Beckett referred to the camera eye as 'ferociously voracious' in a 1964 preproduction discussion about *Film*, during which he explained that he was looking for cinematic means to stage visual appetite and visual disgust.[14] He was to use the same trope collapsing seeing and eating throughout *Ill Seen Ill Said*. And Beckett's description of the film project as 'extremely unreal' and 'completely unrealistic' reverberates with *Ill Seen Ill Said*'s indictment of 'that old tandem' of the real and its 'counter-poison', both, moreover, equally lying (*Ill* 40).

The old woman in mourning the narrator is observing off and on in 'the madhouse of the skull' (*Ill* 20) is both a ghostly and mythic figment of his imagination and a living figure in his memory as he follows her treks back and forth from room to tomb. In another instance of the association of stone with death, the woman, who is depicted moving from her stone-encircled cabin to a granite tombstone, herself repeatedly takes on the appearance of a stone statue. For Laura Salisbury, the woman's frozen demeanor accompanied by tremors evokes the Parkinson's disease of which Beckett's mother died (Salisbury 2001, 376).

Unlike the pursuing earlier camera eye, *Ill Seen Ill Said*'s observer increasingly shares the distaste for visibility that Beckett attributed to

---

[12] Experimental filmmaker Peter Gidal writes perceptively of blindness as an image of silence and emptiness, including in Beckett's texts (Gidal 2001 [1973], 311–12).

[13] In the original project for *Film*, Beckett cites Berkeley's phrase *Esse est percipi* (to be is to be perceived) and explains that he divided the protagonist into a pursuing eye and a fleeing object (*Film* 11). As noted in Chapter 1, because of his philosophical idealism, Schopenhauer refers to Berkeley (1685–1753) as one of his predecessors (*WWR I* § 1, 24).

[14] The 1964 preproduction discussion of *Film* with Alan Schneider, Boris Kaufman, and Barney Rosset is transcribed in Gontarski 1985, 187–92. Beckett's words cited in this paragraph are found on pages 190–2.

Film's fleeing protagonist. At the midpoint of his narrative, the narrator calls for a fade-out of the figment haunting him along with all else: 'Let her vanish. And the rest. For good'. To this wish he adds the hope that nothing will remain but the void: 'Void. Nothing else. Contemplate that. Not another word. Home at last' (*Ill* 31). The 'home at last' is an intriguing rendering of the French 'rendu enfin' ('arrived at last' or 'there at last'; *Mal* 38). Important to notice here is that the longed for 'void', identified with 'home' – termed 'unspeakable home' in his short poetic piece 'neither' composed a few years earlier – is not the same as 'nothing'. Rather, the narrator intimates an ultimate unbornness to which one returns (home) from one's illusory earthly existence: 'If only all could be pure figment. Neither be nor been nor by any shift to be' (*Ill* 20). As the observer-narrator progressively sees less, words too lessen, so that as is happening with the ghostly chair he is observing: 'It will end by being no more. By never having been. Divine prospect' (52).

As the narrator imagines the woman's eyes soon to be 'two black blanks' in death, leaving nothing to be seen (*Ill* 58), he envisages his gluttonous eye's own farewell, in an echo of Schopenhauer, by making the world disappear. In the synechdochal guise of the voracious eye, the frequent stand-in for the writer (as is Mouth), he grants himself enough final moments to 'devour all. Moment by glutton moment. Sky earth the whole kit and boodle', followed by one last moment 'to breathe that void. Know happiness' (59). The figure is to keep enough breath to witness the void and contemplate the 'home at last' envisioned at the midpoint of the narrative.[15]

What this happiness may consist of, besides witnessing the voiding of the empirical world, is announced in the paragraph preceding the final farewell, in which the hope to be free of earthly traces and of the attachment to illusion resonates with Mahāyāna thought (and Schopenhauer's presentation of it): 'Absence supreme good and yet. Illumination then go again and on return no more trace. ... Of what was never. And if by mishap some left then go again. For good again. So on. Till no more trace. On earth's face' (*Ill* 58).[16] More clearly, in the French text, each 'going' is hoped to be final, but if a trace remains, another round

---

[15] The synechdochal 'voracious eye' in this late fiction recalls Beckett's associating the gluttonous eye to birds of prey throughout his oeuvre. In the early 'The Vulture', it is compared to the poet's art; in the first of the *Texts for Nothing*, it appears in the narrator's image of the 'eye ravening patient in the haggard vulture's face' (*CSP* 102), whereas the expression 'eagle the eye' occurs in the fizzle 'For to End Yet Again' (*CSP* 245). My thanks to Paul Lawley for pointing out these linkages.

[16] 'Traces' was the piece's title in composition; the title was changed to *Mal vu mal dit* only at the time of galley proofs (Cohn 2005, 363).

of life and death results until complete detachment from the illusory world is attained. The French term *illusion* (*Mal* 74, 75), which Beckett translates as 'what was never', points more directly to Mahāyāna's view of the illusory nature of the world and the end of *saṃsāric* cycles of rebirths to be attained by detachment and the purification of karmic traces. In the final paragraph of Beckett's late fiction, the anticipated 'happiness' would then suggest the coming 'home' to the 'void', or *śūnyatā*, the liberation from *saṃsāra*. Still, the narrator's 'and yet' in 'Absence supreme good and yet' is not to be ignored. It leaves room for doubt.

Variations on the Unborn

Ill Seen Ill Said's 'neither be nor been nor by any shift to be' (20) is a description of what the Buddha and Schopenhauer termed the *unborn*. This timeless reality is to be distinguished from other guises of being unborn, such as are intermittently imagined by the narrating voices of Beckett's postwar trilogy, who are contained, as they repeat, in a head, a belly, or a womb, or 'nowhere in particular' (*Ma* 221; *Un* 352). As if lingering between two rebirths, they are uncertain whether they are dead or alive and imagine themselves as embryos heading for birth against their will or, alternatively, they portray themselves as spectral beings to be reborn into a worse place than before (*Ma* 227). This resistance to the cycle of births and rebirths leads to intimation of being 'nowhere', slipped in after the containing locations above in *The Unnamable*, and by Malone's claim, 'I shall never get born and therefore never get dead' (*Ma* 225), a possibility whose consonance with the Buddhist *unborn* is explored below to help elucidate the theme of unbornness in Beckett's texts.

If, in these fictions, the specters in the enwombed and entombed space of writing are unable to be born and unable to die, it's all the same to the narrator of *The Unnamable*: 'Mahood I couldn't die. Worm will I ever get born? It's the same problem' (*Un* 352). Ultimately, it all comes down to a dream or 'all lies' (363, 411). It is then all a phantasmagoria, a game of illusion, of the narrator's invention or rather the invention of the 'voluble shades' ('ces fantômes parlants' in the original French; *Un* 374; *In* 179) who say 'always the same wrong thing said always wrong' (*Un* 374). Ultimately, he is not to be found in the same space as his prompters and proxies, who try to saddle him with a belief in a world of their devising. 'I was elsewhere', Malone too insists (*Ma* 268). It is a matter of two worlds akin to Nāgārjuna, Plato, and Schopenhauer. But how are we to conceive of this insistent 'elsewhere'?

The 'unborn', is a theme that surfaces in *The Unnamable*, as embryo-like, the narrator-character feels he is without a mouth and an ear, while insisting that the 'voluble shades', which beset him with their words and stories, are intent on bringing him to birth. Addressing himself in a dream to imaginary 'living bastards', he reassures them with the promise, 'you'll see, you'll never be born again, what am I saying, you'll never have been born' (*Un* 379). The future perfect is the closest available tense for the promise of not having been born precluding birth, death, and rebirth. The mention of 'pidgin bullskrit' (378) in the text preceding the narrator's promise of an end to rebirth, or rather the promise of an escape from birth itself, suggests that Beckett associates the concept of the *unborn* with Eastern thought as did Schopenhauer. The deriding of Sanskrit as 'pidgin bullskrit' for comic effect would then be another instance of the hints Beckett scatters in his writing to screen important themes. In translating from the French, Beckett would appear to strengthen the Indian reference by translating 'du petit nègre' (*In* 187), a devalued form of pidgin, into 'pidgin bullskrit'. A similar vision of the *unborn* and emptiness appears in the tenth of the *Texts for Nothing*: 'No, no souls, or bodies, or birth, or life, or death, you've got to go on without any of that junk, that's all dead with words' (*CSP* 142).

The Buddha's view of the *unborn* is cited in the Udāna (6; 7.1–3), a collection of *suttas* of the Buddhist Pāli Canon, the oldest Buddhist scriptures of the Theravāda tradition: 'There is, O monks, an unborn, an unbecome, an unmade, an unconditioned: if, O monks, there were not here this unborn . . . , there would not here be an escape from the born, the become, the made, the conditioned' (qtd. in Loy 1996, 23). Later Mahāyāna *sūtras*, such as the Tathāgatagarbha Sūtra of circa 200 CE, describe this *unborn* as 'pure, eternal, immanent in all beings and only accidentally defiled by adventitious passions' (qtd. in Conze 1968, 27). To discover this unconditioned reality within one's own mind, Conze explains, became the purpose of meditation (28). Pointing out that the terms commonly used to describe *śūnyatā* are the same as for the *unborn*, David Loy contends that, as stated in the Buddha's words, the *unborn* refers to a state prior to the duality of life and death and all dualisms that Mahāyāna considers mistaken views or an illusion (Loy 1996, 22, 23). As mentioned earlier, the Sanskrit word *tathāgatagarbha* for the *unborn*, literally 'the womb' or 'the embryo' or 'the inner sanctum' of the Buddha, refers to an immanent space that enables sharing in the enlightened 'Buddha-nature' even in one's lifetime and eventually attaining enlightenment (Williams and Tribe 2000, 160–6; P. Williams 2009, 116).

To what extent can the claim be justified that the topos of the unborn, nonduality, and the aesthetics of emptiness, circling through Beckett's first novel to his last works, are consonant with the Buddhist *unborn*? *Dream*'s interval between terms becomes, as previously noted, the emptiness between words in *The Unnamable*, which would be 'a blessed place to be, where you are'. The emptiness of this place is evoked in a string of negatives of being without speech, thought, feeling, hearing, knowing, and saying (*Un* 374). The emptiness so defined is strikingly similar to the description of *śūnyatā* in the Heart Sūtra: 'In emptiness there is no form, nor feeling, nor perception, nor impulse, nor consciousness; no eye, ear, nose, tongue, body, mind; no forms, sounds, smells, tastes, touchables or objects of mind', that is, the conditioning five *skandhas* are nonapplicable. The Heart Sūtra continues with a list of contraries in what Conze terms its 'dialectics of emptiness': 'there is no decay and death, no extinction of decay and death; there is no suffering, no origination, no stopping, no path; there is no cognition, no attainment, and no non-attainment' (qtd. in Conze 1959b, 163).

The relation of emptiness to the *unborn* is further theorized in the Mind or One Mind teaching of Sino-Japanese Buddhism. Paul Williams ascribes this teaching to the *Dasheng qixinlun* or *Awakening of Faith in the Mahāyāna*, a treatise dating from the sixth century CE, which is thought to be possibly the work of Paramārtha, an Indian Buddhist missionary to China and translator of Buddhist texts into Chinese. In the *Awakening of Faith* tradition, Williams writes: 'The essential nature of the Mind is unborn, imperishable, beyond language. Differentiation (i.e. phenomena) arises through illusion, fundamental ignorance of one's true nature', which is emptiness (P. Williams 2009, 116). Accordingly, the Mind, as conceived in this tradition, has two aspects: an essential nature, also defined in terms of 'Suchness or Thusness, that is the Absolute Reality itself' and the Mind as phenomena (116).

The narrators of the postwar trilogy struggling with their imprisoned condition of death in life or life in death and cruel tales of a hellish existence repeatedly evoke an emptiness and peace that resonate with the *unborn*. Malone's view of the two parts of his mind, as previously cited – a hellish/purgatorial part, on the one hand, and an asylum of quietude, on the other – corresponds to the view of the Mind in *The Awakening of Faith*. In Williams's presentation, the originally enlightened Mind is free from thoughts and analogous to empty space or a mirror in which the world appears only as a reflection, whereas the nonenlightened and delusory part of the Mind is identified with mental turmoil. Only when freed of thoughts is the Mind returned to its original state of stillness (P. Williams 2009, 117). Not surprisingly, in the spirit of Buddhist denial of the duality of opposites, Fazang, the Buddhist thinker and scriptural commentator active in China in the seventh century, holds that the two aspects of Mind are not different in essence, as they include each other (P. Williams 2009, 116). In their consonance, Malone's two states and those of the Mind envisioned in *The Awakening of Faith* tradition, despite cultural differences and views on an eventual enlightenment, help us to understand the topos of unbornness in Beckett's oeuvre.

Not only Malone's 'great calm' as against the turmoil in his head, but a poem Beckett wrote two years before his death on completion of his final prose fiction *Stirrings Still* resonates with the theme of the return to an original stillness in Sino-Japanese Buddhism. In the concluding part of this prose fiction, the narrator envisions the possibility of his doppelgänger already being 'where never till then' (*CSP* 264), a vision taken up in the later poem beginning with, 'go where never before / no sooner there than there always' (*CP* 223). At the same time, as mentioned in Chapter 2, this late poem evokes Schopenhauer's stand that if we consider life to be a dream and death an awakening, then death is not a transition to a completely new and foreign state but 'a retreat to one that is originally ours' (*PP II* § 139, 246). This return to where one has always been corresponds to his view of our immanent timelessness (245) and thinking of ourselves as '*unborn*' (*WWR II* ch. 41, 504).

Schopenhauer and Beckett's concept of the unborn concurs further in intriguing ways with the numerous sermons of the seventeenth-century Japanese Rinzai Zen Master Bankei Yōtaku, in which he used the ordinary language of his large lay audiences to address them. For Bankei, if the *unborn* (Japanese *fushō*) is the ultimate reality beyond the cycles of birth and death of *saṃsāra*, it differs from *nirvāṇa* in being immanent in all humans at birth in the guise of an inborn 'Buddha-mind', that is, the Mind in its original state (Bankei 1984, 34–6).

Congruent with the *Awakening of Faith* tradition, Bankei emphasizes that the *unborn* is an unconscious wisdom: 'What we call a "thought"', he maintains, 'is something that has already fallen one or more removes from the living reality of the Unborn' (34), and he warns against creating illusions by fixing onto memories (49) or falling into illusion as the result of defilements of desires, passions, and the clinging to self (61, 67). Similar to attaining *nirvāṇa*, then, in this life, living in the *unborn* is the way out of the suffering of existence. The *unborn*, is, for Bankei, too, the origin to which one returns but which one has never left (36).

To demonstrate the unconscious nature of the Buddha-mind or Buddha-nature, Bankei gives examples in his sermons of the kind of dissociative, or automatic, states outside of conscious awareness that Beckett personifies as proxies that represent him when walking or cycling or writing, while he is absent. (See Chapters 4 and 6.) Bankei, in fact, gives the same example of walking without thinking while taking one step after another (40) to convince his audience of their no-self status and their abiding in the *unborn*. Paul Williams, moreover, observes that Yogācāra assimilates the Buddha-nature with the substratum consciousness or *ālayavijñāna*, which is considered the Buddhist version of the unconscious (P. Williams 2009, 103, 318 n. 29). (See the last section of Chapter 8 for the congruence of the *unborn* with Zen *mushin* (no-mind) and its attraction for artists.)

There are further parallels between *The Unnamable*'s intimations of unbornness and the Buddhist *unborn*, as presented in Bankei's sermons. The narrator's puzzling claim – 'I alone am immortal, what can you expect, I can't get born' (*Un* 383) – echoes Schopenhauer's already cited 'we can only think of ourselves as *immortal* to the extent that we think of ourselves as *unborn*' (*WWR II* ch. 41, 503–4; emphasis in the original). The narrator's claim is further buttressed by the narrator depicting his no-self as 'far' and 'absent', of being outside of space and time and words, far from the stories and proceedings he is made to relate. He blames his prompters for their use of reason and concept of time from which he would prefer to be freed: 'if only they'd stop committing reason, on them, on me, on the purpose to be achieved, and simply go on, with no illusion about having begun one day or ever being able to conclude' (*Un* 384). As noted, Beckett's words to Alec Reid a few years later about *Waiting for Godot* reinforce this view of a state beyond reason similar to Bankei's wisdom of the *unborn*: 'The end is to give artistic expression to something hitherto almost ignored – the irrational state of unknowingness wherein we exist, this mental weightlessness which is beyond reason' (qtd. in Reid 1962, 136). The Western and Eastern mystical and philosophical thinkers aware of the limits of rationalism justify Beckett's 'almost' in 'almost ignored'.

Malone's admission that he has no answers to the questions of birth and death and his indifference to knowing whether he was born or not echo Bankei's assertion that the unborn Mind is unconcerned with birth or death and makes no distinction between being born or not being born (Bankei 1984, 120, 121). Further, for Bankei, to live in the *unborn*, or the Buddha-mind, one is spared transmigration (85), whereas the anguish and the reiterated suffering of being born, and perhaps in a worse state than before, belong to the everyday world and its illusions. In Bankei's view, since the physical body is born, it must necessarily die, but the *unborn* Buddha-mind has its home only temporarily in the body (81). Schopenhauer's will that has negated willing, thereby setting aside the everyday world of illusion and attaining a state comparable to an Indian-inspired timelessness, to which Beckett too alludes throughout his oeuvre, has striking affinities with Bankei's description of the *unborn*.

The family resemblances, then, between Beckett's topos of unbornness and the Buddhist teaching of the *unborn* are many, beginning with *Dream*'s poetics of emptiness and asylum in the mind, freed from desire, will, and thought, pain, turmoil, and the illusion of self and nonself, a place where in the company of the 'never-to-be-born' (among other shades), Belacqua experiences quietude, 'real pleasure'. The resonances continue with the allusions to unbornness in *Watt*, the postwar trilogy and the late *Ill Seen Ill Said*'s 'neither be nor been nor by any shift to be' (*Ill* 20) and 'Void. Nothing else. Contemplate that. Not another word. Home at last' (31).

A different interpretation of the Buddhist *unborn* from that presented in the Tathāgatagarbha Sūtra or in Bankei's recorded sermons is briefly explored by Paul Davies to understand Beckett's fascination with this topos. Davies sees similarities between Beckett's imaginative unbornness and the Platonic tradition of the soul descent as well as the Tibetan Buddhist Dzogchen view of the *unborn* (Davies 2000, 20–1, 80–3, 217). In his view, the *unborn* is similar to an unrealized soul descent into embodiment, a descent which by its fixity is likened to death. Beckett's hostility to birth, Davies surmises, is owing to this constraint as compared to the fluid state of creative awareness, which is the Dzogchen conception of the *unborn* (82, 217).

Because of the interest of modernists in Neoplatonism and because critics have been encouraged by Beckett's allusions to it to read his fiction from a Platonic or Neoplatonic perspective, it is worthwhile to contrast the Neoplatonic return to a divine origin with Beckett's obsessive theme of unbornness and the Buddhist *unborn*.[17] The descent of the soul, a belief shared by many ancient cultures, received well-known elaboration by Plato and particularly the Egyptian-born Greek-speaking Plotinus (204/5–70

---

[17] Eyol Amiran is another critic, besides Davies and others already mentioned, who views Beckett's fiction from a Platonic or Neoplatonic perspective. See Amiran 1993, 123–5, 149–60ff. For Amiran, Beckett's fiction stages the soul's Neoplatonic 'pilgrimage to unity' (16).

CE). Generally, Neoplatonic philosophers between the third and sixth centuries viewed 'the human soul as a voyager with its ultimate aim the re-ascent to its divine origins' (Vassilopoulou and Clark 2009, 319). From reading Inge's *Christian Mysticism*, Beckett would have had an introduction to Plotinus (Inge 1899, 91–8), and from Windelband, he learned that Plotinus is considered 'the true founder of Neoplatonism', whose *Enneads* – six books, each consisting of nine treatises – were edited by his biographer and disciple Porphyry of Tyre (Windelband 1901, 218). Among Beckett's 1930s notes on the history of Western philosophy, there are several pages on Porphyry's *On the Life of Plotinus and the Arrangement of His Work* (Frost and Maxwell 2006, 92–3).

No less than the different realities of the *unborn* and the illusory world of *saṃsāra*, the descent of the soul tradition pits an absolute timelessness against a devalued empirical existence. Depending on the interpretation of the descent doctrine, the body is sanctified by the descent of the soul into it, or, as emphasized by the Pythagoreans, Plato, and the Gnostics (among others), the soul has fallen from its transcendent home into imprisonment and entombment in the body. In *Enneads* IV.8.1 and 4, Plotinus quotes Plato's depictions of the soul 'in fetters', 'entombed in the body', 'in prison', and in a cave.[18] Unlike the *unborn*'s wisdom, however, which is immanent from birth and in which recollection plays no role, Plato held that prior to incarnation the soul has knowledge of the eternal world of Ideas, which it loses at birth and seeks to recover (Fleet 2012, 138–9). For Plotinus, in *Enneads* IV.8.4, on the other hand, some part of the soul always remains in the nobler world: the soul has two lives, one 'there' and the other 'here', and he describes the soul as 'pregnant when it has been filled with God', a state that 'is its first and its last' by becoming again 'what it was'. In contrast to the soul's return to its source, for Plotinus, life 'here' is 'a sinking, a defeat, a failure of the wing' (*Enneads* VI.9.9). If the soul's part in the sensory 'here' has mastery, he maintains, it hinders access to what the higher part of the soul is contemplating in the transcendent 'there' (*Enneads* IV.8.8). In the view of Plotinus, all embodied reality of the 'here' is but a remote image of the intelligible Platonic Ideas that have their source in the first principle. To this unnamable 'One' the soul aspires to return via the intellect (Gerson 2018, § 2–4). It is obvious that the thought of Plotinus resonates with Beckett's contrast between a woeful 'here' and the 'there' of an 'unspeakable home', the arriving elsewhere

---

[18] Quotations from the *Enneads* follow the pattern of book number, treatise number, and section number(s). Quotations are from Plotinus 1956.

where one has always been. Plotinus' teaching also has a family resemblance to the later Sino-Japanese Buddhist tradition of two aspects of Mind. Nevertheless, with these family resemblances come major differences.

In Beckett's postwar *nouvelles*, discussed in Chapter 5, the narrator-character at one point envisages his temporary shelters in terms of the Platonic/Neoplatonic tradition that sees in embodied reality a distant and futile copy of an ideal realm. For the narrator of the novellas, however, there is no transcendent realm of which the material refuges he inhabits are distant copies; they are rather deficient simulacra for the mystic retreat in the mind familiar since *Dream*, where it is depicted as 'assumption upside down', a downward immanent movement as opposed to the Platonic and Plotinian ascent to a transcendent source. Nevertheless, both Schopenhauer's *saṃsāric* penal colony and the state of dispossession and semblance of Beckett's creatures, their falling and failing bodies, their entombed and imprisoned existence, resonate with the Platonic/Plotinian description of the fallen existence that is the soul's in its earthly prison. In the sixth of the *Texts for Nothing*, for instance, the narrator imagines he is in the company of 'keepers' so as to make him think he is 'a prisoner, frantic with corporeality' (*CSP* 122–3).

The question of an Indian influence on Plotinus has been a matter of speculation since the time of the intellectual excitement caused by the Eastern Renaissance in the nineteenth century, and it continues to be debated into the twenty-first. The interest in this question was piqued by Porphyry's brief biography *On the Life of Plotinus*, which Beckett consulted in the early 1930s, in which the disciple of Plotinus recounts that his master joined a Roman military campaign against Persia in order to satisfy his interest in Persian and Indian thought. Unable to reach India, owing to the defeat of the Roman expedition, he eventually settled in Rome where he composed his *Enneads* (Porphyry 1935, § 3).

In his 1928 *La Philosophie de Plotin*, the French historian of philosophy Émile Bréhier argued for an Upanishadic influence on Plotinus. For Bréhier, the Upanishadic identity of the *ātman* with *brahman* is in consonance with the reunion of the soul with the first principle, or the One, in Plotinus, both realizable in this life by the practice of meditation (Bréhier 1982 [1928], 124–31). As we know, Inge ultimely denied an Indian influence, contending that Upanishadic, Buddhist, and Platonic views of a spiritual world in comparison to which the phenomenal world is only a shadow or an illusion were parallel movements (Inge 1926, 8–9). At the beginning of the twenty-first century, similar to Bréhier, however, Plotinus specialist Joachim Lacrosse affirms that, if not an overt influence, Indian thought was an 'incitative' source (a relay) for the philosophical thought of Plotinus and Porphyry, a conclusion based on six centuries of interest in Indian philosophy in the Greek and Roman world, beginning with the 326 BCE meeting of Alexander the Great's army with Indian ascetics, and favored by commercial and diplomatic contacts (Lacrosse 2009, 104–13). Moreover, the Buddhist doctrine of the *unborn* as the immanent Buddha-nature in all sentient beings bears some resemblance to the Upanishadic and Plotinian oneness with a divine first principle to which Bréhier and Lacrosse draw attention.

As a matter of fact, there was some concern among Mādhyamika Buddhists that the doctrine of the *tathāgatagarbha* resembles too closely the Upanishadic oneness of *ātman* with *brahman/Ātman*, so that some Mādhyamika thinkers downgraded it from an absolute to a relative truth, a provisional means to attract people who were destabilized by the concept of *anātman* (no-self). To avoid the resemblance to the *Ātman*, the *tathāgatagarbha* was insistently interpreted in terms of *śūnyatā* (Cornu 2001, 584). Alternatively, the *tathāgatagarbha* can be understood as one of those instances in which Upanishadic and Buddhist notions both derive from a common tradition but are differently interpreted, one in the sense of fullness, the other of emptiness.

The question now becomes to what extent Beckett's painful and illusory 'here' in contrast to a timeless 'there', the 'great calm' of *Malone Dies*, *The Unnamable*'s 'unborn' or 'blessed place, where you are', the reiterated allusions to 'elsewhere' and 'beyond', the 'unspeakable home' of 'neither' and of *Ill Seen Ill Said*, and the poetic 'no sooner there than there always' converge with the 'there' of the Plotinian/Neoplatonic doctrine of a return to the One, the Upanishadic oneness of *ātman* and *brahman*, the Buddhist immanent *unborn*, and the Schopenhauerian Indian-inspired timeless realm that follows the negating of the will.

There are no doubt traces of each of these philosophic views in Beckett's 'elsewhere'. Yet, the ones most apposite to the Beckettian ultimate emptiness of self and world are the Buddhist and Schopenhauerian *unborn* with which, as we have seen, Beckett's later works are repeatedly in consonance. The Neoplatonic and Christian mystic union with the divine within, both transcendent and immanent, although involving an emptying of self and world, ends in an ecstatic oneness with the divine or of being divine that is similar to the identity of *ātman* and *brahman*. To claim that Beckett embraces the Neoplatonic ascent of the soul via the intellect to the divine, one has to ignore the insistence in his writings on an ultimate emptiness in which you are 'bereft of thought, and feel nothing, hear nothing, know nothing, say nothing, are nothing, that would be a blessed place to be, where you are' (*Un* 374) or the call for the 'Void. Nothing else. Contemplate that. Not another word. Home at last' (*Ill* 31). Rather than a pregnant fullness, his writings invoke a pregnant emptiness confluent with Buddhist *śūnyatā*.

In conclusion, this chapter continued to explore the dynamic confusion of birth and death, the prebirth and postmortem states, time and timelessness, and the karmic cycles of birth, death, and rebirth and the 'perhaps' of 'a way out' in Beckett's oeuvre. Probed in detail is the Beckettian concept of the unborn, beyond birth and death in its affinities with both Platonic and Neoplatonic philosophy and Schopenhauerian and Buddhist thought, with each positing an illusory and fallen existence, on the one hand, and, on the other, an ultimate and timeless realm, in which 'no sooner there than there always'. My argument for Beckett's congruence with the Buddhist view is based on his emphasis from his first novel through his late texts on emptiness rather than on a return to the One or Eckhart's attainment of 'oneness and blessedness in your soul's spark' (*DW* 48). Rather, in the view of the narrator in *Ill Seen Ill Said*, 'home at last' corresponds to the unborn – 'neither be nor been nor by any shift to be' – and the 'void, nothing else', resonating with the Buddhist *unborn* envisioned in terms of *śūnyatā*.

CHAPTER 8

Dreaming 'all away' in the Final Texts

In holding to his 'can't and must' to the end, Beckett composed his last prose piece *Stirrings Still* with difficulty from 1983 to 1987.[1] In a letter to Avigdor Arikha and Anne Atik of 27 April 1984, Beckett tells of 'My old head nothing but sighs (of relief?) of expiring cells. A last chance at last. I'll try . . .. Ineffable departure. Nothing left but try & eff it' (*LSB IV* 639). Perhaps because Beckett viewed the piece as 'a last chance', it is less tentative in its poetic evocation of cycles of death and rebirth and the hoped-for *nirvāṇic* 'threshold of final extinction' (*EB* 36) or the 'true end' to 'time and grief and self so-called' of *Stirrings Still* (*CSP* 265).

The images lingering from one of Beckett's texts to the next link *Stirrings Still* (among other writings) to Beckett's penultimate short play of 1982 *Nacht und Träume* (Night and Dreams). They are companion pieces. The same setting, a dark room with the only light coming from a high-up window, and the same opening posture of a male figure sitting at a table with his head resting on his hands lead into a dream-within-a-dream sequence in the teleplay and either dreams or out-of-body *bardo* visions in the prose piece. The dreams and visions of the personas in a darkened room associate these late pieces with the earlier mindscapes situated in the timelessness outside consciousness, the site of imaginative and creative contemplation.

In Beckett's late fiction and drama, the setting of a dimly lit room with one high window is, then, an increasingly minimal version of earlier skullscapes. In *Worstward Ho*, 'one dim black hole mid-foreskull' replaces the former (more realistic) two openings leading into and out of 'the hell of all' (*Worst* 44). The single opening or window evokes Yeats's 'eye of the mind', the inner, or spiritual, eye that permits seeing beyond the everyday

---

[1] In an act of solicitude for his American publisher Barney Rosset, who had been dismissed from Grove Press by its new owners, Beckett enabled him to use *Stirrings Still*, which he dedicated to him, to start a new publishing company.

Figure 8.1   Head of Buddha, ca. fourth century CE, Gandhāra school, Northern Indus Valley, stucco with traces of paint. Metropolitan Museum of Art, New York

real.[2] It is known to Upanishadic, Buddhist, and Western mystic and poetic traditions. See Figure 8.1. In Beckett's last works, taking over from the 'filthy eye of flesh' (*Ill* 30, 35), the eye of the mind is at home in the spiritual dark of unseeing.

Nacht und Träume

Beckett's late play for television takes its name from the Schubert lied for voice and piano of 1825, with lyrics by the Austrian poet Matthäus von Collin. As we know, Beckett was particularly fond of Schubert's music, having told his cousin, the composer John Beckett, that it seemed to him 'more nearly pure spirit than that of any other composer' (qtd. in Zilliacus 1976, 38). Both in the play's first dreaming sequence and its repeat, as the dreamer drifts into his dream, a male off-voice first softly hums the last seven bars of the Schubert lied, then quietly sings the last line 'Holde Träume kehret wieder', the poet's words, no doubt heard from within,

---

[2] In *Happy Days*, Beckett cites Yeats's first line of *At the Hawk's Well*, 'I call to the eye of the mind' (*HD* 58).

entreating the night's 'fair dreams' to return. These are the only sounds, barely heard, throughout the mimed action in dimmed lighting. The lied is, then, a soothing lullaby, replacing the calming voice of the reader of bedtime stories in other texts, to calm the fear of night in its resemblance to death.

Referring to both Beckett's written script of the teleplay and the 1983 production he directed at the Süddeutscher Rundfunk (SDR) in Stuttgart, my discussion will focus on the play's dream within a dream. The play's 'characters' are the dreamer (A), his dreamt self (B), and dreamt right and left hands (R) and (L) standing synecdochically for an invisible someone in the play's 'dark beyond' (*CSPL* 305).[3] The dreamer first sees his dreamt self in the same posture as his own but reversed, as if in a mirror, until the dreamt self raises his head. This doubling in itself, recapitulates Beckett's previous twin mirror images exploring the 'self' and 'second self', as they are termed in *Stirrings Still* (*CSP* 261), or the 'I am me' and 'I am not me'. Mirror images, in fact, are among the preferred Buddhist examples of *śūnyatā*, the image in the mirror being but an illusion. In this teleplay, then, all is illusory, the dreamlike tele-images and the dream within a dream. They are there and not there.[4]

The dreamer's dream is shown twice, the first time on the upper right side of the screen, the second time in close-up and slow motion. See Figure 8.2. The dreamer (A) dreams of his dreamt self (B) dreaming of consolations descending from the 'dark beyond': L resting 'gently' on B's bowed head in a gesture of the laying on of hands, and R holding a cup 'gently' to his lips, 'gently' wiping his brow with a cloth, and then joining B's upheld hand, each gesture, James Knowlson submits, alluding to iconographic images. He mentions two: Albrecht Dürer's *Praying Hands* drawing, a copy of which used to hang in Beckett's bedroom in Cooldrinagh, and the Veil of Veronica identified by Beckett himself as the cloth used to wipe Christ's brow on the Way of the Cross (Knowlson 1996, 599–600). An iconographic source for the cup – a chalice on-screen – was discovered by Graley Herren in sixteenth-century paintings in the National Gallery of London depicting a chalice-bearing angel descending toward the humanly suffering Christ in the Garden of Gethsemane to comfort him in his agony (Herren 2001, 54–70).

---

[3] Because Beckett's script for *Nacht und Träume* is only one and one-half pages long (*CSPL* 305–6), further page references are dispensed with for this piece.

[4] See Herren 2000, 186–7, for an exploration of text and spectator counterpoint in *Nacht und Träume*, the recorded on-screen performance mirroring the viewer's gazing at phantom tele-images, the shades or doubles of the recording process.

Figure 8.2   *Nacht und Träume,* directed by Samuel Beckett, SDR, Stuttgart, 1983.
Photo © SWR/Hugo Jehle

This last image joins the others in Beckett's inner store of pictorial images depicting Christ's Passion, on which he would draw throughout his writings, from *Watt* to *Catastrophe* (the latter play written the same year as *Nacht und Träume*) – the Crowning with Thorns, the Man of Sorrows, the Way of the Cross, the Veil of Veronica, the Crucifixion, the Man Who Died, and Christ in the Tomb – to associate his creatures with them, sometimes openly, sometimes not. In suggesting that the dreamer's dreamt mirror image resembles the suffering Christ, Beckett is reprising the scene in which Sam sees himself mirrored in Watt identified with an icon of Christ crowned with thorns (*W* 159).[5] Further, whereas *Watt* is saturated

---

[5] It is no coincidence that the the iconographic references to Christ's Passion began to appear in the texts Beckett composed during and after World War II. The scene in *Watt*, in which Sam sees himself mirrored in Watt who resembles, so Sam maintains, Hieronymus Bosch's *Christ Mocked* (*The Crowning with Thorns*) in London's National Gallery, takes place at 'a high barbed wire fence' surrounding Watt's and Sam's two asylum gardens (*W* 156). The barbed wire was bound to evoke the detention camps of the war, as Morin (2017, 162) also points out. Intriguingly, Bosch's painting depicts a mild and pale Christ absent from the scene in which he is encircled by four ferocious tormentors, whereas a painting with the same theme, formerly thought to be by Dirk Bouts, which

with religious symbols, as is *Nacht und Träume*, the perplexing last line in *Watt*'s addenda: 'No symbols where none intended' intimates that, paradoxically, the symbols are there and not there, tentatively there only to be erased so that, ultimately, they are empty. And in *Nacht und Träume*? There too, they are something and nothing, existing only in a dream within a dream further denaturalized by the dreamlike televised images.

Nacht und Träume shares the *mise en abyme* structure of some of Beckett's previous plays for television. In his intricate analysis of *Ghost Trio*, written soon after it was first televised in 1976, Peter Gidal, insisting on its constructed nature and distancing techniques, focuses from the outer rectangular frame of the television screen, to the second frame of the visual narrative in a rectangular room filled with rectangular shapes, to the third frame of the interior of the protagonist's boxlike mind and the music issuing from a cassette recorder (Gidal 1979, 53). In both *Ghost Trio* and *Nacht und Träume* (and in other texts), Beckett, however, adds a fourth to these three embedded frames. In the two plays, it is in the guise of off-screen spaces: the 'dark beyond' in *Nacht und Träume*, and in *Ghost Trio*, a door leading to an empty corridor ending in darkness (*CSPL* 252).

In a ghostly reprisal of *Waiting for Godot* and its messenger(s) appearing in the play's two acts, in *Ghost Trio*, a young boy arrives from the outer darkness to faintly shake his head twice in response to the silent question of the waiting male figure (*CSPL* 253–4). If in the teleplay, his arriving from outer darkness hints that the messenger comes from another world, Beckett said as much for this figure in his earlier play. 'Remember, you're not from here. You're not from this earth', he admonished nine-year-old Louis Beckett Clutchey who was playing the role of the boy messenger in the 1984 San Quentin Drama Workshop production of *Waiting for Godot*, with whose rehearsals in London Beckett was assisting (qtd. in Kędzierski 2017, 123). The allusions to angel messengers in Beckett's writing from *Molloy*, *Godot*, *Ghost Trio*, and (possibly) *Nacht und Träume* can be seen as teasingly intimating a beyond about which nothing is certain, in the manner of (post)modern negative allegory.[6]

Beckett, by his own admission, introduced 'teasers' into *Nacht und Träume*. He made the remark about the descending hands, which he decided should be a woman's but of a size to be possibly taken for a

---

perhaps was hanging nearby when Beckett viewed the Bosch, portrays a Christ with bloodied face and hands and thorns in his scalp that corresponds to Sam's description of Watt (*W* 159).

[6] On negative allegory, see Uhlmann 2009, 17–26.

man's, leaving their gender ambiguous.[7] In my view, another teaser is B's 'gaze up at invisible face' following the consoling gestures of the hands descending from 'the dark beyond'. How could spectators suspect that he is gazing up at an invisible face without having read the script? At its best, his gaze could be taken in the sense of *A Piece of Monologue*'s 'staring beyond'. In fact, some descriptions of the production omit this gaze entirely, whereas other exegetes, depending on the script, have speculated on whose face it may be. But, these teasers, to my mind, are best left unknowable, joining others about the beyond.

Shortly after completing *Nacht und Träume* and while struggling with *Stirrings Still*, Beckett gave an explanation for the meticulous construction of his texts. What matters to him, Beckett told Shainberg, is 'the pleasure in making a satisfactory object'. And as already mentioned, the excitement of writing for him, he went on to explain, is a combination of 'metaphysics and technique' (qtd. in Shainberg 1987, 134). The metaphysics is hinted at in this teleplay by the off-screen 'dark beyond' as it had been earlier in his *Monologue* by the off-stage 'beyond that black beyond' and the 'else-where' of previous texts. The suffering and misery from which a way out is imagined takes the form of the repeated identification of Beckett's ceatures with icons of the *kenōtic* Christ's Passion along with the traumas of a *saṃsāric* hellish condition and turmoil in the mind recalling the Buddha's first truth of universal suffering.

The dream of Christian consolation descending from a 'dark beyond', which the dreamt dreamer tries to pierce with his upward gaze, contrasts with the faint voice from deep within in *Stirrings Still*, the path of meditation, announcing the awakening from the life dream into an elsewhere where the figure has always been. What these visions have in common is the beyond as unknowable, unsayable, which Beckett, no less than Schopenhauer, explores in his writings in both their Christian and Eastern versions. Even if it is in part teasingly, Beckett has positioned the viewers of his late teleplay and the readers of his last prose piece in the same unknowingness about a beyond.

Because many commentators of *Nacht und Träume* feel uneasy about the religious sentimentality of the consoling gestures it stages, Beckett appears to have overestimated the distancing effect of the media frame and the dream-within-a-dream structure to offset the sentimental pull to

---

[7] See Beckett's preproduction letter of 5 August 1982 to Reinhart Müller-Freienfels, the artistic director of the SDR (*LSB IV* 587–8). In a letter to the artistic director six days earlier, Beckett referred to the genderless hands as 'one of our numerous teasers' (qtd. in *LSB IV* 588, n. 3).

identify with the dreamer's need for consolation. Or perhaps he did not want to entirely mask this need as he had not in *Ohio Impromptu* the year before in repeatedly drawing attention to the calming effect of storytelling. Missing, in any case, are many of the devices Beckett would draw on to minimize a possible effect of sentimentality or pathos in his other works, including humor, irony, parody, swearing, erasure, and the foregrounding of media illusion.

Stirrings Still

In *Company*, the narrator compares the mind closing to the closing of a single window of 'a dark empty room' leaving 'nothing more'. The 'nothing more', however, is qualified by an exception: 'Pangs of faint light and stirrings still. Unformulable gropings of the mind. Unstillable' (*Co* 23). On a card of 7 July 1987, Beckett explained to John Calder that the title *Stirrings Still* refers to this passage in *Company* (Van Hulle 2011, 96), which Beckett's French title for this last fiction *Soubresauts* (twitches, shudders) would confirm.[8] Yet, the two clashing meanings of the title's 'still' – 'ongoing' and thus 'unstillable', on the one hand, and on the other, 'at rest' or 'stilled' – reverberate to suggest the impatient waiting for the twitches in the mind to subside and, at the end of *Stirrings Still*, 'stir no more'.

In the tripartite *Stirrings Still*, narrative point of view is projected through a third-person persona 'he', eclipsing the first person. Beckett's search for the 'non-pronounial', as told Shainberg at the time he was composing this last fiction (Shainberg 1987, 134) – a search familiar since the postwar trilogy – results in the avoidance not only of 'I' but also of 'he' whenever possible throughout the piece. And the narrated figure's end is told in the distancing technique as that of an other. The pleasure of making a 'satisfactory object' and the excitement of joining technique to metaphysics results in this late piece in occluded images of sublime poetry.

Recalling the earlier *Texts for Nothing*, *Stirrings Still* consists of fragmentary stabs at effing the ineffable, or in Beckett's words in his letter to Arikha and Atic, 'the ineffable departure'. Indeed, Beckett thought of his work in progress as a collection of fragments. If we heed his mention, in one of the *Stirrings Still* manuscripts, of more than one attempt to tell the figure's end

---

[8] As Sam Slote points out, 'translation' may not be quite accurate in referring to *Soubresauts*, since Beckett switched between English and French in his preparatory drafts of his last prose piece (Slote 2015, 124). The card to Calder is not in *LSB IV*.

(UoR MS 29351/1) and his referring to more than one 'tale of his end' (qtd. in Bryden, Garforth, and Mills 1998, 175), then there appear to be four stabs at telling it, instead of three, as one would expect from the piece's tripartite division. In the first part, the first paragraph is one such account of the figure's death, followed by six paragraphs that make up a second narrative. The manuscripts verify that these two fragments were drafted separately.[9] The second and third parts of *Stirrings Still*, then, consist of a one-paragraph narrative each. If one were to give the narratives titles, the two stories of the first part could be 'No Light, No Dark' and 'Reappearances', whereas those of the second and third parts correspond to 'Boundlessness' and 'where never till then'.[10]

In this last piece of fiction, commentators have once more found multiple reverberations with Beckett's previous work, and if still more such reiterations are probed in the discussion that follows, these, as Steven Connor aptly maintains, redefine earlier texts as much as they are defined by them (Connor 2007 [1988], 5).

After hesitating between the present and past tense, Beckett decided on the past tense for the four stories about death of *Stirrings Still*.[11] The two that make up the first part begin similarly with a variation on an out-of-body vision: 'One night as he sat at his table head on hands he saw himself rise and go'. In the first story, it is unclear whether the figure is envisioning his death in a dream or in a near-death *bardo* experience. The passing from life to near-death to death is evoked in terms of light and dark, proceeding from the figure's own light going out, leaving a mysterious light coming from the high window, until it goes out, leaving him in the dark, until the dark goes out. The light and dark contrary so poetically exploited throughout Beckett's oeuvre here unravels into a dimension beyond light and dark, evoked in the 'beyond that black beyond' of *A Piece of Monologue* (*CSPL* 269). If the extinguishing of the light is a familiar motif, the extinguishing of the dark startles. The unearthliness of this state is apparent from the portrayal of the figure, who earlier, would stand on a stool at the window to look up at the sky, avoiding looking down to see the earth below.

---

[9] The two early fragments are found in UoR MS 2935/1/4 and UoR MS 2935/3/2 respectively. See also Bryden et al. 1998, 176, 178. The many drafts of *Stirrings Still* were consulted in digital form, along with their transcriptions by Dirk Van Hulle.

[10] No doubt the placing of four stories into three parts is to be explained by Beckett's attachment to the number three.

[11] Because *Stirrings Still* covers only a few pages, *CSP* 259–65, the first part being the longest at a little over two pages, page references for this piece are omitted, but in which of the three parts the quoted passages occur is noted.

Rather, on his stool, he would stand 'high above the earth' (imagined visible below the window) to gaze at the cloudless and unchanging sky whose faint light was not of the kind he remembered from the time of alternating days and nights. This foretaste of timelessness is seen through 'a clouded pane' giving but a partial vision, reminiscent of the biblical seeing 'through a glass darkly', but also a near-equivalence of the veil of *māyā*.[12] The final extinction of both light and dark that follows intimates the timelessness, beyond day and night, dark and light, birth and death. Evoked, too, is perhaps the plenum void prior to time, there being no time before the origin of the universe at the Big Bang nor before creation in many creation stories, in which dark and light emerge together.[13]

The figure's gazing out of the window is anticipated in an early draft in dramatic form. In Beckett's 'Super Conquérant' notebook (UoR MS 2934), which contains several manuscript drafts of *Stirrings Still*, the first page, dated 1 August 1984, is followed by brief scenes of a short play featuring two characters W and M, gender not specified. The given time is a few strokes away from midnight on New Year's Eve, as, in a reprise of the forgetfulness of *Happy Days*, W and M begin their ritual of taking turns reciting their favorite Shakespeare sonnets, only to find they can no longer recall the words. In a variation on the skullscape of *Endgame*, in a dark, bare room, M is standing at the sole window, reporting what he sees to W, sitting on a wooden bench. The gazing out of the window by the figure in the first story of *Stirrings Still* is most likely derived from this skit, but without the comic touches introduced into the latter. These briefly sketched scenes, then, contain some of the themes Beckett will develop in the tales of his last prose fiction. It is noteworthy that he would work some of these out in dramatic form echoing his earlier dramas. (Another

---

[12] See 1 Corinthians 13.12, to which Beckett alludes in *Molloy* (Mo 62). The figure's mystic vision of a cloudless and unchanging sky resonates with Beckett's 1929 story 'Assumption', in which the protagonist 'hungered to be irretrievably engulfed in the light of eternity, one with the birdless cloudless colourless skies, in infinite fulfillment' (*CSP* 7), with the difference that there is no inkling of 'fulfillment'. Similar wording appears in a sonnet addressed to Smeraldina in 'Sedendo et Quiescendo' inserted into *Dream* (70), where, however, it is mocked, in an allusion to Alfred de Musset, as 'some of the finest Night of May hiccupsobs' (*Dream* 70). See also Lawlor and Pilling 2012, 342.

[13] Peter Gidal's silent fifteen-minute experimental film *No Night No Day* (1997) effects a similar 'distension from any nature', in Gidal's words. 'What darkness the film will have … will not be connected to nature's night', he writes, 'equally light will be unconnected to "day" as a lived concept and reality' (Gidal 1998). His interest appears to be to explore what light and dark might be outside of empirical categories. See also Dirk Van Hulle's description of the 'dynamic process' of abstraction in Beckett's later writing, 'a movement from the concrete *toward* the abstract' (Van Hulle 2004, 487), a process discernible in *Stirrings Still*'s fading light and dark imagery.

theme from the playlet draft found its way into the second part discussed further on.)[14]

The second tale, covering the remainder of the first part of *Stirrings Still*, describes not one but many departures and returns. The figure sees (in the past tense) his out-of-body double rise and go, on 'unseen feet' and always from behind. It is tempting to follow Beckett in distinguishing between the dreamer and his dreamt self in *Nacht und Träume* by calling the persona at the table A, and B his 'own other', or doppelgänger.[15] B's comings and goings, under A's observation, recall the memories that surface without summons during the near-death and out-of-body experiences depicted in other Beckett texts, and they are similarly a mixture of imagination and autographical recollections. Hence, A sees B in the same hat and coat as when he himself walked the back roads. Time and signs of suffering intrude with the metonymic far-off striking of a clock and cries fading in and out. In an early draft, dated July 1984, Beckett refers to far-off lamentations (UoR MS 2935/3/1).

Seeing B get up with difficulty from the table and move slowly, as would be the case of someone enfeebled by age, A could only determine that B has gone because he appears in a different place from where he himself is seated at the table. At this point, the narrative takes an intriguing turn. A's doppelgänger appearing at a different place is compared to other disappearances and reappearances while A is seated at his table, pointing to the cyclic existence of Beckett's creatures in the postwar novels. Where A is seated at his table, moreover, is given as the same place he occupied when Darly died and others before and after him.

Darly refers to Dr. Arthur Darley (Darly in the text), with whom Beckett worked in 1946 at the Irish Red Cross Hospital at Saint-Lô.[16] Beckett's untranslated fifteen-line poem 'Mort de A.D.' was most likely written shortly after the death of his friend of tuberculosis at age forty in September 1948. This particular breach of the boundary between fiction and autobiography in Beckett's last fiction is not unknown in modernist writing, Proust, for example, having similarly attributed one of his own

---

[14] The drafts of the skit are found on pages 1v and 2 and 3r of UoR MS 2934. To give an idea of the extraordinary effort Beckett put into his final fiction, and the difficulty he experienced in writing at this stage of his life, there are thirty-four manuscript drafts listed for *Stirrings Still / Soubresauts* in Bryden et al. 1998, 175–82. Of these, the 'Super Conquérant' notebook is only one.

[15] The expression 'own other' is found in *Rockaby* (*CSPL* 281). In a note of 21 October 1986 to André Bernold, Beckett in fact refers to the 'second self' of *Stirrings Still* as a doppelgänger (*LSB IV* 679).

[16] Beckett wrote both Darly and Darley in his drafts. He explained in a letter to Alan Mandell of 21 May 1987 about 'Darly': 'Here without "e" simply "the beloved"' (*LSB IV* 688).

friends, killed in 1914, to his protagonist in *À la recherche du temps perdu* (Proust 1988 [1923], 168). Both writers are commemorating a lost friend by name in their fictions and at the same time raising uncertainty about the status of their texts as fiction or autography.

Beckett's elegy for his friend, written nearly forty years earlier, fits well into the musings of his persona in *Stirrings Still*. Taking a closer look at this poem will show what reverberates between the two meditations on time and death and cyclic existence. In fact, it appears that the image of a man at his table goes back to the earlier poem, although the head-on-hands posture is already Belacqua's in *Dream* (4).[17] Glued to his old ink-stained board ('vieille planche'), the elegy's speaker mourns the death of his friend and the deadly nature of time ('temps mourant'). Echoing Stéphane Mallarmé's early sonnet 'Brise marine' ('Sea Breeze'), with its temptation of flight from the everyday at the risk of shipwreck, the poet questions his own possibilities of flight from time's fatality ('être là à ne pas fuir et fuir et être là'), intimating that writing itself offers one possible, if temporary, release.[18] The allusion to Mallarmé is further strengthened by the final four lines of Beckett's elegy depicting the poet drinking in, above the storm, the sin/guilt of irrevocable/unforgivable time ('la coulpe du temps irrémissible'), while clinging to the old wood, a witness to the cyclic departures and returns we find reiterated in *Stirrings Still*.[19]

In mourning for those gone before, *Stirrings Still*, together with several of Beckett's other late texts, corresponds to the French literary genre of *tombeau*, a memorial for the dead. There are the farewells in *Worstward Ho* to the shades of both parents, evoking particularly the child's hand in the old man's, as they walk without receding from view, and the long farewell to the maternal 'figment' in *Ill Seen Ill Said*. Additionally, in his final prose piece, Beckett, it would seem, is composing his own *tombeau* as a writer. That Beckett did not exclude the possibility of being reborn as a writer – if only in jest – is evident in his letter to the Haydens of 30 December 1969, in which, describing himself overwhelmed by mail to answer (owing to the award of the Nobel Prize in October), he finds it impossible to work, so

---

[17] On the function of the postmodernist topos of the writer at his desk to break fictional illusion, see McHale 2004 [1987], 198.

[18] That in *Stirrings Still*, Beckett had 'Mort de A.D.' in mind is evident from his referring to 'the same old board as when Darly died' in some of his drafts, but changing 'board' to 'table' in the final text (UoR MS 2935/1/5; qtd. in Bryden et al. 1998, 176). Beckett alludes to Mallarmé's poem in *Dream* (3, 12).

[19] 'Mort de A.D.' is collected in *CPS* 116. The word *coulpe* (guilt), containing the word *coupe* (goblet or glass), would seem to account for the verb *boire* (to drink) in these lines.

that he concludes, 'Je ne vois pas de solution à moins de renaître' ('I see no solution short of being reborn'; *LSB IV* 216).

Because the topos of rebirth is a recurrent one in Beckett's works, it is not unexpected to find it reiterated in his final meditation on time and dying and what comes after. In fact, several drafts, pertaining to reincarnation, but which were not transferred into the final text of *Stirrings Still*, support the allusions to cycles of rebirth in the second narrative of the first part. In several drafts, faint voices come out of the darkness to read to the figure lying in bed. In one draft, catching a sentence concerning Mr. Knott, the figure feels 'he has heard it somewhere before no doubt in the course of some previous incarnation to judge by his experience of the latest now coming to a close' (UoR MS 2935/2/2, 2r; also qtd. in Davies 1994, 232–3).[20]

Toward the beginning of the second tale, A, head on hands, is torn between 'half hoping' for an end to B's cycles of reappearances and 'half fearing' that they would end, while waiting to see whether or not he (A) would be 'again waiting for nothing again'. Waiting for nothing recalls not only the Godot who never appears but the unattainable nothingness he mentions in a draft of *Stirrings Still* (UoR MS 2935/1/5), reminiscent of the 'evermost almost void' of *Worstward Ho* (43). The reluctance of A to contemplate the end of cycles of existence for his 'second self' can, as usual, be read in more than one way. Bent over his writing table, the figure may be reluctant to let go of writing. In this connection, at the time he was composing *Stirrings Still*, Beckett told Shainberg that 'writing was the only thing that made life bearable' and explained that, for him, not being able to write and writing each have their own painfulness (Shainberg 1987, 133). Additionally, the passage echoes the uncertainty of *Ill Seen Ill Said*'s 'Absence supreme good and yet' (*Ill* 58).

By the end of this narrative, however, A has changed his mind about the half hope of another existence in this world for his doppelgänger, as he contemplates an escape from the strokes of the clock and the cries, the suffering and imprisonment in time. Wavering between the possibility of continuing cycles and an end to the lamenting and reappearances, the fragment ends with a call for patience, 'till the one true end to time and

---

[20] In a subsequent draft, Beckett tried out several other words for 'incarnation' (UoR MS 2935/2/3). Paul Davies (1994, 233) and Andy Wimbush (2020, 248–51) both draw attention to the subject of reincarnation in the drafts. They too hold that the allusion to rebirth remains available in less explicit form in the published text.

grief and self and second self his own', a line repeated with variation at the end of the third and final part.

In the second part's story (the third story in my counting), the doppelgänger appears to be walking in a dream or a near-death or an afterlife landscape. Pictured outside the mind-room, he continues to hear the cries and clock as before, whereas his steps make no sound. Stilling his ears, he observes that he is in a field, which, unlike the green pastures with fences or other boundaries that he knew from the past, is rather a boundless wintry landscape, with the gray of the hoar grass verging on white. Such a boundless psycho-landscape recalls others in Beckett's works, among which the poetic 'Ash grey all sides earth sky as one all sides endlessness' (*CSP* 198) in *Sans / Lessness* (French, 1969; English, 1970). In *Company*, the seemingly last recalled scene tells of walking again in memory in a snow-covered mountain pasture, where in spring lambs are said to scamper (*Co* 35). The ghostly white terrain of *Ill Seen Ill Said* and the allusion to Schubert's lieder cycle *Winterreise* in Beckett's last play *What Where* – 'It is winter. / Without journey'. (*CSPL* 316) – further assimilate the nearness of death with wintry landscapes.

If the field in *Stirrings Still* is a vision of paradise, it counters paradisiacal landscapes such as the idyllic eternal spring of Dante's Earthly Paradise (*Purgatorio*, cantos 28–9). Rather, the boundless and desolate field of the second part intimates the mystics' paradise identified with both an inner and outer desert[21] and the Eckhartian 'calm wastes' of *The Lost Ones*, a fading into an infinite emptiness, 'a boundless void' (*Worst* 47).

In its emphasis on silence, stillness, and white on white, the last part of the dramatic skit at the beginning of the 'Super Conquérant' notebook, anticipates the dream or vision of the mystical landscape of the second part. While looking out the window, M describes a landscape covered in snow, the white crest of the waves, and an overcast sky, reporting that everything is as strange as ever (UoR MS 2934, 3r). Recalled, it would seem, are not only Clov's description of what he sees out of the window – 'Zero' and 'GRRAY' (*End* 4, 29, 31) – but even more so *Bing / Ping*'s 'white planes shining white one only shining white infinite but that known not' evoking visions of the infinite and its unknowability (*CSP* 195).[22]

---

[21] See McGinn 1994, 160–1.

[22] Beckett's original title for *Bing* was 'Blanc' (white) (Cohn 2005, 298). The skit and *Bing / Ping*'s vision recall white-on-white paintings, such as the 1918 *Suprematist Composition: White on White* by Kazimir Malevich (1879–1935), for whom white was the color of infinity (www.moma.org/collection/works 80385). And Robert Ryman's 1989 illustrated edition of Beckett's *Nohow On* consists of six white-on-white aquatints signed by the artist and Beckett.

Troubled by the eerie boundless landscape in which B in the second part of *Stirrings Still* finds himself, he turns his attention from outside to inside to meditate. The likelihood that he is in a dreamlike state is intimated by the allusion at this point to Walther von der Vogelweide (c. 1170–c. 1230) – political poet and *Minnesänger* – who portrays himself deep in thought in his poem 'Ich saz ûf eime steine' (I sat on a stone), his head in one hand, whereas there was no stone, B reports, on which to sit to meditate in this vast and boundless field.[23] In alluding to Walther in the near-death or afterlife settings of *Stirrings Still*, Beckett may be indirectly alluding to his 1934 quatrain 'Da tagte es' (Then dawn broke), whose title cites the German equivalent of the Provençal *alba*, the 'Tagelied' (song of lament at dawn): 'redeem the surrogate goodbyes / the sheet astream in your hand / who have no more for the land / and the glass unmisted above your eyes' (*CP* 22).

There is some controversy about whose 'Tagelied' Beckett had in mind in composing his 1934 elegy. He could have been alluding to the genre in general and the line 'da tagte es' that appears in such songs. On later annotating his copy of the 1935 collection *Echo's Bones and Other Precipitates*, Beckett, however, surmised, 'Walther von der Vogelweide?' for 'Da tagte es' (Van Hulle and Nixon 2013, 84).[24] That, in *Stirrings Still*, Beckett may be obliquely alluding to his early poem, addressed to a 'you' without given gender, is attested by his poetically weaving together a number of separations and departures – the lovers' awakening and parting at dawn in medieval *albas*, such as Walther's; the farewells waved on a boat about to sail; and the journey into death – which reiterate the mourning theme of the first part's second story.

Beckett's particular fondness for 'Da tagte es' is apparent when he chose it, along with 'The Vulture', a poem about the poet's art, from his 1935 collection of poems *Echo's Bones*, to possibly represent him in the *Great Book of Ireland*. In November 1989, during the last visit of his artist friends Louis and Anne Madden le Brocquy – the former the illustrator of *Stirrings Still* – Beckett recited the two poems from memory, asking Louis, who would also illustrate the chosen poem in the *Great Book of Ireland*, to

---

[23] Walther made a previous appearance in 'The Calmative', evoked when the protagonist finds a stone seat to sit on and crosses his legs in imitation of the posture described in the medieval poet's 'Ich saz ûf eime steine' (*CSP* 71).

[24] Thanks are due Mark Nixon for helpful information about Beckett's notetaking on Walther von der Vogelweide. During his six-month trip through Germany in 1936–7, Beckett sent a volume of Walther's poems home, a sign of his fondness for the medieval poet (Van Hulle and Nixon 2013, 84–5).

choose between the two. His choice fell on 'Da tagte es' (Cronin 1997, 589; Le Brocquy 2017, 100). About 'the sheet astream in your hand', Anne Madden le Brocquy recounts, Beckett explained that it is the sheet [hand-kerchief?] 'held in *her* hand'; the sail of the boat heading out to sea; and also the winding sheet (qtd. in Le Brocquy 2017, 100; emphasis added). The 'her' in 'her hand' most likely refers to Beckett's cousin Peggy Sinclair (the model for Smeraldina of the 'supreme adieu' with which *Dream* begins), who died of tuberculosis a month before Beckett's father in 1933.[25] Yet, still another reading suggests itself for this elegy written shortly after the 'Echo's Bones' story with its allusions to rebirth, *nirvāṇa*, and a dreamlike existence. Could the awakening from a dream that is implied by the allusion to a 'Tagelied' not also intimate Schopenhauer's vision of death as an awakening from a life dream? As you will recall, the philosopher's vision corresponds to the Buddha's consolatory thought of *nirvāṇa*, which in the Heart Sūtra is evoked in terms of an awakening. The poem's mysterious last line 'the glass unmisted above your eyes' most likely alludes to the glass of 1 Corinthians 13.12 unmisted on awakening from the dream of existence.

The second part of *Stirrings Still*, as did the first, evokes the trials of old age by picturing B disoriented in space and worried about being in his right mind. Having found no help from what remained of his mind as he stood still meditating, he resigns himself to not knowing where he is, how he got there, where he is going, and how to find his way back to where he may have come from. His lostness echoes that of Beckett's creatures particularly in the postwar fiction, while simultaneously suggesting the figure's search for a way back 'home'.

At the end of the second part, B's state of resignation, pictured as both 'unknowing' and without a wish to know, and, moreover, without 'any wish of any kind nor therefore any sorrow', resonates unmistakably with the Buddha's indictment of desire and grasping as the source of suffering. The words of an end to wishing and therefore an end to sorrow, however, are followed by the restriction, reminiscent of the compassion of the *bodhisattvas*, 'except that he would have wished the strokes to cease and the cries for good and was sorry that they did not'.

The theme of 'where never before', reviewed in Chapter 7, is explored in the third and final part of *Stirrings Still*. The doppelgänger, moving once

---

[25] For John Pilling, 'Da tagte es' commemorates the death of Beckett's father (Pilling 1976, 136; Lawlor and Pilling 2012, 29). There is no critical agreement on this point, whereas the poem 'Malacoda' following 'Da tagte es' in *Echo's Bones*, is recognized as alluding to the funeral of Beckett's father and the grief of his mother.

more through the hoar grass at the end of the second part, is in the third
pictured standing still and bowed down, listening to a faint voice from
'deep within', only partially heard, with a word missing after the exclam-
atory beginning: 'oh how . . . it were to end where never till then'. A faint
inner voice, of which only fragments are audible, recapitulates the topos of
the voice, as first broached in *Watt*, arriving from an out-of-awareness
region of the mind. His senses stilled, the figure is here entirely immersed
in the 'profounds of mind. Of mindlessness', in the words of *Ohio
Impromptu*, congruent with Buddhist meditation and Zen no-mind.

Beckett entered a six-line poem 'Brief Dream' (*CP* 224) into the last
pages of the 'Super Conquérant' notebook, following on a passage dated
Ussy, July 86 (UoR MS 2934, 8r), the poem's title implying the dreamlike
nature of going 'where never till then' (*CP* 224, l. 3). The poem, with
some variation, is incorporated into the final part of Beckett's last prose
piece. The words B hears faintly from within about possibly ending 'where
never till then' prompt the question in his mind about already being there,
which, on additional reflection, he decides must be so, and without the
possibility of getting out of it. Left uncertain, owing to the missing word, is
how this being endlessly in the hereafter is something to be hoped for or
not. After completing *Stirrings Still* in June 1987, Beckett composed the
four-line poem 'go where never before / no sooner there than there always'
(*CP* 223, ll. 1–2), comprising both the earlier 'Brief Dream' and the
further reflections recorded in the third part of his last prose piece.[26]
The meditation on the 'never till then' of an afterlife and the question of
already being there before death is answered by the 'no sooner there than
there always' of the later poem, a summing up in poetic terms of the
immanent timelessness of the Buddha's *unborn*, its embrace by
Schopenhauer, and, following him, by the author throughout his
writing life.

After introducing the paradox of already being where never before, the
third part of *Stirrings Still* reiterates the hesitations between repeated
rebirths and 'stir[ring] no more' in the second tale of the first part.
Beyond such 'hubbub in the mind' – recalling Malone's – only the fading
fragment 'oh to end' is heard at the end of the third part, varying the first

---

[26] The poem 'go where never before' is a translation of the French 'Là' (there) written shortly before its
translation into English. Both versions of the poem remained unpublished in Beckett's lifetime,
whereas 'Brief Dream' appeared in the Irish press on 13 April 1989, Beckett's eighty-third and last
birthday (Lawlor and Pilling 2012, 471).

part's 'one true end to time and grief and self and second self' with 'Time and grief and self so-called. Oh all to end'.

We find, then, five decades after *Dream*, recapitulated in *Stirrings Still* and its manuscript drafts, the elements projected into Belacqua's retreat in the dark of the mind: the end of desire and grief and self and time, a topos resonating with the Buddhist *unborn* emptiness that gives access to the *nirvāṇic* end to *saṃsāra* about which Beckett read in Schopenhauer before composing his first novel. Unlike *Dream*, however, where the retreat is a temporary release associated with Schopenhauer's view of artistic contemplation and generativity, in Beckett's final piece of fiction, it is a whispered call for a lasting liberation, the 'one true end' to suffering and time and the illusory self. And further, the regret that the laments or cries will not cease with the figure's own end mark this final meditation with a compassion absent from *Dream*.

If read linearly, *Stirrings Still* concludes with the call for 'Oh all to end', but reading Beckett's texts as proceeding from a beginning to an end is something he, more often than not, frustrates by his paradoxical, contrapuntal, and endlessly reverberating constructions. In his final fiction, the end-is-in-the-beginning trope takes us back to the first tale's vision of timelessness and emptiness, with no light, no dark.

In scrutinizing the upward or downward directions in which the figures in *Nacht und Träume* and *Stirrings Still* look for solace, we find, in the former, the figure, bowed over his hands, dreaming of his double – identified with the suffering *kenōtic* Christ – who is dreaming in turn of forms of consolation descending from above. In *Stirrings Still*, reminiscent of the character in 'Assumption', the story written in 1929, the dreaming figure recalls his former contemplation of the sky to escape from earthly sorrows. As we have seen, Beckett reversed this ascending direction beginning with *Dream*'s 'assumption upside down', while also suggesting in his letter to Axel Kaun that the two directions are paradoxically the same. In the second and third parts of *Stirrings Still*, solace is evoked in the form of a meditative descent into the mind from which issue the fragments of a voice outside of consciousness – the 'unformulable gropings of the mind' (*Co* 23) – and the perhaps of the 'one true end' in the silence where one has always been.

Beckett's unflinching depictions of miseries inflicted by the 'human predicament', from which solace or a way out is sought, are tied as much to cycles of birth, death, and rebirth as to personal and historical traumas and losses. Even when rendered from the distance of humor, the 'nothing is funnier than unhappiness', or from the ideal real of *sub specie aeternitatis*, 'the world's woes', as seen through Beckett's eyes, generate powerful textual effects for readers and audiences. If the icons of the *kenōtic* Christ's human agonies, to which Beckett alludes time and again, call visual images of suffering to mind as do the allusions to the *saṃsāric* hellishness of the 'real' tied to historical and contemporary terrors, these are not countervailed by the comforting beliefs in divine redemption or mercy. Rather, he imagined performative effects to situate readers and audiences against the domineering and ideological dicta and roles intensifying torments and miseries, calling indirectly for the solidarity and compassion that the Buddha and Schopenhauer taught as an ethical imperative following from the connectedness among all living beings. And for his texts, he envisioned calming effects and stories to tell of an elsewhere that is 'perhaps' the way out and also a way back 'home', even though the telling is always suspended, leaving his creatures close to the 'Void. Nothing else. Contemplate that. Not another word. Home at last' (*Ill* 31). The role of writing in the attempted way back is once again emphasized in *Stirrings Still* by the persona at his writing table seeing his doppelgänger – harking back to the 'internus homo' (from Thomas à Kempis) of the Belacqua saga[27] – appear and disappear and appear again while wondering about the possibility 'to stir no more' and a 'true end' to suffering and the illusions of time and self, beyond the temporary relief found in writing and contemplation beyond thought.

Unlike the commentators who maintain that Beckett denies a way out, the many allusions to an elsewhere and a beyond that pervade his late drama and fiction do not close the door to a final liberation. Affirmed it may not be, but neither is it denied. Hence, in Beckett's 'neither', which he wrote for composer Morton Feldman, declaring that 'there was only one theme in his life',[28] the search for asylum in this shadow world, whether inward or outward, is compared to two lit refuges whose doors beckon, close, and beckon again, until absence from self and world suspends the search in stillness, leaving an unfading unearthly light on the 'unspeakable home' to which neither self nor world is gateway

---

[27] On the 'internus homo', see *DN* #578 and *MPTK* 40.

[28] In his biography, Knowlson describes the origin of 'neither' in a meeting between the avant-garde composer Morton Feldman and Beckett in Berlin in September 1976. Over lunch, after Feldman showed Beckett a score he had composed on lines of Beckett's *Film* scenario, Beckett, declaring that 'there was only one theme in his life', wrote the beginning of 'neither' on the sheet, sending Feldman the rest of the sixteen-line piece ten days later (Knowlson 1996, 556–7; *LSB IV* 436–7). Feldman's one-act 'anti-opera' *Neither* for soprano and orchestra was premiered in May 1977 by the Rome Opera.

(*CSP* 258). Such an unearthly light lingering in later works precedes a final beyond of light and dark. For Beckett, there is no knowing what the 'unspeakable home' may be, as the Buddha and Schopenhauer repeatedly assert in referring to the unknowable *nirvāṇa* only in terms of the liberation from grasping and thus from suffering and cycles of existence.

In response to the exegetes who find that Beckett's texts deny transcendence, there is, in speaking of his writing, Beckett's own insistence on the spiritual 'ideal real', the metaphysics of his own experience, the other dimension of his theatrical space, and the 'perhaps'.[29] It could be that 'transcendence' is thought of as implying necessarily a theistic transcendence. Such was in fact my meaning on suggesting in conversation with Beckett that the lack of a belief in transcendence results in increased laughter. Beckett, unaware of my intended meaning, disagreed with my comment, remarking that we had been laughing quite a bit during our conversation and yet we surely have 'transcendent principles' (qtd. in Moorjani 2017, 41). Whether Beckett was thinking of the Proustian ideal real, or the Buddha and Schopenhauer's 'beyond all knowledge', or Simone de Beauvoir and Jean-Paul Sartre's active and transformative stance toward a determining facticity (biological, social, and so on), none of these imply a theistic transcendence, while exemplifying what Beckett termed 'transcendent principles'.

Paul Davies argues that *Stirrings Still* is largely congruent not only with Buddhism but with other mystical traditions (Davies 1994, 233–7). Of these, Neoplatonic and Christian mysticisms have been explored throughout this study owing to the family resemblances between them and the Buddha and Schopenhauer's teachings, as the philosopher that Beckett read again and again maintained. My arguments in favor of the greater family resemblance of Beckett's writing with the Buddha's teachings, some partly overlapping with Upanishadic thought, have been voiced throughout this study as strand after strand of resemblance twined into his texts strengthened into a strong thread winding through his writing.

---

[29] At the end of her fine study focusing on technology and the body in Beckett's oeuvre, Ulrika Maude, for instance, agreeing with many Beckett scholars, concludes that 'Beckett's work denies all forms of transcendence' (Maude 2010, 137). There can be no doubt that the body plays a major role in Beckett's double focus on the empirical and the metaphysical but so does 'a way out'. Accordingly, Andy Wimbush, too, sees a 'paradisiacal side' in Beckett's late prose, derived, he maintains, from the writings of Christian Quietists and the teachings of Schopenhauer, Buddhism, and Greek Pyrrhonism (2020, 213). As a matter of fact, the convergence between the skepticism of Pyrrho, who accompanied Alexander the Great to India in the fourth century BCE, and the Buddha's is such that some scholars of Hellenism trace Pyrrhonism to the tetralemma and Buddhist teachings (Romm 2020, 31).

In summary, where Beckett's 'perhaps' of a beyond self and time and the illusory life dream parts ways with Upanishadic and Neoplatonic and Christian mysticism is in his resolute envisioning of the way out in terms of a positive void, which, as this study has argued, aligns his work with Buddhist philosophy. Thus, the absolute silence beyond silence that is the Upanishadic *Ātman* has no name for the followers of the Buddha. As Murti contends, the difference between the Upanishadic and Buddhist paths to desirelessness consists in the Upanishadic aim of realizing 'the plenitude of our being', whereas the Buddha, 'impressed by the negative aspect of the highest trans-states as devoid (*śūnya*) of intellect, conscious-ness etc.', conceived of a new negative path (Murti 1955, 19). And mystic visions of the soul emptied of self and world, an emptiness likened to a silent desert or wasteland are not, for Beckett, a preliminary for the advent of divinity or the union with the One of other religious and mystical traditions. In agreement with mystics before and after him, Eckhart, for instance, reminds his audience that, 'When I preach I am in the habit of speaking about detachment, and of how a person [*mensche*] should get rid of self and all things' in order to be 'in-formed back' into God (*DW* 53; *MEW I* 564; *CMW* 152; translation modified). Rather, Beckett's obsession with unbornness and the undoing of birth resonates with the Buddhist concept of an immanent and ultimate *unborn* to which one returns without ever having left it. And, finally, it is the Buddha's path via meditation to the ultimate liberation that is alluded to in *Stirrings Still* as the persona, deeply immersed in the mindlessness beyond thought, hears the whispered call to go into that elsewhere where one has always been, beyond desire, self, and time and the suffering they inflict, a call seemingly answered in circling back to the beginning's vision of the 'one true end' of a return to a timeless emptiness. It is a vision anticipated in *Watt* by Arsene's intuition of 'sites of a stirring beyond coming and going, of a being so light and free that it is as the being of nothing' (*W* 39). It nevertheless leaves regrets about the lamentations left behind.

'Comment dire' / 'What Is the Word'

But the last word, or rather lack of a word, is Beckett's. His final text, the poem 'Comment dire' / 'What Is the Word' (*CP* 226–9), written in French in September and October 1988, was begun in the Hôpital Pasteur and completed in the retirement home where he spent the last year of his life. There are seven drafts of the text in his 'Sporting-Herakles' notebook – UoR MS 3316/1 – that bear witness to the difficulty of putting the elements together after Beckett had been felled in July 1988 by what appears to be a stroke or a sequel of the emphysema from which he was suffering. Ruby Cohn, finding traces of aphasia in the text, reports that Beckett only slowly regained speech and mobility in the hospital. On her request, Beckett later translated the poem into English for performance by actor Joe Chaikin, who suffered aphasia after an operation (Cohn 2005, 382–3).

Recalling Beckett's earlier poem 'Roundelay' (1976) and the round song in *Waiting for Godot* and *The Unnamable*, 'What Is the Word' circles from end to beginning, the last line repeating the title and appearing throughout as a refrain.[30] As we know, Beckett's fondness for circular patterns and echoic repetitions is apparent throughout his writing. Imagining Beckett's pleasure in the repetition of the word 'what' in translating his last round-poem into English brings to mind the much puzzled-over painting of a circle in *Watt*, 'broken at its lowest point', and of a dot floating in pictorial space (*W* 128). This painting triggered Watt's musings about possible relationships between the dot and circle 'in boundless space, in endless time' (129), some of which suggest a parody of mystic contemplations of divinity. Watt's attention, however shifts to ruminations on ways to reunite the dot with the circle, a coming home conceived of as a re-enwombing in nothingness. For this reason, it mattered to Watt that the circle's breach was 'below and nowhere else. It is by the nadir that we come, said Watt, and it is by the nadir that we go' (130).

The painting of the dot and broken circle with its 'nadir' – meaning both 'lowest point' and 'zero' – is the most abstract of the simulacra imagined by Beckett throughout his oeuvre for the 'being of nothing', in Arsene's words. In fact, for Yasunari Takahashi, the painting in *Watt* and Beckett's circular patterns evoke the Zen art of the *ensō* – circles hand-drawn with an ink brush in one breath that may be broken and accompanied or not by dots – which, interpreted as symbols of *mushin* (no-mind), are associated with enlightenment (Takahashi 2001, 38).[31] The further associations of Zen circles with infinity and the *unborn* are

---

[30] Enoch Brater draws attention to 'What Is the Word' as a round-poem, in which the last line repeats the first line, in this case, the title. Additionally, for him, Beckett's poem recalls the longer ballade form, with its identical refrain at the end of three stanzas and the envoi of four to five lines (Brater 1994, 165, 170). Beckett's unrhymed poem is then a free adaptation of these poetic forms, with the 'what is the word' refrain occurring eight times (twice as often as in a ballade), in addition to the title.

[31] On first meeting Beckett in 1971, Takahashi brought him a book on Zen art; an *ensō* by Yamada Mumon, broken below like that shown in Figure 8.3, is reproduced in Takahashi 2001, 37.

Figure 8.3   Kazuaki Tanahashi, *Miracles of Each Moment*, 2014, *ensō*, acrylic on canvas.
Image courtesy of the artist

apparent in an *ensō* by Zen Master Yamada Mumon (1900–88), entitled
Fushō (*Unborn*) in reference to Bankei (Seo 2007, 36–7).[32] Hence,
Beckett's 'mindlessness' at the end of *Ohio Impromptu*, reprised in
Stirrings Still, in congruence with Zen *mushin* (no-mind), presupposes a
mind emptied of conscious content to arrive at the dissociative state of
Bankei and Beckett's unaware walking and the creative modes of imaginative writing, composing of music, or drawing of a Zen circle, and
beyond these, of meditative immersion in the *unborn*. Contemporary
Zen artist and scholar Kazuaki Tanahashi (b. 1933), who entitled many
of his *ensō* paintings *Miracles of Each Moment*, speaks, in no-mind terms of
moments lived in meditation beyond thought (Tanahashi 2015, n.p.).

   In 'What Is the Word', aligning a small number of words in free verse
form, Beckett focuses in the first half of the fifty-three-line poem on the
'here': 'folly seeing all this this this here –' (line 19), while switching to
'there' (line 33) in the second half and the 'folly' of the need for a 'glimpse'

---

[32] In her study *Ensō: Zen Circles of Enlightenment*, Audrey Yoshiko Seo reports that at the time zero
was invented in Ancient India, it was first represented by a dot, 'the point from which all things
emerged', which developed into a small empty circle identified with the void (Seo 2007, 2–3).
Unlike an *ensō* however, the circle in *Watt*'s painting is not hand-drawn but 'obviously described by
a compass' (*W* 128), a surprising detail for a painting.

of an unknowable 'over there what −' (line 50).[33] In his translation into English, Beckett doubled the length of the corresponding French line (49) by introducing additional distancing expressions, including 'afaint afar away', alluding, as often pointed out, to the final lines of *Finnegans Wake*, whose circling back to the beginning adds to the poignancy of this final tribute to Joyce added into the English translation of Beckett's final round-poem.[34] In fact, the poem is a line longer in English than in French, Beckett having added line 37, 'afar away over there −', which has no equivalent in 'Comment dire'.

On one level, 'Comment dire' / 'What Is the Word' can be read as staging a frustrating experience of aphasia, akin to the search for the right word in conversation, which is commonly signaled by filler phrases such as 'comment dire' or 'what is the word'. The dashes that come at the end of the poem's lines, both in the French and English versions, with the exception of the last one of each, appear to play a similar role of hesitation. Alternatively, Beckett having termed the dashes *traits de désunion* (marks of separation) in a metacomment to a draft in his 'Sporting-Herakles' notebook, the dashes could be taken as intensifying the unbreachable distance between words and the unsayable.[35]

The folly, then, attributed to the need to glimpse a distant 'what', shifts the interpretation of aphasia into another dimension. In the French version, the final 'comment dire', without a dash, implies the absence of an answer, whereas in the English version, the last 'what is the word', minus the dash, can be read as no longer questioning what the word may be but rather declaring that the looked-for word is 'what' itself, a question asking to be filled left empty. In the round of coming and going, the final emptiness once more intimates the 'perhaps' of an end to the folly of the here and, in further attunement with the Buddha and Schopenhauer, the folly of needing to put into words the inexplicable there.

---

[33] 'Comment dire' is found in *CP* 226–7, followed by 'What Is the Word' on pages 228–9.

[34] See, for instance, Lawlor and Pilling 2012, 474.

[35] The *traits de désunion* comment is found in UoR MS 3316/1, 2v, also quoted in Van Hulle 2011, 102. In a confusion common to both French and English between the terms *trait d'union* (hyphen) and *tiret* (dash), Beckett's *traits de désunion* puns on the French term for hyphen (*trait d'union*) but in the sense of a dash (*tiret*) to emphasize the separating function attributed to dashes as compared to the joining nature of hyphens.

References

PUBLISHED WORKS BY SAMUEL BECKETT

Beckett's Dream Notebook, ed. by John Pilling (Reading: Beckett International Foundation, 1999).

Bing (Paris: Éditions de Minuit), 1966.

The Collected Poems: A Critical Edition, ed. by Seán Lawlor and John Pilling (New York: Grove Press, 2012).

Collected Shorter Plays (New York: Grove Press, 1984).

Comment c'est (Paris: Éditions de Minuit, 1961; 1964 ed.).

Company (New York: Grove Press, 1980).

The Complete Short Prose, 1929–1989, ed. by S. E. Gontarski (New York: Grove Press, 1995).

Le Dépeupleur (Paris: Éditions de Minuit, 1970).

Disjecta: Miscellaneous Writing and a Dramatic Fragment, ed. by Ruby Cohn (New York: Grove Press, 1984).

Dream of Fair to Middling Women, ed. by Eoin O'Brien and Edith Fournier (New York: Arcade Publishing, 1992).

Echo's Bones, ed. by Mark Nixon (New York: Grove Press, 2014).

Eleutheria (Paris: Éditions de Minuit, 1995).

Endgame (New York: Grove Press, 1958).

Film: Complete Scenario/Illustrations/Production Shots (New York: Grove Press, 1969).

Fin de partie, suivi de Acte sans paroles (Paris: Éditions de Minuit, 1957; 1967 ed.).

Happy Days (New York: Grove Press, 1961).

How It Is (New York: Grove Press, 1964).

Ill Seen Ill Said (New York: Grove Press, 1981).

L'Innommable (Paris: Éditions de Minuit, 1953; 2016 ed.).

The Letters of Samuel Beckett, vol. I: 1929–1940, ed. by Martha Dow Fehsenfeld and Lois More Overbeck (Cambridge: Cambridge University Press, 2009).

The Letters of Samuel Beckett, vol. II: 1941–1956, ed. by George Craig, Martha Dow Fehsenfeld, Dan Gunn, and Lois More Overbeck (Cambridge: Cambridge University Press, 2011).

The Letters of Samuel Beckett, vol. III: 1957–1965, ed. by George Craig, Martha Dow Fehsenfeld, Dan Gunn, and Lois More Overbeck (Cambridge: Cambridge University Press, 2014).

The Letters of Samuel Beckett, vol. IV: 1966–1989, ed. by George Craig, Martha Dow Fehsenfeld, Dan Gunn, and Lois More Overbeck (Cambridge: Cambridge University Press, 2016).

Malone Dies, in *Three Novels* (New York: Grove Press, 1956), 177–288.

Mal vu mal dit (Paris: Éditions de Minuit, 1981).

Molloy, in *Three Novels* (New York: Grove Press, 1955), 7–176.

More Pricks than Kicks (London: Calder & Boyars, 1970).

Murphy (New York: Grove Press, 1957).

Nouvelles et Textes pour rien (Paris: Éditions de Minuit, 1958; 2013 ed.).

Pas moi, in *Oh les beaux jours suivi de Pas moi* (Paris: Éditions de Minuit, 1963–1974), 79–95.

Premier amour (Paris: Éditions de Minuit, 1970).

Proust (New York: Grove Press, 1957).

The Unnamable, in *Three Novels* (New York: Grove Press, 1958), 289–414.

Waiting for Godot (New York: Grove Press, 1954).

Watt (New York: Grove Press, 1959).

Worstward Ho (New York: Grove Press, 1983).

ARCHIVAL AND OTHER MATERIALS BY SAMUEL BECKETT

'Beckett on *Film*' (edited transcript of 1964 preproduction discussions with Alan Schneider, Boris Kaufman, and Barney Rosset), in *The Intent of Undoing in Samuel Beckett's Dramatic Texts*, by S. E. Gontarski (Bloomington: Indiana University Press, 1985), 187–92.

Lecture notes taken in Beckett's 1931 course on Racine and the Modern Novel, at Trinity College Dublin, by Rachel Burrows (formerly Dobbin), Trinity College Library Dublin, MIC 60.

Manuscripts of 'Comment dire' / 'What Is the Word', Beckett International Foundation, University of Reading, MS 3316/1, viewed in online digital edition, transcribed by Dirk van Hulle, The Beckett Digital Manuscript Project, www.beckettarchive.org.

Manuscripts of *Stirrings Still*, Beckett International Foundation, University of Reading, MS 2934 and MS 2935, viewed in online digital edition, transcribed by Dirk van Hulle, The Beckett Digital Manuscript Project, www.beckettarchive.org.

Notes on Heinrich Zimmer's *Maya: Der indische Mythos* (Stuttgart: Deutsche Verlags-Anstalt, 1936), reproduced in *The Personal Library of James Joyce: A Descriptive Bibliography*, by Thomas E. Connolly, University of Buffalo Studies 22 (Buffalo, NY: University of Buffalo, 1955), 42–7.

'Sottisier' notebook, Beckett International Foundation, University of Reading, MS 2901.

Typescript of *Not I* entitled 'Analysis', University of Reading, MS 1227/7/12/1, and typescript entitled 'NOT I – synopsis', University of Reading, MS 1227/7/12/10, reprinted in *Theatre of Shadows: Samuel Beckett's Drama 1956–1976*, by Rosemary Pountney (Gerrards Cross: Colin Smythe 1998 [1988]), 245, 247.

WORKS BY OTHER AUTHORS

Abbott, H. Porter (1996), *Beckett Writing Beckett: The Author in the Autograph* (Ithaca: Cornell University Press).

——— (2008), 'I Am Not a Philosopher', in *Beckett at 100: Revolving It All*, ed. by Linda Ben-Zvi and Angela Moorjani (New York: Oxford University Press), 81–106.

——— (2009), 'Immersions in the Cognitive Sublime: The Textual Experience of the Extratextual Unknown in García Márquez and Beckett', *Narrative* 17.2: 131–42.

——— (2013), *Real Mysteries: Narrative and the Unknowable* (Columbus: Ohio State University Press).

Abe, Masao (1990), 'Kenosis and Emptiness', in *Buddhist Emptiness and Christian Trinity: Essays and Exploration*, ed. by Roger Corless and Paul F. Knitter (New York: Paulist Press), 5–25.

Ackerley, Chris (1998), *Demented Particulars: The Annotated* Murphy, special issue, *Journal of Beckett Studies* 7.1–2.

——— (2000), 'Samuel Beckett and Thomas à Kempis: The Roots of Quietism', *Samuel Beckett Today/Aujourd'hui* 9: 81–92.

——— (2004), 'The Uncertainty of Self: Samuel Beckett and the Location of the Voice', *Samuel Beckett Today/Aujourd'hui* 14: 39–51.

Ackerley, Chris, and S. E. Gontarski (2004), *The Grove Companion to Samuel Beckett: A Reader's Guide to His Works, Life, and Thought* (New York: Grove Press).

Adelman, Gary (2003), 'Fearful Symmetry: Beckett's *The Lost Ones*', *Journal of Modern Literature* 26.2: 164–9.

——— (2004), *Naming Beckett's Unnamable* (Lewisburg PA: Bucknell University Press).

Adorno, Theodor W. (2000a [1966]), *Negative Dialectics*, trans. by E. B. Ashton (London: Routledge).

——— (2000b [1998]), *Metaphysics: Concept and Problems*, ed. by Rolf Tiedemann, trans. by Edmund Jephcott (Cambridge: Polity Press).

——— (2010), 'Notes on *The Unnamable*', trans. by Dirk Van Hulle and Shane Weller, *Journal of Beckett Studies* 19.2: 172–8.

Amiran, Eyal (1993), *Wandering and Home: Beckett's Metaphysical Narrative* (University Park: Pennsylvania State University Press).

Anzieu, Didier (1985), *Le Moi-peau* (Paris: Dunot).

App, Urs (1998), 'Schopenhauers Begegnung mit dem Buddhismus', *Schopenhauer-Jahrbuch* 79: 35–58.

——— (2010), 'Schopenhauers Nirwana', in *Die Wahrheit ist nackt am schönsten: Arthur Schopenhauers philosophische Provokation*, ed. by Michael Fleiter (Frankfurt a. M.: Institut für Stadtgeschichte/Societätsverlag), 200–8.

——— (2014), *Schopenhauer's Compass: An Introduction to Schopenhauer's Philosophy and Its Origins* (Wil: UniversityMedia).

Arnold, Dan (2014), *Brains, Buddhas, and Believing: The Problem of Intentionality in Classical Buddhist and Cognitive-Scientist Philosophy of Mind* (New York: Columbia University Press).

(n.d.), 'Madhyamaka Buddhist Philosophy', in *Internet Encyclopedia of Philosophy*, www.iep.utm.edu/b-madhya/.

Bachelard, Gaston (1973 [1942]), *L'Eau et les rêves: essai sur l'imagination de la matière* (Paris: José Corti).

(2009 [1957]), *La Poétique de l'espace*, 10th ed. (Paris: Presses universitaires de France).

Badiou, Alain (1995), *Beckett: l'increvable désir* (Paris: Hachette).

(2003), *On Beckett*, ed. by Alberto Toscano and Nina Power (Manchester UK: Clinamen Press).

Bair, Deirdre (1978), *Samuel Beckett* (New York: Harcourt Brace Jovanovich).

Baker, Phil (1997), *Beckett and the Mythology of Psychoanalysis* (Houndmills: Macmillan Press).

Bakhtin, Mikhail M. (1981), *The Dialogic Imagination: Four Essays*, ed. by Michael Holquist, trans. by Caryl Emerson and Michael Holquist (Austin: University of Texas Press).

Baldwin, Hélène L. (1981), *Samuel Beckett's Real Silence* (University Park: Pennsylvania State University Press).

Bankei Yōtaku (1984), *The Unborn: The Life and Teachings of Zen Master Bankei 1622–1693*, trans. and comm. by Norman Waddell (New York: North Point Press).

Barthes, Roland (1953), *Le Degré zéro de l'écriture* (Paris: Éditions Gonthier).

(1967), 'The Death of the Author', trans. by Richard Howard, *Aspen: The Magazine in a Box* 5–6: n. p., www.ubu.com/aspen/aspen5and6/threeEssays .html.

Beaty, Roger E., M. Benedek, P. J. Silvia, and D. L. Schacter (2016), 'Creative Cognition and Brain Network Dynamics', *Trends in Cognitive Sciences* 20.2: 87–95.

Begam, Richard (1996), *Samuel Beckett and the End of Modernity* (Stanford: Stanford University Press).

(2007), 'Beckett's Kinetic Aesthetics', *Journal of Beckett Studies* 16.1–2: 46–63.

Ben-Zvi, Linda (1980), 'Samuel Beckett, Fritz Mauthner, and the Limits of Language', *PMLA* 95.2: 183–200.

(1984), 'Fritz Mauthner for Company', *Journal of Beckett Studies* 9: 65–88, www.english.fsu.edu/jobs/num08/Num9Ben-Zvi.htm.

(1986), *Samuel Beckett* (Boston: Twayne Publishers).

(2017), 'Memories of Meeting Beckett', in *Beckett in Conversation 'yet again' / Rencontres avec Beckett, 'encore'*, ed. by Angela Moorjani, Danièle de Ruyter, and Sjef Houppermans (Leiden: Brill/Rodopi), 63–9.

Beplate, Justin (2005), 'Who Speaks? Grammar, Memory, and Identity in Beckett's *Company*', *Journal of Modern Literature* 29.1: 153–65.

Bersani, Leo, and Ulysse Dutoit (1993), *Acts of Impoverishment: Beckett, Rothko, Resnais* (Cambridge, MA: Harvard University Press).

Bignell, Jonathan (2010), 'Into the Void: Beckett's Television Plays and the Idea of Broadcasting', in *Beckett and Nothing: Trying to Understand Beckett*, ed. by Daniela Caselli (Manchester: Manchester University Press), 125–42.

Bion, Wilfred R. (1967), 'The Imaginary Twin', in *Second Thoughts: Selected Papers on Psycho-Analysis* (New York: Jason Aronson), 3–22.

    (1989 [1977]), *Two Papers: The Grid and Caesura* (London: Karnac Books).

Bixby, Patrick (2009), *Samuel Beckett and the Postcolonial Novel* (New York: Cambridge University Press).

Blanchot, Maurice (1943), *Faux pas* (Paris: Gallimard).

    (1950 [1941]), *Thomas l'obscur*, new ed. (Paris: Gallimard).

    (1953), 'Où maintenant? Qui maintenant?', *Nouvelle Nouvelle Revue Française* 1.10: 678–86.

    (1979 [1953]), 'Where Now?, Who Now?', an abridged translation by Richard Howard of the 1953 article, in *Samuel Beckett: The Critical Heritage*, ed. by L. Graver and R. Federman (London: Routledge), 116–21.

    (1993 [1969]), *The Infinite Conversation*, trans. by Susan Hanson (Minneapolis: University of Minnesota Press).

    (2001), *Faux Pas*, trans. by Charlotte Mandell (Stanford, CA: Stanford University Press).

Bowles, Patrick (1994), 'How to Fall: Notes on Talks with Samuel Beckett', *PN Review 96* 20.4: 24–38.

    (2006), 'Patrick Bowles on Beckett in the Early 1950s', in *Beckett Remembering Remembering Beckett: A Centenary Celebration*, ed. by James and Elizabeth Knowlson (New York: Arcade Publishing), 108–15. (Excerpted from Bowles 1994.)

Brater, Enoch (1994), *The Drama in the Text: Beckett's Late Fiction* (New York: Oxford University Press).

Bréhier, Émile (1982 [1928]), *La Philosophie de Plotin* (Paris: Librairie philosophique J. Vrin).

Brown, Llewellyn (2011), 'Voice and Pronouns in Beckett's *The Unnamable*', *Journal of Beckett Studies* 20.2: 172–96.

Bryden, Mary (1998), *Samuel Beckett and the Idea of God* (Houndmills: Macmillan Press).

Bryden, Mary, Julian Garforth, and Peter Mills (1998), *Beckett at Reading: Catalogue of the Beckett Manuscript Collection at the University of Reading* (Reading: Whiteknights Press and the Beckett International Foundation).

Buning, Marius (1990), 'Samuel Beckett's Negative Way: Intimations of the *Via Negativa* in His Late Plays', in *European Literature and Theology in the Twentieth Century: Ends of Time*, ed. by David Jasper and Colin Crowder (London: Macmillan), 129–42.

    (2000), 'The *via negativa* and Its First Stirring in *Eleutheria*', in *Samuel Beckett Today/Aujourd'hui* 9: 43–54.

Butler, Lance St. John (1984), *Samuel Beckett and the Meaning of Being: A Study in Ontological Parable* (London: Macmillan Press).

Calder, John (2001), *The Philosophy of Samuel Beckett* (London: Calder Publications).

Campbell, Julie (2005), 'The Entrapment of the Female Body in Beckett's Plays in Relation to Jung's Third Tavistock Lecture', *Samuel Beckett Today/Aujourd'hui* 15: 161–72.

(2012), 'Allegories of Clarity and Obscurity: Bunyan's *The Pilgrim's Progress* and Beckett's *Molloy*, *Samuel Beckett Today/Aujourd'hui* 24: 89–103.

Carpenter, Amber (2014), *Indian Buddhist Philosophy: Metaphysics as Ethics* (London: Routledge).

Caselli, Daniela (2005), *Beckett's Dantes: Intertextuality in the Fiction and Criticism* (Manchester: Manchester University Press).

Charbonnier, Jean-Michel (2018), 'Le Japon, pays des fantômes', in *Enfers et fantômes d'Asie*, Connaisance des Arts, hors-série (Paris: Société Française de Promotion Artistique), 14–21.

Clément, Bruno (2008), 'Mais quelle est cette voix?', *Samuel Beckett Today/ Aujourd'hui* 19: 89–101.

Coe, Richard N. (1970 [1964]), *Samuel Beckett*, rev. ed. of *Beckett* (New York: Grove Press).

Cohn, Ruby (1980), *Just Play: Beckett's Theater* (Princeton, NJ: Princeton University Press).

(2005), *A Beckett Canon* (Ann Arbor: University of Michigan Press).

Connolly, Thomas E. (1955), *The Personal Library of James Joyce: A Descriptive Bibliography* (Buffalo, NY: University of Buffalo).

Connor, Steven (2007 [1988]), *Samuel Beckett: Repetition, Theory and Text* (Aurora, CO: Davis Group, Publishers).

(2008), '"On Such and Such a Day ... in Such a World": Beckett's Radical Finitude', *Samuel Beckett Today/Aujourd'hui* 19: 35–50.

Conze, Edward (1959a [1951]), *Buddhism: Its Essence and Development* (New York: Harper & Row).

ed. (1959b), *Buddhist Scriptures* (London: Penguin books).

(1968), Introduction, in *On Indian Mahayana Buddhism*, by D. T. Suzuki (New York: Harper Torchbooks), 1–29.

trans. and comm. (2001 [1958]), *Buddhist Wisdom: 'The Diamond Sutra' and 'The Heart Sutra'* (New York: Vintage Books).

Cornu, Philippe (2001), *Dictionnaire encyclopédique du bouddhisme* (Paris: Éditions du Seuil).

Cousineau, Thomas (n.d.), 'L'Amnésie vue par Samuel Beckett' (unpublished paper), https://washcoll.academia.edu/tomcousineau.

Critchley, Simon (2004), *Very Little ... Almost Nothing: Death, Philosophy, Literature*, 2nd ed. (London: Routledge).

Cronin, Anthony (1997), *Samuel Beckett: The Last Modernist* (New York: HarperCollins Publishers).

Cross, Stephen (2013), *Schopenhauer's Encounter with Indian Thought: Representation and Will and Their Indian Parallels* (Honolulu: University of Hawai'i Press).

Dällenbach, Lucien (1989), *The Mirror in the Text*, trans. by Jeremy Whiteley with Emma Hughes (Chicago: University of Chicago Press).

Dauer, Dorothea W. (1969), *Schopenhauer as Transmitter of Buddhist Ideas* (Bern: Herbert Lang).

Davies, Paul (1994), *The Ideal Real: Beckett's Fiction and Imagination* (London: Associated University Presses).

— (2000), *Beckett and Eros: Death of Humanism* (Houndmills: Palgrave Macmillan).

— (2001), 'On Beckett's Metaphysics of Non-Location: Vagrancy, Void and Formless Fire', *Samuel Beckett Today/Aujourd'hui* 11: 399–407.

Davis, Bret W. (2004), 'Zen after Zarathustra: The Problem of Will in the Confrontation of Nietzsche with Buddhism', *Journal of Nietzsche Studies* 28: 89–138.

Deleuze, Gilles (1990 [1969]), *The Logic of Sense*, ed. by Constantin V. Boundas, trans. by Mark Lester with Charles Stivale (New York: Columbia University Press).

— (1997a [1992]), 'The Exhausted', trans. by Anthony Uhlmann, in *Essays Critical and Clinical* (Minneapolis: University of Minnesota Press), 152–74.

— (1997b), 'He Stuttered', in *Essays Critical and Clinical*, trans. by Daniel W. Smith and Michael A. Greco (Minneapolis: University of Minnesota Press), 107–14.

— (2000 [1986]), 'The Brain Is the Screen: An Interview with Gilles Deleuze', in *The Brain Is the Screen: Deleuze and the Philosophy of Cinema*, ed. by Gregory Flaxman (Minneapolis: University of Minnesota Press), 365–74.

Denham, Robert D. (2011), 'Northrop Frye and Giordano Bruno', in *The Educated Imagination: A Website Dedicated to Northrop Frye*, 1–11, http://bit.ly/denhamRD.

Dennett, Daniel C. (1991), *Consciousness Explained* (New York: Back Bay Books/Little Brown and Company).

Dennis, Amanda (2015a), 'Radical Indecision: Aporia as Metamorphosis in Beckett's *The Unnamable*', *Journal of Beckett Studies* 24.2: 180–97.

— (2015b), 'Poets of Their Own Acts: Tactics, Style and Occupation in Beckett's *Nouvelles*', *Samuel Beckett Today/Aujourd'hui* 27: 43–55.

Derrida, Jacques (1972 [1967]), 'Freud and the Scene of Writing', trans. by Jeffrey Mehlman, *Yale French Studies* 48: 73–117.

— (1989), 'How to Avoid Speaking: Denials', trans. by Ken Frieden, in *Languages of the Unsayable: The Play of Negativity in Literature and Literary Theory*, ed. by Sanford Budick and Wolfgang Iser (New York: Columbia University Press), 3–70.

— (1995), *Sauf le nom (Post-Scriptum)*, trans. by John P. Leavey, Jr., in *On the Name*, ed. by Thomas Dutoit (Stanford: Stanford University Press), 35–85.

— (2009 [1992]), '"This Strange Institution Called Literature": An Interview with Jacques Derrida', trans. by Geoffrey Bennington and Rachel Bowlby, in *Acts of Literature*, ed. by Derek Attridge (New York: Routledge), 33–75.

Deussen, Paul (1907 [1898]), *Die Philosophie der Upanishads*, vol. 1, part 2 of *Allgemeine Geschichte der Philosophie*, 2nd ed. (Leipzig: F. A. Brockhaus).

De Vos, Laurens (2018), 'The Observer Observed. The Promise of the Posthuman: Homeostasis, *Autopoiesis* and Virtuality in Samuel Beckett', *Journal of Beckett Studies* 27.2: 245–60.

Dewey, Russell A. (2018), *Psychology: An Introduction* (*Psych Web* online text), https://psywww.com/intropsych/.

Driver, Tom (1979 [1961]), 'Beckett by the Madeleine', *Columbia University Forum* (Summer 1961): 21–25, rpt. in *Samuel Beckett the Critical Heritage*, ed. by L. Graver and R. Federman (New York: Routledge), 217–23.

Eckhart, Meister (1993), *Werke*, 2 vols., ed. and comm. by Niklaus Largier, trans. into modern German by Josef Quint (vol. 1) and Ernst Benz et al. (vol. 2) (Frankfurt a. M.: Deutscher Klassiker Verlag).

(1994), *Selected Writings*, trans. by Oliver Davies (London: Penguin Books).

(2009), *The Complete Mystical Works of Meister Eckhart*, trans. and ed. by Maurice O'C. Walshe, revised with a foreword by Bernard McGinn (New York: Crossroad Publishing).

Edelglass, William (2009), 'The Bodhisattva Path: Śāntideva's Bodhicaryāvatāra', in *Buddhist Philosophy: Essential Readings*, ed. by William Edelglass and Jay L. Garfield (New York: Oxford University Press).

Esslin, Martin (1986), 'Samuel Beckett – Infinity, Eternity', in *Beckett at 80/ Beckett in Context*, ed. by Enoch Brater (New York: Oxford University Press), 110–23.

Facco, Enrico, and Christian Agrillo (2012), 'Near-Death Experiences between Science and Prejudice', *Frontiers in Human Neuroscience* 6: 1–7.

Feldman, Matthew (2006), *Beckett's Books: A Cultural History of Samuel Beckett's 'Interwar Notes'* (London: Continuum).

(2009), '"Agnostic Quietism" and Samuel Beckett's Early Development', in *Samuel Beckett: History, Memory, Archive*, ed. by Seán Kennedy and Katherine Weiss (New York: Palgrave Macmillan), 183–200.

Flasch, Kurt (2015), *Meister Eckhart: Philosopher of Christianity*, trans. by Anne Schindel and Aaron Vanides (New Haven: Yale University Press).

Fleet, Barrie, trans. (2012), Introduction and Commentary, in *Enneas IV.8: On the Descent of the Soul into Bodies*, by Plotinus (Las Vagas: Parmenides), 13–42, 69–189.

Foster, Paul (1989), *Beckett and Zen: A Study of the Dilemma in the Novels of Samuel Beckett* (London: Wisdom Publications).

Foucault, Michel (1969), 'Qu'est-ce qu'un auteur?', *Bulletin de la Société française de philosophie* 63.3: 73–104.

Freud, Sigmund (1955 [1920]), *Beyond the Pleasure Principle*, in *The Standard Edition of the Complete Psychological Works*, vol. 18, ed. and trans. by James Strachey (London: Hogarth Press), 1–64.

(1959 [1908]), 'Creative Writers and Day-Dreaming', in *The Standard Edition of the Complete Psychological Works*, vol. 9, ed. and trans. by James Strachey (London: Hogarth Press), 142–53.

(1961 [1925]), 'A Note upon the "Mystic Writing-Pad"', in *The Standard Edition of the Complete Psychological Works*, vol. 19, ed. and trans. by James Strachey (London: Hogarth Press), 227–32.

Frost, Everett, and Jane Maxwell (2006), '*Notes diverse[s] holo*: Catalogues of Beckett's Reading Notes and Other Manuscripts at Trinity College

Dublin, with Supporting Essays', *Samuel Beckett Today/Aujourd'hui* 16: 13–181.

Garfield, Jay (2011), 'Mindfulness and Ethics: Attention, Virtue and Perfection', Lecture, University of Hamburg, Numata Centre for Buddhist Studies, https://info-buddhism.com/Mindfulness-and-Morality-J-Garfield.html.

Garforth, Julian A. (2004), 'Samuel Beckett, Fritz Mauthner, and the *Whoroscope* Notebook: Beckett's Beiträge zu einer Kritik der Sprache', *Journal of Beckett Studies* 13.2: 49–68.

Gendronneau, Paul (1922), *De l'influence du bouddhisme sur la figuration des enfers médiévaux* (Nîmes: P. Gallion et Bandini).

Gerson, Lloyd (2018), 'Plotinus', in *The Stanford Encyclopedia of Philosophy*, ed. by Edward N. Zalta, https://plato.stanford.edu/archives/fall2018/entries/plotinus.

Gibson, Andrew (2002), 'Beckett and Badiou', in *Beckett and Philosophy*, ed. by Richard Lane (Houndmills: Palgrave), 93–107.

(2015), 'Beckett, Vichy, Maurras, and the Body: *Premier Amour* and *Nouvelles*', *Irish University Review* 45.2: 281–301.

Gidal, Peter (1979), 'Samuel Beckett's *Ghost Trio*', *Artforum* 17.9: 53–7.

(1986), *Understanding Beckett: A Study of Monologue and Gesture in the Works of Samuel Beckett* (London: Macmillan).

(1998), Note on *No Night No Day*, www.film-makerscoop.com/catalogue/peter-gidal-no-night-no-day.

(2001[1973]), 'Beckett & Others & Art: A System', *Samuel Beckett Today/Aujourd'hui* 11: 303–14.

Gide, André (1968 [1925]), *Les Faux-monnayeurs* (Paris: Livre de poche).

(1981 [1923]), *Dostoïevski: articles et causeries* (Paris: Gallimard).

Gillette, Kyle (2012), 'Zen and the Art of Self-Negation in Samuel Beckett's *Not I*', *Comparative Drama* 46.3: 283–302.

Gontarski, S. E. (1985), *The Intention of Undoing in Samuel Beckett's Dramatic Texts* (Bloomington: Indiana University Press).

Graham, Daniel W. (2017), 'Heraclitus', in *Internet Encyclopedia of Philosophy*, www.iep.utm.edu/heraclit/.

Haeckel, Ernst (1911 [1882]), *A Visit to Ceylon*, trans. by Clara Beel, 3rd ed. (New York: Peter Eckler Publisher), https://archive.org/details/visittoceylon00haecuoft.

Hamilton, Clarence H. (1950), 'The Idea of Compassion in Mahayana Buddhism', *Journal of American Oriental Society* 70.3: 145–51.

Hartman, Geoffrey (1977), Letter, in *PMLA* 92 (March): 307–8.

Harvey, Lawrence E. (1970), *Samuel Beckett: Poet and Critic* (Princeton, NJ: Princeton University Press).

(2006), 'On Beckett, 1961–2', in *Beckett Remembering Remembering Beckett*, ed. by James and Elizabeth Knowlson (New York: Arcade Publishing), 133–7.

Hayman, David (1962), 'Quest for Meaninglessness: The Boundless Poverty of *Molloy*', in *Six Contemporary Novels: Six Introductory Essays in Modern*

Fiction, ed. by William O. S. Sutherland (Austin University of Texas), 90–112.

Herren, Graley (2000), 'Splitting Images: Samuel Beckett's *Nacht und Träume*', *Modern Drama* 43.2: 182–91.

—— (2001), '*Nacht und Träume* as Beckett's Agony in the Garden', *Journal of Beckett Studies* 11.1: 54–70.

Hesla, David H. (1971), *The Shape of Chaos: An Interpretation of the Art of Samuel Beckett* (Minneapolis: University of Minnesota Press).

Hill, Leslie (1990), *Beckett's Fiction: In Different Words* (Cambridge: Cambridge University Press).

Holmes, Ken (n.d.), 'Karma and the Wheel of Life', in *Teaching Archive of Kagyu Samye Ling*, n.p., www.samyeling.org/buddhism-and-meditation/.

Horn, Laurence R. (1989), *A Natural History of Negation* (Chicago: University of Chicago Press).

Hutcheon, Linda (1985), *A Theory of Parody: The Teachings of Twentieth-Century Art Forms* (New York: Methuen).

Inge, William Ralph (1899), *Christian Mysticism: Considered in Eight Lectures Delivered before the University of Oxford* (London: Methuen).

—— (1926), *The Platonic Tradition in English Religious Thought: The Hulsean Lectures at Cambridge 1925–1926* (London: Longmans, Green and Co.)

Jacquart, Emmanuel (1997), 'Beckettisimo: Beckett virtuose de l'écho. *Fin de partie* et l'essence du bouddhisme', *Samuel Beckett Today/Aujourd'hui* 6: 31–42.

Jones, David Houston (2011), *Samuel Beckett and Testimony* (Houndmills: Palgrave Macmillan).

Joyce, James (1968 [1939]), *Finnegans Wake* (New York: Viking Press).

Juliet, Charles (1986), *Rencontre avec Samuel Beckett* (Montpellier: Éditions Fata Morgana).

Kalupahana, David (1976), *Buddhist Philosophy: A Historical Analysis* (Honolulu: University Press of Hawai'i).

Keatinge, Benjamin (2015), 'Breakdown or Breakthrough?: Deleuzoguattarian Schizophrenia and Beckett's Gallery of Moribunds', in *Deleuze and Beckett*, ed. by S. E. Wilmer and Audrone Zukauskaitė (Houndmills: Palgrave Macmillan), 81–96.

Kędzierski, Marek (2017), 'Bothering Him with My Questions…', in *Beckett in Conversation, 'yet again'/Rencontres avec Beckett, 'encore'*, ed. by Angela Moorjani, Danièle de Ruyter, and Sjef Houppermans (Leiden: Brill/Rodopi), 116–27.

Keene, Donald (1990), *Nō and Bunraku* (New York: Columbia University Press).

Keown, Damien (2001 [1992]), *The Nature of Buddhist Ethics* (Houndmills: Palgrave Macmillan).

Kirishima, Keiko (1990), 'Le Théâtre de Beckett et le théâtre de Nô', *Critique* 46.519–20 (Special Issue Samuel Beckett): 690–91.

Klee, Paul (1996), *Gedichte*, ed. by Felix Klee (Zurich: Arche Verlag).

Klossowski, Pierre (1969), *Nietzsche et le cercle vicieux* (Paris: Mercure de France).

Knowlson, James (1983), 'Beckett's "Bits of Pipe"', in *Samuel Beckett: Humanistic Perspectives*, ed. by Morris Beja, S. E. Gontarski, and Pierre Astier (Columbus: Ohio State University), 16–25.

(1996), *Damned to Fame: The Life of Samuel Beckett* (New York: Simon and Schuster).

Körte, Konrad (2017), 'Beckett Listens: Sound Production for the 1977 *Geistertrio*', in *Beckett in Conversation, 'yet again'/Rencontres avec Beckett, 'encore'*, ed. by Angela Moorjani, Danièle de Ruyter, and Sjef Houppermans (Leiden: Brill/Rodopi), 107–15.

Krance, Charles, ed. (1993), *Samuel Beckett's Company/Compagnie and A Piece of Monologue/Solo: A Bilingual Variorum Edition* (New York: Garland Publishing).

Kügler, Peter (2005), 'The Meaning of Mystical 'Darkness'', *Religious Studies* 41.1: 95–105.

Kundert-Gibbs, John Leeland (1999), *No-Thing Is Left to Tell: Zen/Chaos Theory in the Dramatic Art of Samuel Beckett* (London: Associated University Presses).

Kuzma, Joseph (n.d.), 'Maurice Blanchot (1907–2003)', in *The Internet Encyclopedia of Philosophy*, n.p., https://iep.utm.edu/blanchot/.

Lacrosse, Joachim (2009), 'Plotinus, Porphyry, and India: A Re-Examination', in *Late Antique Epistemology*, ed. by Panayiota Vassilopoulou and Stephen R. Clark (Houndmills: Palgrave Macmillan), 103–17.

Laplanche, Jean, and Jean-Bertrand Pontalis (1973), *Vocabulaire de la psychanalyse*, 4th ed. (Paris: Presses universitaires de France).

Lawley, Paul (1983), 'Counterpoint, Absence and the Medium in Beckett's *Not I*', in *Modern Drama* 26: 407–14.

(1989), 'The Difficult Birth: An Image of Utterance in Beckett', in *'Make sense who may': Essays on Samuel Beckett's Later Works*, ed. by Robin J. Davis and Lance St. J. Butler (Totowa NJ: Barnes and Noble Books), 1–10.

(2002), '*That Time* and the Dynamics of Being', in *Other Becketts*, ed. by Daniella Caselli, Seven Connor, and Laura Salisbury (Tallahassee, FL: Journal of Beckett Studies Books), 173–86.

(2015), 'Krapp at the Hawk's Well: Beckett, Yeats, and Joyce', *Modern Drama* 58.3: 370–90.

(n.d.), 'Hedda's Children', https://plymouth.academia.edu/PaulLawley.

Lawlor, Seán, and John Pilling (2012), Commentary, in *The Collected Poems of Samuel Beckett*, ed. by Seán Lawlor and John Pilling (New York: Grove Press), 253–489.

Le Brocquy, Anne (2017), 'Come back soon!', in *Beckett in Conversation, 'yet again'/Rencontres avec Beckett, 'encore'*, ed. by Angela Moorjani, Danièle de Ruyter, and Sjef Houppermans (Leiden: Brill/Rodopi), 91–101.

Le Juez, Brigitte (2009), *Beckett before Beckett*, trans. by Ros Schwartz (London: Souvenir Press).

Levinas, Emmanuel (1974), *Totalité et infini: essai sur l'extériorité*, 4th ed. (The Hague: Martinus Nijhoff).

Locatelli, Carla (1990), *Unwording the World: Samuel Beckett's Prose Works after the Noble Prize* (Philadelphia: University of Pennsylvania Press).

Lodge, David (1979 [1968]), 'Some Ping Understood', *Encounter* 30.2 (Feb. 1968): 85–9; rpt. in *Samuel Beckett: The Critical Heritage*, ed. by L. Graver and R. Federman (London: Routledge), 291–301.

Loy, David (1996), 'The Nonduality of Life and Death', in *Lack and Transcendence: The Problem of Death and Life in Psychotherapy, Existentialism, and Buddhism* (Atlantic Highlands, NJ: Humanities Press International), 1–29.

Magessa O'Reilly, Edouard (2006), '*Molloy*, Part II, Where the Shit Hits the Fan: Ballyba's Economy and the Worth of the World', *Genetic Joyce Studies* 6 (online journal), www.geneticjoycestudies.org.

Magnani, Lorenzo (2009), *Abductive Cognition: The Epistemological and Eco-Cognitive Dimensions of Hypothetical Reasoning* (Berlin Springer-Verlag).

Masson, André (1949), 'Divagations sur l'espace' [Ramblings about Space] – Pages de journal (1936–1938)', *Les Temps Modernes* 44: 961–72.

Matoba, Junko (2000), 'Religious Overtones in the Darkened Area of Beckett's Later Short Plays', *Samuel Beckett Today/Aujourd'hui* 9: 31–41.

(2003), *Beckett's Yohaku: A Study of Samuel Beckett's Empty Space on Stage in His Later Shorter Plays* (Tokyo: Shinsui-sha).

Maude, Ulrika (2010), *Beckett, Technology and the Body* (New York: Cambridge University Press).

Mauthner, Fritz (1912 [1901]), *Zur Sprachwissenschaft*, vol. 2 of *Beiträge zu einer Kritik der Sprache*, 2nd ed. (Stuttgart: J. G. Cotta'sche Buchhandlung Nachfolger), www.archive.org.

(1912 [1902]), *Zur Grammatik und Logik*, vol. 3 of *Beiträge zu einer Kritik der Sprache*, 2nd ed. (Stuttgart: J. G. Cotta'sche Buchhandlung Nachfolger), www.archive.org.

(1921 [1901]), *Zur Sprache und zur Psychologie*, vol. 1 of *Beiträge zu einer Kritik der Sprache*, 3rd ed. (Stuttgart: J. G. Cotta'sche Buchhandlung Nachfolger), www.archive.org.

McGinn, Bernard (1994), 'Ocean and Desert as Symbols of Mystical Absorption in the Christian Tradition', *The Journal of Religion* 74.2: 155–81.

McHale, Brian (2004 [1987]), *Postmodernist Fiction* (London: Routledge).

McLeod, Beryl Rosay (1992), 'Buddhism, T. S. Eliot and *The Four Quartets*', *Journal for the Study of Religion* 5.1: 3–16.

McMahan, David L. (2008), *The Making of Buddhist Modernism* (New York: Oxford University Press).

McMillan, Dougald, and Martha Fehsenfeld (1988), *Beckett in the Theatre: An Author as Practical Playwright and Director* (New York: Riverrun Press).

Moorjani, Angela (1982), *Abysmal Games in the Novels of Samuel Beckett* (Chapel Hill: University of North Carolina Press). Reissued 2018.

(1992), *The Aesthetics of Loss and Lessness* (Houndmills: Macmillan).

(1996), 'Mourning, Schopenhauer, and Beckett's Art of Shadows', in *Beckett On and On . . .*, ed. by Lois Oppenheim and Marius Buning (London:

Associated University Presses), 83–101, https://umbc.academia.edu/AngelaMoorjani.

(2000), *Beyond Fetishism and Other Excursions in Psychopragmatics* (New York: St. Martin's Press).

(2003), 'Diogenes Lampoons Alexandre Kojève: Cultural Ghosts in Beckett's Early French Plays', in *Drawing on Beckett: Portraits, Performances, and Cultural Contexts*, ed. by Linda Ben-Zvi (Tel Aviv: Assaph Books), 69–88, https://umbc.academia.edu/AngelaMoorjani.

(2004), 'Peau de chagrin: Beckett and Bion on Looking Not to See', *Samuel Beckett Today/Aujourd'hui* 14: 25–38, https://umbc.academia.edu/AngelaMoorjani.

(2008), '"Just Looking": Ne(i)ther-World Icons, Elsheimer Nocturnes, and Other Simultaneities in Beckett's *Play*', in *Beckett at 100: Revolving It All*, ed. by Linda Ben-Zvi and Angela Moorjani (New York: Oxford University Press), 123–38, https://umbc.academia.edu/AngelaMoorjani.

(2009), 'André Gide among the Parisian Ghosts in the "Anglo-Irish" *Murphy*', *Samuel Beckett Today/Aujourd'hui* 21: 209–222, https://umbc.academia.edu/AngelaMoorjani.

(2017), 'Recollecting Sam-ness and Watt-ness', in *Beckett in Conversation, 'yet again'/Rencontres avec Beckett, 'encore'*, ed. by Angela Moorjani, Danièle de Ruyter, and Sjef Houppermans (Leiden: Brill/Rodopi), 35–45.

Morin, Emilie (2017), *Beckett's Political Imagination* (New York: Cambridge University Press).

Murti, Tirupattur R. V. (1955), *The Central Philosophy of Buddhism: A Study of the Mādhyamika System* (London: George Allen and Unwin).

Nagao, Gadjin M. (1979), 'From Mādhyamika to Yogācāra: An Analysis of MMK, XXIV.18 and MV, I.1–2', *Journal of the International Association of Buddhist Studies* 2.1: 29–43.

Nāgārjuna (2013), *Nāgārjuna's Middle Way: Mūlamadhyamakakārikā*, trans. and comm. by Mark Siderits and Shōryū Katsura (Somerville, MA: Wisdom Publications).

Nájera, Elena (2007), 'Wittgenstein versus Mauthner: Two Critiques of Language, Two Mysticisms', in *Papers of the 30th IWS* [International Wittgenstein Symposium], ed. by H. Hrachovec, A. Pichier, J. Wang (Kirchberg am Wechsel: ALWS Austrian Ludwig Wittgenstein Society), www.wittgensteinrepository.org.

Nietzsche, Friedrich (1994 [1887]), *On the Genealogy of Morality*, ed. by Keith Ansell-Pearson, trans. by Carol Diethe (Cambridge: Cambridge University Press).

Nixon, Mark (2011), *Samuel Beckett's German Diaries 1936–1937* (London: Continuum).

(2014), Introduction and Annotations, in *Echo's Bones* by Samuel Beckett (New York: Grove Press), ix–xx, 53–109.

Noda, Yubii (2016), 'Paul Klee's *Chinese Picture* and *Chinese II*', *Zwitscher-Maschine: Journal on Paul Klee* 2: 79–92, www.zwitscher-maschine.org.

Nosthoff, Anna-Verena (2018), 'Beckett, Adorno, and the Hope for Nothingness as Something: Meditations on Theology in the Age of Its Impossibility', *Critical Research on Religion* 6.1: 35–53.

O'Brien, Eoin (1986), *The Beckett Country: Samuel Beckett's Ireland* (Dublin Black Cat Press in association with New York: Riverrun Press).

(1987), 'Zone of Stones: Samuel Beckett's Dublin', *Journal of the Irish College of Physicians and Surgeons* 16.2: 69–77.

(1992), Foreword, in *Dream of Fair to Middling Women*, by Samuel Beckett, ed. by Eoin O'Brien and Edith Fournier (New York: Arcade Publishing), xi–xx.

Okamuro, Minako (2009), 'Beckett, Yeats, and Noh: *...but the clouds...* as Theatre of Evocation', *Samuel Beckett Today/Aujourd'hui* 21: 165–77.

Perloff, Marjorie (2005), '"In Love with Hiding": Samuel Beckett's War', *The Iowa Review* 35.1: 76–103.

Pilling, John (1976), *Samuel Beckett* (London: Routledge and Kegan Paul).

ed. (1999), *Beckett's Dream Notebook* (Reading: Beckett International Foundation).

(2003), *Companion to* Dream of Fair to Middling Women, special issue, *Journal of Beckett Studies* 12.1–2.

(2006), 'Beckett and Mauthner Revisited', in *Beckett after Beckett*, ed. by S. E. Gontarski and Anthony Uhlmann (Gainesville: University Press of Florida), 158–66.

Plato (1937), *The Timaeus, in Plato's Cosmology*, trans. and comm. by Francis Macdonald Cornford (London: Routledge and Kegan Paul).

Plotinus (1956), *The Enneads*, trans. by Stephen MacKenna, 2nd ed., revised by B. S. Page (London: Faber).

Plümacher, Olga (1888 [1883]), *Der Pessimismus in Vergangenheit und Gegenwart: Geschichtliches und Kritisches*, 2nd ed. (Heidelberg: Georg Weiss Verlag).

Porphyry (1935), *On the Life of Plotinus and the Arrangement of His Work*, trans. by Stephen MacKenna and B. S. Page (London: P. L. Walker), www.sacred-texts.com.

Pothast, Ulrich (2008), *The Metaphysical Vision: Arthur Schopenhauer's Philosophy of Art and Life and Samuel Beckett's Own Way of Making Use of It* (New York: Peter Lang).

Pountney, Rosemary (1998 [1988]), *Theatre of Shadows: Samuel Beckett's Drama 1956–1976* (Gerrards Cross: Colin Smythe).

Proust, Marcel (1983), Letter to Robert Dreyfus, 10 Nov. 1910, in *Correspondance, 1910–1911*, vol. 10 of 21 vols., ed. by Philip Kolb (Paris: Plon), 207–8.

(1988 [1923]), *La Prisonnière*, in vol. 3 of *A la recherche du temps perdu* (Paris: Gallimard-Pléiade), 519–915.

(1989 [1927], *Le Temps retrouvé*, in vol. 4 of *A la recherche du temps perdu* (Paris: Gallimard-Pléiade), 273–625.

Rabaté, Jean-Michel (2016), *Think, Pig! Beckett at the Limit of the Human* (New York: Fordham University Press).

Rank, Otto (1971 [1914]), *The Double: A Psychoanalytic Study*, trans. and ed. by Harry Tucker, Jr. (Chapel Hill: University of North Carolina Press).

(2010 [1924]), *The Trauma of Birth*, translator not given (Mansfield Centre, CT: Martino Publishing).

Red Pine (Bill Porter), trans. and comm. (2001), *The Diamond Sutra: The Perfection of Wisdom* (Berkeley: Counterpoint).

(2004), *The Heart Sutra: The Womb of Buddhas* (Berkeley: Counterpoint).

Reid, Alec (1962), 'Beckett and the Drama of Unknowing', *Drama Survey* 2.2: 130–8.

Rhys Davids, Thomas R. (1910), 'Buddhism', in *The Encyclopaedia Britannica*, 11th ed., vol. 4, 742–9.

Riley, Denise (2004), '"A Voice without a Mouth": Inner Speech', *Qui parle* 14.2: 57–104.

Rodríguez-Gago, Antonia (2017), 'Reminiscences of a Late Friendship', in *Beckett in Conversation, 'yet again'/Rencontres avec Beckett, 'encore'*, ed. by Angela Moorjani, Danièle de Ruyter, and Sjef Houppermans (Leiden: Brill/ Rodopi), 18–26.

Roesler, Layla M. (2012), 'En *Compagnie* d'une métaphysique parodique: Beckett lecteur de Descartes redux', *Samuel Beckett Today/Aujourd'hui* 24: 139–53.

Romm, James (2020), 'What Did India Learn from the Greeks?', review of *The Greek Experience of India: From Alexander to the Indo-Greeks*, by Richard Stoneman, *The New York Review of Books* 67.6 (9 April): 31–2.

Rosen, Steven J. (1976), *Samuel Beckett and the Pessimistic Tradition* (New Brunswick, NJ: Rutgers University Press).

Ruegg, David S. (1969), *La Théorie du Tathāgatagarbha et du Gotra* (Paris: École française d'Extrême Orient).

Ryman, Robert (1989), *Nowhow On* (New York: The Limited Editions Club).

Sakauchi, Futoshi (2008), '*Not I* in an Irish Context', *Samuel Beckett Today/ Aujourd'hui* 19: 371–79.

Salisbury, Laura (2001), '"So the unreasoning goes": The Comic Timing of Trembling in *Ill Seen Ill Said*', *Samuel Beckett Today/Aujourd'hui* 11: 372–81.

(2012), *Samuel Beckett: Laughing Matters, Comic Timing* (Edinburgh: Edinburgh University Press).

Sartre, Jean-Paul (1947), 'L'Homme ligoté: notes sure le *Journal* de Jules Renard', in *Situations, I* (Paris: Gallimard), 271–88.

Sass, Louis (2017), *Madness and Modernism: Insanity in the Light of Modern Art, Literature, and Thought*, rev. ed. (New York: Oxford University Press).

Schaik, Sam van (2018), *The Spirit of Zen* (New Haven: Yale University Press).

Schneider, Alan (1967 [1958]), 'Waiting for Beckett', in *Beckett at 60: A Festschrift*, ed. by John Calder (London: Calder and Boyars), 34–52.

Schopenhauer, Arthur (1889 [1867], *On the Will in Nature*, in *Two Essays*, trans. by Mme. Karl Hillebrand, 4th edition (London: G. Bell). https://archive.org.

(2014 [1818]), *The World as Will and Representation*, vol. 1, trans. and ed. by Judith Norman, Alistair Welchman, and Christopher Janaway (Cambridge: Cambridge University Press).

(2015 [1851]), *Parerga and Paralipomena: Short Philosophical Essays*, vol. 2, trans. and ed. by Adrian del Caro and Christopher Janaway (Cambridge: Cambridge University Press).

(2018 [1844]), *The World as Will and Representation*, vol. 2, trans. and ed. by Judith Norman, Alistair Welchman, and Christopher Janaway (Cambridge: Cambridge University Press).

Sebastian, C. D. (2016), *The Cloud of Nothingness: The Negative Way in Nāgārjuna and John of the Cross* (New Delhi: Springer India).

Seo, Audrey Yoshiko (2007), *Ensō: Zen Circles of Enlightenment* (Boston: Weatherhill).

Shainberg, Lawrence (1987), 'Exorcising Beckett', *Paris Review* 29.104 (fall): 100–36.

Shields, Paul (2001), 'Beckett's Labour Lost: *Company* and the Paradox of Creation', *Samuel Beckett Today/Aujourd'hui* 11: 478–85.

Shulman, David (2020), 'Buddhist Baedekers', review of *Creating the Universe: Depictions of the Cosmos in Himalayan Buddhism*, by Eric Huntington, *The New York Review of Books* 67.5 (March 26): 36–8.

Siderits, Mark, and Shōryū Katsura, trans. and eds. (2013), *Nāgārjuna's Middle Way: Mūlamadhyamakakārikā* (Sommerville, MA: Wisdom Publications).

Simmer-Brown, Judith (2001), Preface, in *Buddhist Wisdom,* trans. and expl. by Edward Conze (New York: Random House–Vintage Spiritual Classics), xv–xxvi.

Stewart, Paul, and David Pattie, eds. (2019), *Pop Beckett: Intersections with Popular Culture* (Stuttgart: ibidem).

Slote, Sam (2015), 'Bilingual Beckett: Beyond the Linguistic Turn', in *The New Cambridge Companion to Samuel Beckett*, ed. by Dirk Van Hulle (New York: Cambridge University Press), 114–25.

Spretnak, Charlene (2014), *The Spiritual Dynamic in Modern Art: Art History Reconsidered, 1800 to the Present* (New York: Palgrave Macmillan).

Stutley, Margaret, and James Stutley (1977), *Harper's Dictionary of Hinduism: Its Mythology, Folklore, Philosophy, Literature, and History* (New York: Harper & Row).

Suzuki, Daisetz T. (1957), *Mysticism, Christian and Buddhist* (New York: Harper), www.sacred-texts.com/bud/mcb.

Takahashi, Yasunari (1982), 'The Theatre of the Mind: Samuel Beckett and the Noh', *Encounter* 58.4: 66–73.

(1983), 'Qu'est-ce qui arrive? Some Structural Comparisons of Beckett's Plays and Noh', in *Samuel Beckett: Humanistic Perspectives*, ed. by Morris Beja, S. E. Gontarski, and Pierre Astier (Columbus: Ohio State University Press), 99–106.

(2001), 'On "Mindlessness": Beckett, Japan, and the Twentieth Century', *Samuel Beckett Today/Aujourdhui* 11: 37–41.

Takebe, Yoshiko (2011), 'The Effect of Translated Plays: Samuel Beckett and Japanese Theatre', [The Japanese Association of] *Interpreting and Translation Studies* 11: 113–22, http://jaits.jpn.org/home/kaishi2011/pdf/09_Takebe.pdf.

Tanahashi, Kazuaki (2015), 'If Each Moment Is Complete Why Do We Need Practice?' (Video interview excerpt), SAND Anthology, vol. 5, www.archive.scienceandnonduality.com.

Touret, Michèle (2006), 'Y a-t-il un événement dans le texte?', *Samuel Beckett Today/Aujourd'hui* 17: 15–34.

Trezise, Thomas (1990), *Into the Breach* (Princeton, NJ: Princeton University Press).

Trinh, Xuan Thuan (2016), *La Plénitude du vide* (Paris: Éditions Albin Michel).

Tucker, David (2012), *Samuel Beckett and Arnold Geulincx: Tracing 'a literary fantasia'* (London: Bloomsbury Publishing).

Ueda, Shizuteru (2004 [1977]), '"Nothingness" in Meister Eckhart and Zen Buddhism: With Particular Reference to the Borderlines of Philosophy and Theology', in *The Buddha Eye: An Anthology of the Kyoto School and Its Contemporaries*, rev. ed., ed. by Frederick Frank (Bloomington, IN: World Wisdom), 157–69.

Uhlmann, Anthony (1999), *Beckett and Poststructuralism* (Cambridge: Cambridge University Press).

—— (2006), 'Samuel Beckett and the Occluded Image', in *Beckett after Beckett*, ed. by S. E. Gontarksi and Anthony Uhlmann (Gainesville: University Press of Florida), 79–97.

—— (2009), 'Negative Allegory: Buning on Allegory and the *Via Negativa*', *Samuel Beckett Today/Aujourd'hui* 21: 17–26.

Van Hulle, Dirk (2004), '("Hiatus in MS"): *Watt* and the Textual Genesis of *Stirrings Still*', *Samuel Beckett Today/Aujourd'hui* 14: 483–94.

—— (2009), 'The Urge to Tell: Samuel Beckett's *Not I* as a *Texte Brisé* for Television', *Journal of Beckett Studies* 18. 1–2: 44–56.

—— (2011), *The Making of Samuel Beckett's 'Stirrings Still'/Soubresauts' and 'Comment Dire'/'what Is the Word'*, The Beckett Digital Manuscript Project, module 1 (Brussels: University Press Antwerp ASP/UPA).

—— (2012), '"Eff it": Beckett and Linguistic Skepticism', in *Beckett/Philosophy*, ed. by Matthew Feldman and Karin Mamdani (Sofia, BG: University Press St. Klimmt Ohridski), 221–37.

Van Hulle, Dirk, and Mark Nixon (2013), *Samuel Beckett's Library* (Cambridge: Cambridge University Press).

Van Hulle, Dirk, and Shane Weller, eds. (2014), *The Making of Samuel Beckett's L'Innommable/The Unnamable*, The Beckett Digital Manuscript Project, module 2 (Brussels: University Press Antwerp ASP/UPA).

Vassilopoulou, Panayiota, and Stephen R. Clark, eds. (2009), *Late Antique Epistemology: Other Ways to Truth* (Houndmills: Palgrave Macmillan).

Verdi, Richard (1985), *Klee and Nature* (New York: Rizzoli).

Viévard, Ludovic (2002), *Vacuité (śūnyatā) et compassion (karuṇā) dans le bouddhisme madhyamaka* (Paris: Collège de France/Diffusion de Boccard).

Vivekananda, Swami (Narendranath Datta) (1958 [1896]), 'Maya and Illusion', in *The Complete Works*, 9th ed., vol. 2 of 12 vols. (Calcutta: Advaita Ashrama), 88–104.

Waldron, William S. (2003), *The Buddhist Unconscious: The ālaya-vijñāna in the Context of Indian Buddhist Thought* (London: Routledge).

Warrilow, David (1986), 'La musique, pas le sens', *Revue d'esthétique*, Special Samuel Beckett Issue, ed. by Pierre Chabert (Paris: Privat), 251–3.

Weber-Caflisch, Antoinette (1994), *Chacun son dépeupleur: sur Samuel Beckett* (Paris: Éditions de Minuit).

Weller, Shane (2005), *A Taste for the Negative: Beckett and Nihilism* (London: Modern Humanities Research Association and Maney Publishing).

(2008), '"Gnawing to be naught": Beckett and Pre-Socratic Nihilism', *Samuel Beckett Today/Aujourd'hui* 20: 321–33.

(2009), '"Some Experience of the Schizoid Voice": Samuel Beckett and the Language of Derangement', *Forum for Modern Language Studies* 45.1: 32–50.

(2010), 'Adorno's Notes on *The Unnamable*', in *Journal of Beckett Studies* 19.2: 179–95.

Westerhoff, Jan (2009), *Nāgārjuna's Madhyamaka: A Philosophical Introduction* (New York: Oxford University Press).

Williams, Duane (2016), 'Feminist Theology and Meister Eckhart's Transgendered Metaphor', *Feminist Theology* 24.3: 275–90.

Williams, Paul (2009), *Mahāyāna Buddhism: The Doctrinal Foundation*, 2nd ed. (London: Routledge).

Williams, Paul, with Anthony Tribe (2000), *Buddhist Thought: A Complete Introduction to the Indian Tradition* (London: Routledge).

Wilson, Ann (1990), '"Her Lips Moving": The Castrated Voice of *Not I* ', in *Women in Beckett*, ed. by Linda Ben-Zvi (Chicago: University of Illinois Press), 190–200.

Wimbush, Andy (2013), 'Biology, the Buddha and the Beasts: The Influence of Ernst Haeckel and Arthur Schopenhauer on Samuel Beckett's *How It Is*', in *Encountering Buddhism in Twentieth-Century British and American Literature*, ed. by Lawrence Normand and Alison Winch (London: Bloomsbury), 123–38.

(2020), *Still: Samuel Beckett's Quietism* (Stuttgart: ibidem).

Windelband, Wilhelm (1901), *A History of Philosophy*, vol. I, rev. ed., translated by James H. Tufts (New York: Macmillan).

Wittgenstein, Ludwig (1958 [1953]), *Philosophical Investigations*, trans. by G. E. M. Anscombe, 2nd ed. (Oxford: Basil Blackwell).

Wolosky, Shira (1989), 'Samuel Beckett's Figural Evasions', in *Languages of the Unsayable: The Play of Negativity in Literature and Literary Theory*, ed. by Sanford Budick and Wolfgang Iser (New York: Columbia University Press), 165–84.

Wynands, Sandra (2007), *Iconic Spaces: The Dark Theology of Samuel Beckett's Drama* (Notre Dame, IN: University of Notre Dame Press).

Zilliacus, Clas (1976), *Beckett and Broadcasting: A Study of the Works of Samuel Beckett for and in Radio and Television* (Abo, FI: Abo Akademi).

Zimmer, Heinrich (1936), *Maya: Der indische Mythos* (Stuttgart: Deutsche Verlags-Anstalt).

Index

Printed in the United States
by Baker & Taylor Publisher Services